W9-BWJ-309

Witchcraft, Magic, and Religion in 17th-Century Massachusetts

Richard Weisman

The University of Massachusetts Press   *Amherst, 1984*

BF
1576
. W42
1984
Cop. 2

Copyright © 1984 by
The University of Massachusetts Press
All rights reserved
Printed in the United States of America

Library of Congress Cataloging in Publication Data

Weisman, Richard.
  Witchcraft, magic, and religion in seventeenth-
century Massachusetts.

  Bibliography: p.
  Includes index.
  1. Trials (Witchcraft)—Massachusetts. 2. Witch-
craft—Massachusetts. 3. Massachusetts—History—
Colonial period, ca. 1600–1775. 4. Witchcraft.
I. Title.
KFM2478.8.W5W44 1984   345.744'0288   83-15542
ISBN 0–87023–415–3   347.4405288

Fordham University
LIBRARY
AT
LINCOLN CENTER
New York, N. Y.

For my mother,
for my father in memoriam,
and for my wife.

WITHDRAWN
FROM
COLLECTION

FORDHAM
UNIVERSITY
LIBRARIES

Witchcraft, Magic, and Religion
in 17th-Century Massachusetts

Contents

Acknowledgments   ix

Preface   xi

1   Introduction   1

2   The Crime of Witchcraft in Massachusetts Bay:
Historical Background and Pattern of Prosecution   7

THE SOCIAL MEANING OF WITCHCRAFT IN SEVENTEENTH-CENTURY MASSACHUSETTS BAY

3   Witchcraft and Puritan Beliefs   23   *Beliefs*

4   Witchcraft and Magic   39

5   The Interrelationship between Popular
and Theological Meanings of Witchcraft   53

WITCHCRAFT AND COMMUNITY

6   The Identification of the Malefic Witch   75   *Who*
Harmful Evil

7   The Official Response to Popular Demands   96   *why*

WITCHCRAFT AND THE STATE

8   The Salem Witchcraft Prosecutions:
The Framework for Official Initiative   117

9   The Salem Witchcraft Prosecutions:
    The Discovery of Conspiracy   132

10 The Salem Witchcraft Prosecutions:
    The Invisible World at the Vanishing Point   160

11 Witchcraft in Historical and Sociological Perspective   184

    APPENDIXES

A   List of Legal Actions against Witchcraft
    Prior to the Salem Prosecutions   191

B   List of Defamation Suits Involving Witchcraft
    in Seventeenth-Century Massachusetts Bay   204

C   List of Persons against Whom Legal Actions
    Were Initiated during Salem Prosecutions   208

D   List of Confessors during Salem Prosecutions   217

E   List of Allegations of Ordinary Witchcrafts by Case   219

F   List of Persons Diagnosed as Afflicted in
    Seventeenth-Century Massachusetts Bay   222

    Notes   225

    Bibliography   251

    Subject Index   263

    Name Index   265

Acknowledgments

I AM SURE that I am not alone among those who have engaged in a lengthy project to have occasionally cursed the world for its indifference to the creative process and for its recognition of the creative product only. If I can now look upon these moments with some amusement, it is because there were people who gave me support and criticism when I needed it. Among those who offered encouragement and/or helpful comments on earlier drafts of this manuscript are Jean Burnet, Kai Erikson, Robert Middlekauff, E. William Monter, and Stephen Nissenbaum. Most recently, I am grateful to Barbara Palmer for her careful and painstaking editorial assistance and to Pam Campbell for her assistance on that part of the manuscript that remained after Ms. Palmer's work was completed.

There are several others to whom I owe a special debt of gratitude. I thank my friend and colleague, Cynthia Zimmerman, not only for her continued support and helpful insights but also for reminding me not to lose sight of why I was doing this project. I thank my former teacher David Matza for his wholehearted encouragement in the earlier stages of this manuscript and for embodying the highest ideals of scholarship in his own work. I have benefited immeasurably from the thoughtful and constructive advice of my friend Donald Evans, professor of philosophy and United Church minister. The generosity and support of John Demos, fellow voyager to the world of witchcraft belief, has been an unexpected gift that I can only hope my project deserves.

I owe the deepest thanks to my wife, Maureen Cooper, whose sane and sensible outlook helped me to keep this project in perspective and whose respect for my creative process was my greatest resource.

Preface

I BEGAN THIS project about a decade ago in order to address the issue of why collective action against witchcraft had ended so abruptly in Europe and its colonial derivatives in the seventeenth century. My initial plan was to approach this puzzle through what seemed to be an unusually strategic point of entry into the history of witchcraft. Apart from their dramatic and literary possibilities, the Salem witchcraft prosecutions were among the very few recorded occasions in which the same officials who had participated in the conviction and execution of persons for witchcraft endeavored to posthumously invalidate and reverse their own findings. I anticipated that a community undergoing so drastic a shift between acceptance and rejection of witchcraft beliefs would make visible to itself and to future generations the various interests and assumptions that had sustained those beliefs. Hence, my seventeenth-century subjects would write their own sociology, albeit with some editorial assistance.

But as I probed more deeply into the legal, theological, and narrative records that had survived into the twentieth century, my hopes for rapid enlightenment began to fade. For one thing, the Salem prosecutions seemed historically out of place in terms of my earlier calculations. The colonists had been comparatively inactive in their pursuit of witches prior to the Salem trials. Why did the decline of witchcraft prosecutions occur just after the most dramatic increase in such prosecutions? I was not at all satisfied with explanations that spoke of these events as instances of collective hysteria or mass delusion, and I vowed that I would resort to such diagnostic tools only if my sociological imagination failed me completely.

For another, I found my seventeenth-century sources not only singularly disinclined to think about witchcraft as protosociologists but often unhelpful and even evasive in their pronouncements on the subject. Not until much later in the project did I learn that silences about an event of public concern can be as revealing as any text. Even more disconcerting, I discovered that the anomalies that troubled me did not appear to trouble most of the writers and scholars who had preceded me in this topic. I could only conclude either that I was the victim of my own preconceptions or that I drew my inspiration from a different muse.

Eventually, I was able to return to my original concerns, but not before I had come to understand the historical context of Massachusetts witchcraft in terms quite different from those with which I had begun. I credit my belated reawakening in no small measure to Keith Thomas's study of popular beliefs in sixteenth- and seventeenth-century England in *Religion and the Decline of Magic*. From Thomas's work, I learned that by the time that English beliefs in witchcraft had been transplanted to the shores of New England, there had already occurred a collapse in consensus over the meaning of the supernatural. What this implied was that witchcraft was not to be regarded as a unitary phenomenon but rather as a collection of conflicting beliefs and interests. I found that this conflict-oriented approach seemed to make sense of the curious pattern of prosecution in New England in a way that my previous approach did not. The elaboration of this perspective thus became a central part of the present study.

No less important to this reappraisal was my growing conviction that a crucial gap existed in the literature of New England witchcraft that I could not afford to ignore. For the vast majority of scholars, the history of witchcraft in New England was synonymous with the history of the Salem prosecutions. The few articles and texts that dealt with witchcraft prior to Salem or in jurisdictions other than Massachusetts were directed primarily to audiences with antiquarian interests. Indeed, John Demos's *Entertaining Satan*, which, unfortunately, did not come out until this work was already in press, is the first extended work to have done scholarly justice to these pre-Salem expressions of witchcraft belief.

The problem with this emphasis, however understandable, was that it entailed a risk of misinterpreting not only the overall pattern of prosecution but also the pattern exhibited by the Salem trials themselves. It was only when the Salem trials were situated in the larger context of seventeenth-century colonial witchcraft prosecutions that one could more confidently distinguish what were conventional expressions of the idiom of witchcraft from what were departures from this idiom. I concluded that it was for lack of historical perspective that it was so difficult to resolve whether the Salem trials represented merely an escalation of earlier patterns of prosecution or a different pattern altogether. Because these issues seemed so fundamental, a reconsideration of witchcraft belief in Massachusetts in light of its own history became another objective of the study.

But I do not think that, even with these changes in perspective, I could have undertaken an interpretation of this particular expression of witchcraft belief without first acquiring some familiarity with the language of covenant theology. From the writings of Perry Miller especially, but also from a later generation of historians of Puritan thought, I learned to better appreciate the distinctive style of discourse in terms of which contemporaries deliberated the major issues of their society. I also discovered that among these narrators, diarists, and preachers were the reflective and articulate voices I had been listening for earlier but had been unable to hear.

The chapters in this work have been organized in relation to the overall goal of explicating the social processes underlying support and resistance to collective action against witchcraft in seventeenth-century Massachusetts. After an introduction in chapter 1, the first task is to describe in historical overview the data to be analyzed in the remainder of the study. Thus, in chapter 2, the form and pattern of legal actions against witchcraft in Massachusetts Bay are situated in relation to the form and pattern of legal actions in England and in Continental Europe. From this comparison, it becomes possible to formulate the dimensions of New England witchcraft in terms of broad sociohistorical units of analysis.

The main body of the work is divided into three sections. In the first section, entitled "The Social Meaning of Witchcraft in Seventeenth-Century Massachusetts Bay," an attempt is made to explicate the logic and meaning of the two major interpretive frameworks in terms of which the category was understood by inhabitants of Massachusetts Bay. Chapter 3 is concerned with theological interpretations of witchcraft. Chapter 4 focuses on the relationship between witchcraft and magic. Chapter 5 discusses the interrelationships between these two interpretations of witchcraft.

The second and third sections of this study deal with the sources of support and resistance to collective actions against witchcraft prior to the Salem trials and during the Salem trials respectively. In "Witchcraft and Community," chapter 6 deals with the identification of the witch in pre-Salem legal actions and chapter 7 analyzes the official response to these identifications. In "Witchcraft and the State," chapters 8 and 9 examine the social processes entailed in the creation of witches during the Salem trials and chapter 10 looks at the aftermath of these trials.

Finally, I cannot refrain from drawing upon my experience in this project to comment on the somewhat tortured relationship that exists between sociology and history. It would seem that each generation of scholars finds it necessary to establish clear boundaries between the two disciplines—a sure sign that these boundaries are tenuous at best. But it would be a mistake to trivialize the anxiety that underlies this continuing preoccupation. Put bluntly, it is a fear that the theoretical range required of a work in sociology is not really compatible with the specific knowledge and understanding expected of the historian. Thus the student in sociology or history who ventures into that other domain runs the risk of producing a hybrid that is not acceptable according to the criteria of either discipline.

This is not because the academic standards that are applied in one field are not in principle respected by the other. The sociological emphasis upon theoretical generalization can no more excuse a superficial and invalid representation of historical reality than the specificity of historical interpretation can justify an insensitivity toward social context. As I have experienced it, the real dilemma is whether to participate in the intellectual tradition of one or the other discipline or to merely use it as a resource. The most frequent resolution has been the latter, in which the sociologist treats as final a particular historical version in order to pursue analytic objectives in sociology. The problem with this choice is that the doing of history is no more static an enterprise than the doing of sociology. One imputes finality to a historical account at one's peril.

I can do no better in responding to this dilemma than to paraphrase Kai Erikson who, as a sociologist, once undertook an academic odyssey similar to my own to seventeenth-century New England. I began this study in order to pursue theoretical objectives derived from a sociological literature. If in the course of this project, however, I have wandered into the domain of the historian to meet these objectives, I can only hope that I have not produced that dreaded hybrid that has haunted academic trespassers before me.

Note: Unless otherwise stated in the text, the quotations from seventeenth-century sources have been left in their original form.

Witchcraft, Magic, and Religion
in 17th-Century Massachusetts

Introduction

T̲HE WONDER THAT it could happen that, throughout Europe until
the late seventeenth and early eighteenth centuries and until quite
recently in simple societies in Africa, Melanesia, Latin America, and
North America, most of humanity believed in the existence of supernatural adversaries called witches or some other equivalent designa-
tion has been aptly referred to by Marvin Harris as one of the riddles
of culture.[1] But its importance consists as much in the mystery surrounding ourselves as in the mystery surrounding witchcraft. Every
answer to the question of why our historical predecessors believed in
witchcraft is simultaneously an answer to the other equally interesting
question of why we do not believe in witchcraft. Indeed, both questions have absorbed the attention of generations of scholars from a
variety of disciplinary perspectives.

Some of these answers have been more reassuring to a modern audience than have others. For a long time, the dominant view among
historians was that belief in witchcraft was the result of error or delusion or superstition or some combination of these intellectual deficiencies.[2] The obvious corollary was that we who do not believe in
witchcraft were somehow more immune from such defects in cogni-
tion than were our predecessors. Not infrequently, the same scholars
would credit science or the decline of religion or some other conventional benchmark of social progress with our liberation from these false
beliefs.

Other variations on this response have been equally reassuring, but
with greater subtlety. Some students of witchcraft have suggested that
accused witches suffered from mental illness, and others have alleged
that the paranormal experiences reported in the confessions of witches
were induced by hallucinogenic substances.[3] The thrust of these solutions is to concede that belief in witchcraft was based upon subjectively
real perceptions but that historical predecessors lacked the technical

knowledge to explain what caused these perceptions. The corollary of course is that we do not believe because we now possess this technical information, whether from psychiatry or pharmacology or some other branch of knowledge.

I draw attention to these approaches not to revive ancient controversies but rather to situate the concerns of this work. While this study also addresses the riddle of witchcraft, the resources for analysis are recent sociological perspectives on deviance and the delimited historical and cultural setting of seventeenth-century Massachusetts Bay. My objective is to make visible through an intensive case study the social processes involved in the construction of categories of deviance in general and witchcraft in particular. Thus I approach the riddle of witchcraft as a problem of social organization and not as a problem of incomplete knowledge. Some brief remarks are necessary to acquaint the reader with this perspective.

FORMULATION OF THE PROBLEM

Since Emile Durkheim's critique of Cesare Lombroso in *The Division of Labor in Society*, sociologists have been aware, at least in principle, that deviance does not inhere in the act or in the individual but rather is a consequence of the collective imposition of sanctions upon the act. But it was not until some two decades ago that the implications of this perspective were developed to a point that challenged Durkheim's own understanding of deviance. The major theoretical assumptions of this new approach—variously referred to as the labeling or interactionist perspective—as well as its relationship to other schools of deviance have been ably articulated by Howard Becker, David Matza, and Edwin Schur, among others.[4] For present purposes, it is sufficient merely to indicate more precisely how this study constitutes an application of this perspective and its later elaborations to the study of witchcraft.

Perhaps the most fundamental assumption of the interactionist approach is to conceive of deviance not as an individual act but rather as the outcome of a social process. Becker's often quoted proposition, "Social groups create deviance by making the rules whose infraction constitutes deviance and by applying those rules to particular people and labeling them as outsiders," well articulates this premise that deviance is the outcome of an interaction between those members who break a rule and those members who enforce a rule.[5] It is important to understand, though, that Becker's proposition is a statement about the creation of social meanings and not a statement about the causal efficacy of group pressure. To assert that social groups constitute deviance is not to say that deviant actions are caused by a particular social response.[6] It is rather to suggest that acts become instances of deviance only when they are defined as such by groups who are in a position to claim legitimacy for their definitions.

The interactionist perspective is deceptively simple, for what it asserts is both obvious and yet profoundly at odds with our everyday experience.[7] Official and lay audiences typically confront the actions of the deviant as if these actions were external and independent events. The public conception of an action as an instance of burglary, delinquency, hysteria, or some other form of rule-breaking activity is then perceived as a response to something that already happened. Proponents of the interactionist approach challenge this perception by suggesting that conventional and official conceptions of deviance are not to be characterized as mere reactions to external happenings. To the contrary, it is the act of interpretation itself that transforms an event into an instance of deviance. From an interactionist standpoint, it is thus essential to consider not just the rule-breaking act or person but also the interpretive work of others whose rule-making and rule-enforcing practices allow for the possibility of the act.

It is in these terms that the analytic goals of this investigation have been formulated. This study seeks to answer the riddle of witchcraft—that is, the question of how witchcraft could have occurred as a believably real event—by making explicit the unacknowledged social processes in terms of which the category of witchcraft was constructed. In particular, it seeks to demonstrate that what believers took as the external occurrence of witchcraft was a product of their own interpretive work. It also attempts to demonstrate the reflexive character of imputations of witchcraft by showing that what believers took as qualities inherent in the witch were in fact qualities that emerged as a result of the interactions between the witch and themselves. In this manner, the present study addresses the question not only of how specific individuals became identified as witches but also of how the category of witchcraft was itself generated.[8]

PERSPECTIVES ON WITCHCRAFT

It is a curious feature of the literature on witchcraft that Western scholars have been far more appreciative of mystical beliefs in non-European societies than of mystical beliefs in European societies. Thus, where anthropologists can legitimately claim to have demonstrated the comprehensibility of individual and collective responses to witchcraft in the simple societies of Africa and Melanesia, questions about the intelligibility of witchcraft belief remain to be resolved in the historical studies that have investigated the phenomenon in the complex and differentiated societies of postmedieval Europe. These different sensibilities toward witchcraft are evident even in the descriptive vocabularies that have been applied to the subject. Where anthropologists have referred to collective public actions against witchcraft as witchfinding movements in appreciation of their social and political character, historians have referred to such collective actions in Europe and America as witch crazes, witch hunts, witch panics, and so forth in judgment against their allegedly pathological and irrational character.[9] Where anthropologists have discovered coherent patterns in the relationship between witchcraft accusations and the structural conditions in which they arise, historians have tended until recently to conceive of these actions as idiosyncratic cultural manifestations or episodes that somehow occurred without clear connection to their social context.

The continuing challenge for contemporary students of witchcraft is to somehow disentangle those differences between African and European witchcraft that arise from divergent modes of analysis from those differences that are intrinsic to the phenomenon itself.[10] There can be little question that perspectives derived from social anthropology have already been useful in effectively extinguishing the last vestiges of rationalism from the historiography of European witchcraft. No doubt the receptivity of historians to this literature has been in part a by-product of a general resurgence of interest in popular beliefs in postmedieval Europe. Whatever the reason, the classic investigations of Evans-Pritchard and others have demonstrated the value of analyzing witchcraft as a coherent system of beliefs and, incidentally, have put to rest the rationalist conceit that such beliefs are devoid of logic and that they must necessarily collapse before the onslaught of scientific thinking.

Beyond this substantial accomplishment, efforts by anthropologists to situate mystical beliefs within their social context have yielded valuable clues for later historical research. The wealth of existing fieldwork linking witchcraft and related mystical beliefs to political and economic forces suggests the inadvisability of failing to at least search for similar connections between European witchcraft and its social environment. The famed maxim of anthropological investigations that "witchcraft accusations are not random" is a reminder to students of European witchcraft to be sensitive to the web of social relationships within which suspicions of witchcraft arise. Other studies conducted within the framework of the once dominant functionalist model have shown how witchcraft accusations contribute to the stability of the social order by penalizing members who violate social norms and by restricting through fear of accusations members who are socially mobile.[11] The relevance of these studies to the peasant communities of sixteenth- and seventeenth-century Europe has been established by historians.

Until the beginning of the last decade, the differences in how European and African witchcraft had been characterized might well have been attributed to limitations in historical scholarship. The combined effects of isolation from the mainstream of European social history and inattention to the conceptual tools applied in social anthropology had produced a specialized esoteric literature that lagged behind theoretical developments in both history and anthropology. The failure to locate witchcraft in its social and political context, the depreciation of witchcraft beliefs as mere superstition, and the inability to identify patterns in witchcraft accusations were the failures of rationalism and not a true reflection of differences between the phenomenon of witchcraft in Africa and in Western Europe.

Nevertheless, it is now clear in the light of more recent historical scholarship that, even after the elimination of rationalist bias, there are aspects of witchcraft in the complex societies of Western Europe that no amount of theoretical refinement can reconcile with witchcraft in simple societies. It is not just that European witchcraft, together with its New England derivative, was somehow more convulsive, less stabilizing, and bloodier than its African counterpart. These are merely the surface manifestations of a difference that goes to the root of the phenomenon itself.

The historian H. C. Midelfort captures this difference when he observes that sixteenth-century doctrines of witchcraft were "controversial, flexible, and definitely not monolithic."[12] To be sure, it is easy to overestimate the degree of consensus that prevailed in simple societies, and ethnographies abound with instances in which allegations of witchcraft proved controversial and even schismatic with respect to the villages and communities involved.[13] But this does not approach the degree of dissension to be found in Europe. As recent studies have suggested, European witchcraft consisted not in a unified set of beliefs but rather in a composite of disparate and sometimes conflicting beliefs.[14] The result is that disagreement went beyond conflict over the identity of particular witches to conflict over the definition of witchcraft itself. In European witchcraft, considerations of power—the power of one group to impose its definition of the problem of witchcraft on another group—figure far more prominently than in the forms of witchcraft investigated by anthropologists.

Such differences do not of course render the contributions of social anthropology unusable by students of European witchcraft. Certain principles of inquiry that have become associated with anthropological approaches to occult beliefs—in particular, that the logic of witchcraft cannot be understood apart from its social context—remain equally valid for historical research. But the substantive differences between witchcraft in simple societies and witchcraft in complex societies do mean that explanatory models that have been applied so fruitfully in one context are not automatically transferable to the other.

This study builds upon recent historical descriptions of European witchcraft in its formulation of the overall pattern of witchcraft belief in seventeenth-century New England. In its attempt to bring new perspectives to bear on New England witchcraft, it participates in a process begun in the research of John Demos, Paul Boyer, and Stephen Nissenbaum. With reference to the English roots of New England witchcraft, the work of Keith Thomas has been especially helpful.[15]

2

The Crime of Witchcraft in

Massachusetts Bay: Historical Background

and Pattern of Prosecution

THE MULTIDIMENSIONAL character of European witchcraft belief may be illustrated by juxtaposing the conflicting generalizations of George Kittredge and G. L. Burr, perhaps still among the foremost historians of witchcraft in New England:

The belief in witchcraft is the common heritage of humanity. It is not chargeable to any particular time, or race, or form of religion. [Kittredge, *Witchcraft in Old and New England*, p. 372]

Magic is actual and universal . . . but witchcraft never was. It was but a shadow, a nightmare: the nightmare of a religion, the shadow of a dogma. Less than five centuries saw its birth, its vigor, its decay. [Burr, "New England's Place in the History of Witchcraft," p. 192]

It would seem almost as if two different classes of phenomena are encompassed in these formulations; yet it is the case that each of the statements is a partially accurate characterization of European beliefs.

The disagreement between the two men arises from their exclusive concern with one or the other of the two major components of the European response to the problem of witchcraft: its associations with malefic magic and its associations with organized religion. The sorting of these components is particularly important in this study because both figure independently in the Anglo-American constitution of the crime of witchcraft.

As the historian H. C. Lea has amply demonstrated in his collection of statutes and ligatures against witchcraft, the regulation of magical practices has been a feature of virtually all the civilizations of Europe, regardless of their religious orientation.[1] The authority for such regulation has been variously assumed by either secular or ecclesiastical courts with appropriate shifts in emphasis. As an example of secular control, Roman legislation against magic sharply distinguished between good or socially beneficial uses and evil uses, reserving punishment only for the latter.[2] Ecclesiastical prohibitions, on the other hand, from their earliest mention in recorded history to their more recent expression in the seventeenth century, have stressed the illicit more than the potentially malefic uses of magic.[3] Perhaps the best-known injunctions of this type are contained in the Old Testament, in which lawful and unlawful alliances with spiritual powers are distinguished without reference to their outcomes.[4]

Within this framework of social control, in which primary emphasis was placed on the regulation of magic, the label "witchcraft" arose as merely one among many alternative designations for socially disapproved magical practices. In a recent work on European witchcraft, Jeffrey Burton Russell provides a lexicon of perhaps twenty such terms, gathered from medieval ecclesiastical records, that were used more or less interchangeably to refer to witches or magical practitioners.[5] Regardless of the elasticity of these definitions, it is important to note that some form of legal machinery for prosecution of acts of witchcraft and allied practices existed long before the period under consideration in this study.

It was not until the late Middle Ages that a new understanding of witchcraft was disseminated in Continental Europe that transformed both the meaning of the phenomenon and the terms of its social regulation. In this formulation, the supernatural capabilities of the witch—whether used for good or evil employments—were believed to issue from a voluntary pact with the devil. Although elements of this understanding can be traced as far back as the sixth century after Christ,[6] its effective translation into political action was a unique development of the fourteenth and fifteenth centuries.

The seminal work of this school of thought is generally acknowledged by historians to be the *Malleus Maleficarum* composed in 1486 by the German inquisitors Heinrich Institoris and Jakob Sprenger under the authority of a papal bull issued by Innocent VIII in 1484.[7] Institoris, the chief author of the *Malleus*, was a member of the Dominican order and had served as inquisitor for southern Germany prior to the writing of the treatise.[8] Sprenger, also a Dominican, was the inquisitor for the Rhineland. Innocent's pronouncements in 1484 had been delivered in response to a request by the two men for official support for their activities in the face of mounting opposition in the Alps.[9]

The *Malleus* was essentially a work of synthesis rather than of innovation. It used the traditional arguments of medieval scholasticism to demonstrate the existence of a monstrous reality. Three conditions were necessary for the occurrence of witchcraft: the evil intentions of the witch, the assistance of the devil, and the permission of God.[10] But the practice of witchcraft entailed far more than an allegiance with the devil against God, although this in itself made it the most heinous of crimes. Witchcraft embodied the most obscene and blasphemous activities imaginable to the medieval church. The sacrifice of unbaptized infants to Satan, the forming of sexual alliances with male and female demons, and the full devotion of body and soul to evil works were among the routine abominations of this heresy.[11] In the writings of Institoris and Sprenger, witchcraft became the focus of inquisitorial activity against both heresy and unlawful magical practices.

The *Malleus* exerted an enormous influence on both witchcraft theory and social policy toward witchcraft in Continental Europe throughout the sixteenth and seventeenth centuries. The fact that it was reprinted in twenty-nine separate editions in Italy, France, and Germany between 1487 and 1669 gives some indication of its considerable popularity.[12] That its formulations both reflected and shaped the conventional understanding of witchcraft in much of western Europe for almost two centuries has been a matter of consternation to modern historical observers. Undoubtedly, the conferral of papal authorization lent considerable weight to the conclusions of the *Malleus*. By itself, however, this can hardly account for its durability. German Protestants as well as German Catholics were persuaded by its arguments.[13]

The more intriguing possibility is that the descriptions of the inquisitors did in fact correspond to the actual religious practices of certain contemporary heretical sects. The determination of the extent and nature of this correspondence has proved difficult at best, however. The speculations of Margaret Murray and her successors that the inquisitorial texts accurately recorded, albeit prejudicially, the rites of a coexistent pagan fertility cult have met serious criticism.[14] Among other problems, much of the evidence in support of this hypothesis has been drawn from confessions and other testimonies obtained under duress. At the same time, however, it should not be overlooked that extreme heretical movements were prevalent during the period in which the *Malleus* was composed and that at least one such group, the Luciferans of late medieval Austria, celebrated rituals in honor of the devil.[15] Whether or not such movements formed the ontological core for inquisitorial texts to embellish into witchcraft remains an open question.[16]

Probably the most adequate, if incomplete, explanation for the remarkable longevity of the *Malleus* is one that focuses less on the suspects and more on the prosecutors. The legal machinery proposed by the *Malleus* for the prosecution of witchcraft was sufficient in itself to engender the reality it purported to condemn. And it is these specific proposals that are most significant for present purposes because of the contrast they provide with official policy toward witchcraft in England and New England.

The distinctive political accomplishment of the *Malleus* was to extend the application of inquisitorial procedures with regard to heresy to the discovery and prosecution of witchcraft. The problem of witchcraft continued to be understood in secular as well as in theological terms. Indeed, a broad variety of catastrophes—ranging in scope from male impotency to the raising of hurricanes—were attributed to acts of witchcraft. But the *Malleus* proposed that this unrestrained evil be confronted not at the point of its worldly manifestations but rather at its roots in the willing complicity of men and, more often, of women with the subversive design of the devil. In this manner, secular and ecclesiastical concerns were synthesized in the social regulation of witchcraft.[17]

The defining characteristic of the inquisitorial method was its incorporation of accuser, prosecutor, judge, and defense into one official body, thus guaranteeing consensus through each phase of the criminal process.[18] The *Malleus*'s provision of legal defense for the accused in no way altered this monolithic structure since the advocate was cautioned that "if he unduly defends a person already suspect of heresy, he makes himself as it were a patron of that heresy."[19] Under these conditions, the accused witch entered into the inquisitorial process with virtually no legal safeguards.

Although the inquisitorial approach demanded the rigorous proof of confession before sentence was pronounced, the total absence of judicial restraint made the fulfillment of this standard unproblematic. Given the enormity of the offense of witchcraft, judges were encouraged to use torture to elicit confessions, and if the suspect was nonetheless reluctant because of fear of death, the inquisitor was advised to use guile and deceit by falsely promising mercy.[20] Once accused, the suspect was never fully exonerated, not even on the rare occasions in which evidence was insufficient for conviction. At a later date, the trial could be resumed.[21]

Additional structural features helped insure a continuous supply of accusations and denunciations. No restrictions were placed upon the source of accusations; all persons, no matter how demonstrably unreliable, and no matter how personally biased against the accused, were regarded as legitimate informants.[22] Especially valued was the testimony of the convicted witch on the activities of confederates, which thus promoted the expansion of prosecutions.

Overriding these procedures was the power of the state to confiscate the property of the accused witch—whether convicted or not.[23] The immediate effect of this prerogative was to greatly increase the liability of the wealthier classes to formal accusations. Of more lasting importance, the opportunity for financial gain endowed the activities of the witchfinders with a businesslike aggressiveness. The most prestigious inquisitors were also the most productive.

The program of action recommended by the *Malleus* continued to be operative on the Continent—particularly in France and Germany—until well into the seventeenth century, although the authority for prosecution was for the most part assumed by secular courts.[24] The faithful translation of these policies into appropriate legal machinery had several major consequences regarding the discovery of witchcraft. First, though evidence of malefic practice continued in theory to constitute the principal form of incriminating testimony, such considerations were minimized by the effective use of torture to obtain confessions. Second, the use of extreme judicial measures made prosecution virtually coincident with conviction. A recent detailed investigation of witchcraft prosecutions in southwestern Germany reports an acquittal rate of 7.35 percent in one of the more extended campaigns against the offense.[25] Similar proportions are reported by Robert Mandrou for witchcraft prosecutions in sixteenth-century France, and slightly lower proportions are given by E. William Monter for French Switzerland during the same period.[26]

PUBLIC POLICY TOWARD WITCHCRAFT
IN ENGLAND AND NEW ENGLAND

The first English translation of the *Malleus* did not appear until the comparatively late date of 1584.[27] The same date is also significant in the history of English witchcraft as the year of publication of Reginald Scot's *Discoverie of Witchcraft*. Taken together, these two literary events help illuminate the pattern of dissemination of Continental beliefs to England. The fact that an English edition of the *Malleus* was not available until well after its policies had been institutionalized in France and Germany well reflects the English insulation from mainstream Continental beliefs. It is equally significant, however, that the first major work on witchcraft during the reign of Elizabeth constituted a devastating critique of the *Malleus* in terms of both its assumptions and its conclusions.[28]

The importance of Scot's treatise consists less in its immediate impact on English public opinion than in the fact that the literary offensive in England was initiated by an opponent rather than an advocate of Continental beliefs. King James I vehemently criticized the work for its alleged skepticism in his *Daemonologie* of 1597, and later publicists would strongly object to Scot's equivocation on the question of whether or not spirits could assume material form.[29] But it is quite possibly the case that Scot's work gained its partisans among English contemporaries not so much for its exemplary scholarship or reasoned skepticism as for its nationalist rejection of foreign ideas.

The divergence between English and Continental policy is most clearly reflected in the actual terms in which the crime was defined. The earliest English statute specifically concerned with witchcraft was enacted in 1542, and it is clear from the phrasing of its provisions that the legal emphasis was upon maleficium.[30] The felony of witchcraft made it punishable by death to use invocation, conjuration, or sorcery to find money or to waste, consume, or destroy any person "in his body, membres, or goodes" or to provoke anyone to unlawful love or for any other unlawful intent or purpose.

After the statute was repealed in 1547, the legal machinery for action against witchcraft appears to have reverted to ecclesiastical control until the acceptance of a more severe statute enacted in 1563.[31] The most significant modification in this act broadened the felony of witchcraft to include consultation with or invocation of evil spirits with or without maleficium—an apparent shift toward Continental understandings. It is also noteworthy that a distinction was made between maleficium resulting in death and maleficium resulting in injury or loss of property, with the lesser penalty of one year's imprisonment imposed for the latter offense.

A final statute issued under King James I in 1604 gave further weight to Continental definitions in addition to increasing the penalties imposed for maleficium. The prohibitions against communion with evil spirits were more clearly specified to include those who would "consult, covenant with entertaine employ feede or rewarde any evil and wicked spirit to or for any intent or purpose."[32] The phrasing of this act represents the closest point of accommodation between English and Continental legislation.

The New England statutes of Massachusetts Bay and Connecticut—issued in 1641 and 1642, respectively—are less informative about both the scope of the crime and the terms of its definition.[33] The enactments would appear to stress heresy in view of their Old Testament derivation: "If any man or woman be a witch (that is hath or consulteth with a familiar spirit) They shall be put to death." However, since the colonists relied on Mosaic law to justify and to express all capital offenses, the statute would necessarily have conformed to the biblical language regardless of its intended emphasis.[34] The absence of specific direction regarding the grading of penalties merely reflects a general lack of elaboration in early colonial legislation.[35] The eventual revocation of the Massachusetts charter in 1684 compelled the colonists to rely on English law, and several of the criminal indictments of the Salem trials of 1692 specifically refer to the statute of James I.[36]

Nevertheless, despite ambiguities in the formal definition of the offense, it is clear from examination of the actual indictments that the prosecution of witchcraft in England and New England almost invariably had a secular basis. Alan Macfarlane's recent study of witchcraft prosecutions in the county of Essex, England, confirms C. L'Estrange Ewen's earlier conclusion that the overwhelming majority of indictments in sixteenth- and seventeenth-century England were issued for acts of maleficium rather than for errors in belief. Between 1560 and 1680, all but 11 of the 503 indictments issued in Essex included maleficium as part of the offense.[37] An equally pronounced stress upon the harmful nature of witchcraft is apparent from examination of the formal complaints and indictments leading to extended legal action in Massachusetts. Only 7 of 183 such actions include no reference to maleficium.

This emphasis upon the harmful rather than the heretical aspects of witchcraft was bound up with the use of adversary rather than inquisitorial techniques for the discovery of witchcraft.[38] Whereas inquisitorial methods were based on the presumption of guilt, the adversary system was based on the presumption of innocence. In England and New England, the accuser or victim entered the court as a private party whose interests were distinct from the official concerns of prosecution. The right to trial by a jury of peers further divided the spheres of legal authority. Even without the presence of a defense lawyer,[39] it is clear that, within these altered structural relations, disagreements among judge, jury, and complainant were a real possibility.

The use of an adversary system made it unlikely that complaints of malefic practice would be amplified into confessions of heresy. Most significantly, laws prohibiting the use of torture to elicit convictive testimony made the proof of witchcraft far more problematic in England and New England than on the Continent.[40] While these laws were not always strictly enforced, they were nonetheless accepted as norms for ideal judicial conduct. As one prominent minister in Massachusetts expressed it, torture was "an un-English method."[41]

The most conspicuous effect of these legal safeguards was to greatly decrease the likelihood of conviction in witchcraft prosecutions. For the home circuit in England from 1560 to 1700, Ewen indicates that 81 percent of persons indicted for witchcraft escaped execution.[42] For Essex, the area of most intensive prosecution within the home circuit, Macfarlane found that only 48 percent of persons accused of witchcraft were convicted of the crime.[43] And, of sixty-three legal actions entered against witchcraft in Massachusetts and Connecticut prior to the Salem trials, only eighteen, or 28 percent, resulted in convictions. The outcome of the Salem prosecutions presents a more complex distribution, which will be discussed later in the investigation.

Thus the Continental synthesis of secular and theological responses to the problem of witchcraft was never achieved in the Anglo-American constitution of the crime. The elements for such a synthesis were present in the secular concern with malefic practice and in a theological concern with sin and apostasy, the foundations of which will be explored in the following chapter. But the assimilation of magic and sorcery into the theology of witchcraft was impeded both by a formidable intellectual opposition to the earliest manifestations of Continental scholasticism and by a legal system that embodied, at least in rudimentary form, the principles of adversary procedure. This failure to integrate the two components both within the theory of witchcraft and within public policy toward witchcraft will be demonstrated to be of crucial importance in the construction of the crime in seventeenth-century Massachusetts.

LEGAL ACTIONS AGAINST WITCHCRAFT
IN MASSACHUSETTS BAY

The form of legal actions.   Despite several institutional changes in the organization of criminal justice, formal litigation against witchcraft proceeded according to a standard sequence throughout the seventeenth century in Massachusetts Bay. In the first phase of legal action, the plaintiff(s) filed a deposition against the putative witch with one of several inferior courts. This court of first recourse usually consisted of one of the inferior quarterly courts, most often referred to as county courts because they were apportioned one for each county. Each county court was to be comprised of five magistrates, although three were sufficient for a quorum.[44] In the frontier areas of western

Massachusetts, equivalent judicial duties were performed by commissioners' courts or by single magistrates.

The original jurisdiction of these courts was limited to "all civill causes, whereof the debt or damage shall not exceede 10 pounds, and all criminall causes, not concerneing life, member, or banishment."[45] In cases of witchcraft, the function of the lower court was merely to decide whether or not the evidence presented against the witch constituted grounds for capital prosecution. If the decision were affirmative, the case was then referred to a higher court for final judgment.

A well-documented case in 1674 will help to illustrate the above sequence of litigation.[46] The accused witch, Mary Parsons, a married woman, voluntarily presented herself before the Hampshire County Court at Springfield on September 29, 1674, to clear herself of mounting village suspicions of witchcraft. At this session, the husband and the father of a recently deceased woman charged Mary with bewitching the woman to death or, in the veiled language of the document, with murder "by means of some evil instrument." The court was adjourned until November 18, 1674, when it was then readjourned until January 5, 1675,[47] for undisclosed reasons.

On this occasion, the original witnesses against Mary resubmitted their testimony, and new testimony was introduced from other sources. The court also appointed a jury of "soberdized Chast" women to search the suspect for witch's marks.[48] In the light of their findings, together with the preceding testimony, the court set bail at fifty pounds and ordered Mary to appear before the Court of Assistants—a superior court with competence to rule on capital offenses. The one exceptional feature of this case is that Mary's wealthy husband was able to meet bail requirements.

The grand jury of the Court of Assistants, meeting on March 2, 1675, issued an indictment, and Mary was placed in jail without bail until the next session. On May 13, the court reconvened and rendered a verdict of not guilty. Approximately eight months had transpired between the initial appearance of the accused in court and the final verdict.

In purely formal terms, legal action against witchcraft in Massachusetts can not be distinguished from legal action against other capital offenses. The same sequence could be charted for the offenses of murder, rape, or piracy as for witchcraft. Only in the informal spheres of judicial conduct—in the methods of discovery, arrest, and detection and the weighing of evidence—was the special character of the crime perforce acknowledged as, for example, in the flight of a sheriff before the sudden transformation of a suspect into a phantom beast or in the placing of leg fetters on an octogenarian invalid or in the clinical inspection of bodies for the presence of irregular markings and blemishes.

Temporal and geographic distribution of legal actions. Depending on whether one accepts the interpretative frameworks of Kittredge or of Burr, two different expectations arise with respect to the temporal and geographic distribution of witchcraft prosecutions in Massachusetts. For Kittredge, the colonial response to witchcraft was fundamentally a product of the transplantation of European beliefs in folk magic to the North American frontier.[49] For Burr, on the other hand, witchcraft prosecutions in Massachusetts were inextricably linked to the unique theological imperatives of a Puritan state.[50] The two perspectives correspond to different versions of the legal history of the crime.

In the Kittredge thesis, it is argued that witchcraft was essentially a contained phenomenon, that its locus was the community rather than the state, and that its prosecution was routine, infrequent, and unspectacular. From this vantage point, there is a continuity between the pre-Salem and the Salem litigations that overrides differences in scale and intensity. If the pre-Salem cases expressed the sporadic surfacing of endemic village strains, the Salem cases were merely an amplification of the same sorts of tensions to the point of collective hysteria. The apparent aberration of Salem is in fact only a variation on a theme. In this version, colonial witchcraft prosecutions form a unity of belief and action, and their common point of departure is the locality, with its attendant emphasis on malefic magic.

In the Burr thesis, it is the Salem trials rather than their precursors that are given primary emphasis. Here it is asserted that the colonial response to witchcraft was defined by zealous and unrestrained pursuit of malefactors, that the parameters of prosecution were regional rather than local, and that the pattern of legal action forms an index, however crude, of degrees of religious fanaticism. In this rendering, the roots of legal action are sought in the intersections of church and state and in the general social and political conditions of the New England settlement.

An examination of the actual temporal and geographic distribution of legal actions shows that each of the frameworks is at best only partially successful in accounting for the colonial pattern of prosecution. By using table 1, it is possible to broadly distinguish three periods of legal action according to variations in the volume and intensity of prosecution. In the first period, from 1630 to 1639, there is no indica-

Table 1 Temporal Distribution of Legal Actions against Witchcraft in Massachusetts

Dates	Presentments	Number of persons indicted[a]	Convictions	Executions
1630–39	0	0	0	0
1640–49	3	3	2	1
1650–59	12 (2)	10 (1)	4	3
1660–69	5	2	0	0
1670–79	7 (1)	4	0	0
1680–91[b]	10 (10)	5	1	1
1692–93	141 (7)	58	29	19[c]
Total population of known legal actions	178	82	36	24
Residual cases	20	1	...	...
Estimate of true population	198	83	36	24

Note: Figures in parentheses refer to residual cases of witchcraft in which there is evidence of legal action but no identification of accused persons or in which there is identification of accused persons but no clear indication of whether accusation was formal or informal. See App. A for sources in pre-Salem legal actions.
[a] Calculation in terms of number of indictments would yield a higher figure because occasionally several indictments were issued for the same crime.
[b] In the years 1690–91, court records indicate only one legal action, a presentment issued in 1691.
[c] Three other deaths related directly to proceedings: two women died in prison; one man was pressed to death for refusing to place himself on trial.

tion of any formal action against the crime. The second period, from 1640 to 1691, is characterized by a low volume and a low intensity of prosecution. Only seven out of thirty-seven presentments resulted in convictions. Finally, the Salem trials of 1692–93 represent a considerable increase in the volume of prosecution, although the proportion of presentments that resulted in convictions and executions is only slightly higher than that for the second period.

The low frequency of pre-Salem cases per decade conforms to the description set forth by Kittredge, whereas the higher density of prosecutions in 1692 more closely corresponds to Burr's version of the colonial pattern. Nevertheless, it can hardly be argued that the prosecution of witchcraft was unrestrained for either period of legal action.

Through the five decades of prosecution, each phase of the legal process was to some degree independent of the other phases. Presentments did not necessarily result in indictments, nor did indictments invariably produce convictions. Even the progress from conviction to execution was not automatic, although death by hanging was prescribed in colonial law as the penalty for all capital offenses.

Information on geographic distribution similarly fails to yield unequivocal support for either of the two perspectives. By grouping the villages and townships in which legal actions against witchcraft occurred according to their respective counties, it may be shown that witchcraft cases were concentrated in specific geographic centers. Among the pre-Salem cases, the northeastern counties of Essex and Norfolk, which were seated in Salem and Hampton, respectively, together with the frontier county of Hampshire, seated in Springfield, accounted for approximately two-thirds of the known legal initiatives against witchcraft.[51] Even at the most generous estimate, the combined population for these counties could not have exceeded one-third of the total population of the colony for any period during the seventeenth century.[52] The Salem trials reveal an even greater geographic concentration. At least 135 of the 150 recorded legal actions were initiated in Essex County. The remainder of the witchcraft cases for both pre-Salem and Salem litigations originated in the counties of Suffolk and Middlesex, seated in Boston and Cambridge, respectively.[53]

Yet the fact of regional concentration in the total distribution of legal actions does not necessarily imply that individual legal actions were interrelated. The patterns of geographic dispersion differed considerably between the pre-Salem and the Salem prosecutions. In the pre-Salem period, the pattern conforms to what would be anticipated from Kittredge's description of New England witchcraft. Within each decade of legal action from 1640 to 1691, individual cases were scattered over nonneighboring communities. Given this form of geographic spread, it seems reasonable to assume that initiatives for legal action during this period resulted from the independent operation of social processes within the respective localities.

On the other hand, the pattern of dispersion for the Salem trials indicates a clear interconnection between individual legal actions. Virtually all legal actions were concentrated in Essex County. It is also clear that the sequence of legal action between communities was related to factors of geographic proximity. By using table 2, it is possible to describe this geographic flow with some degree of precision. The earliest legal initiatives originated in February and March in Salem Vil-

Table 2 Distribution of Legal Initiatives for Salem Trials by Months by Adjacent Towns

Clusters of Adjacent Towns	Feb.–Mar.	Apr.–May	June–July	Aug.–Sept.	Oct.–Nov.
Salem Village, Salem Town, Beverly, Lynn, Topsfield	6	36	3	1	0
Andover, Rowley, Haverhill		2	9	38	0
Gloucester			1	3	3

Note: Table includes only those towns in which four or more legal actions were initiated.

lage, a partially autonomous section of Salem Township. From there, the accusations spread in April and May to the immediately adjacent communities of Salem Town, Beverly, and Topsfield. In June and July, there were fewer new indictments, in part because the magistrates who had conducted the pretrial hearings were now presiding over the first series of trials. When the court resumed its earlier activity, the new locus of witchcraft accusations was Andover. In August and September legal initiatives extended eastward from Andover to the neighboring towns of Rowley and Haverhill. The final points of activity were the next major communities in this eastward direction, Gloucester and Manchester. These actions occurred from late September to early November.

The descriptive models of Kittredge and Burr are logically consistent if equally one-sided. Where Kittredge has stressed the element of magic in witchcraft belief, Burr has emphasized its theological component. Likewise, whereas Kittredge discovers the locus of activity against witchcraft in the community, Burr traces the initiative to the state.

Yet it is clear that neither framework does full justice to the colonial pattern of legal action. The units of analysis that are applicable to either the pre-Salem or the Salem trials are not applicable to both. In the pre-Salem cases, witchcraft was essentially a community-centered crime in which legal actions were directed against particular individuals. In the Salem trials, legal actions extended between communities and were directed against groups.

Taken together, however, the two frameworks yield the analytic coordinates within which this apparently idiosyncratic pattern of prosecution may be rendered comprehensible. In the remainder of this investigation, it is shown that the curious policy of containment and expansion in the colonial response to the crime was rooted in the conflicting directives of community and state and in the irreconcilable differences between magical beliefs and theological doctrine.

The Social Meaning of Witchcraft in
17th Century Massachusetts Bay

3

Witchcraft and Puritan Beliefs

T HE ROLE OF the New England clergy in the formation of attitudes and policy toward witchcraft has been much discussed in early American historiography, although most frequently in the context of partisan debate. Thus writers unsympathetic to the body of ideas developed within Puritan theology or suspicious of the political power wielded by the Puritan ministers have found in the sermon literature on witchcraft a useful vehicle with which to express their condemnation.[1] Conversely, there has been a tendency among historians who find Puritan thought at least in part congenial either to minimize the importance of theological contributions to witchcraft belief in New England or to portray the clergy as a moderating rather than an aggravating influence upon witchcraft prosecutions.[2] Such discussions, whether in behalf or in criticism of the clergy, have invariably focused upon ecclesiastical participation in the Salem trials.

Yet the historical observer who seeks to situate the theology of witchcraft within the larger body of Puritan beliefs enters a surprisingly unexplored domain of inquiry—and perhaps for ample reason. For, apart from several treatises produced during the latter part of the seventeenth century, the New England clergy are more notable for their absence than their prominence in the contemporary literature on witchcraft. Indeed, their output on this subject was meager even in comparison with that of fellow Puritan divines in England.

Given this literary void, the several sermons and narratives that did in fact deal directly with witchcraft appear all the more conspicuous, and it is easy to exaggerate their importance both with respect to Puritan theology and with respect to the life histories of their authors. The contributions of Increase Mather (1639–1723) and, more particularly, his son Cotton Mather (1663–1728) have thus frequently been credited with defining the ecclesiastical response to witchcraft in New England, and the Mathers themselves have been portrayed as excessively preoccupied with the subject.[3] If the names of these ministers have become closely associated with their works on witchcraft, it is not because of the emphasis they gave to this subject in their own life-times. Although Increase maintained a genuine interest in supernatural occurrences throughout his life, witchcraft received little considera-tion in his writings on these events. Similarly, Cotton's involvement with witchcraft constituted but one episode in a remarkably eventful public career, and his two extended treatises on the subject comprised only a negligible proportion of his total published works.[4]

Accordingly, despite the frequent discussion of witchcraft by suc-ceeding generations of American historians, one might well agree with Perry Miller's assessment of the bearing of the Salem trials and of witchcraft belief in general on the major social events of colonial New England: "the intellectual history of New England up to 1720 can be written as though no such thing ever happened. It had no effect on the ecclesiastical or political situation, it does not figure in the institu-tional or ideological development."[5] And, in the histories produced by the Puritan leaders themselves, from John Winthrop's *Journal* cover-ing the period from 1630 to 1649 through William Hubbard's *General History of New England* published in 1680, the occurrences of witchcraft are given only passing reference.[6] It is a fact with which the researcher must come to terms that the clergy and other intellec-tuals of seventeenth-century New England were more apt to disattend than to emphasize witchcraft as a part of their ecclesiastical history.

If Puritan theology can be adequately interpreted without refer-ence to witchcraft, it remains the case that witchcraft in Massachu-setts cannot be understood outside the context of Puritan theology. It is necessary to appreciate, however, that witchcraft was not of pivotal importance to Puritan dogma but was rather itself a derivative from more crucial assumptions about God, nature, and humanity. Thus it is with these core assumptions rather than with witchcraft that the student must begin if he is to locate his subject matter within Puritan thought.

In the following sections, an attempt is made to show how and in what terms the category of witchcraft was incorporated within the mainstream of Puritan ideas. One of the tasks of such an examination is to demonstrate that the ministers who wrote on the subject, however idiosyncratic their personal style, sought to interpret witchcraft within the confines of established Puritan doctrine and that they were for the most part successful in this undertaking. Another equally important task is to show that, even in the hands of skillful interlocutors, witch-craft fit but uncomfortably within this body of thought.

WITCHCRAFT AND DIVINITY

For Puritan ministers, as for contemporary Christian theologians in general, belief in witchcraft was anchored upon belief in Satan. It is by examining their writings on the relationship between God and Satan that the theological doctrine of witchcraft and its implications for Puritan piety may be most clearly explicated.

As realized in the numerous sermons on the subject, Satan was the formidable and ubiquitous opponent of God. The Reverend Deodat Lawson well summarizes the orthodox formulation of his manifold roles: "Satan is the Adversary and Enemy. He is the Original, the Fountain of Malice, the Instigator of all Contrariety, Malignity, and Enmity."[7] Indeed, as conceived by the clergy, the range of Satan's destructive powers was enormous. He was at least a party to if not the prime mover in all sins of commission and omission against God; he was capable of leading men to despair and suicide and of causing violent pain and sickness.[8] Not the least of his extraordinary powers was his ability to produce natural wonders such as thunder and lightning.[9] In sevententh-century Massachusetts, it was no mere stylistic mannerism to mention the devil as codefendant in virtually all criminal indictments and not just in crimes of witchcraft.

In all his varied activities, whether as tempter or destroyer, Satan enjoyed considerable advantage over his victims. It was not unusual for Puritan ministers to expound at length on the vulnerability of individuals when faced with such an adversary. As Increase Mather explained, any angel, whether of God or fallen from God, as the devil, could "destroy all the men upon the face of the Whole Earth, in a very little time."[10] But, even without this power over nature, Satan had a hold on all humanity by virtue of its fall from grace. According to Samuel Willard, all persons were in their spiritual estate the children of Satan, although in their natural estate they were the children of God.[11] And even though an individual might come to accept God as a regenerate Christian, Satan never fully relinquished his control over the inner workings of human nature. Thus the ministers described the desperate battle Christians must wage in order to defend their souls against a superior foe.

However formidable the worldly activities of Satan, the New England clergy nevertheless firmly adhered to the doctrine that his movements were effectively limited and contained by the infinite and unlimited power of God. As Willard asserted after recounting the awesome powers of the devil, "God is the Supream Governour over the whole World; and though the Devils are risen up in rebellion against him, yet he holds them in his hands, curbs in their rage, and lets it out as and when he pleaseth."[12] More briefly, Lawson wrote of Satan's dependence: "he is absolutely Bounded and Limited by the Power and Pleasure of the Great and Everlasting God."[13] Accordingly, Satan acted not as an independent being in his assaults on humanity but rather by the liberty granted to him by God.

That God should permit such evil in the world was an obvious paradox that by no means escaped the attention of the New England clergy. It is in the curiously ambivalent resolution to this paradox that a fundamental tension arose between Puritan doctrine and Puritan piety, and it is this tension that permeated the theological response to witchcraft. Within the framework of Puritan doctrine, the resolution was really quite simple. Lawson's sermon may again be quoted for the orthodox formulation: "The Sovereign Power of the Great God to rebuke Satan, appears, In that he doth Manage, all his Motions and Operations, to serve his own most Holy Ends, and to advance his own Glory in the winding up."[14] Thus, if God gave leave to Satan to tempt the believing Christian, it was in order that his faith be tested and thereby strengthened. Similarly, God might use Satan as one of his many instruments to punish the disbeliever or to warn the believer to further exert himself. But whether Satan appeared in his characteristic role of tempter or, more directly from God, in the role of destroyer, God's purpose in permitting these worldly manifestations was in some manner to promote the spiritual welfare of humanity.

The more complete and unambiguous the doctrinal resolution to the paradox, however, the less adequate were its implications for Puritan piety, for if God's triumph over his adversary were an absolute certainty and the terms of his victory easily understood, then the believing Christian might have grounds for complacency in aligning himself with the forces of righteousness. If God intended greater piety from his people by granting Satan his freedom, then it might be assumed that the believer could exact protection from God by means of his spiritual exertions.

Nothing could be more antithetical to the form of piety that the Puritan ministers sought to engender among their followers. Far from taking comfort in the triumph of good over evil, the believer was enjoined never to relax in his own struggle to defeat Satan within himself. That God had a design in permitting this struggle must be accepted on doctrinal grounds, but the minister preferred to remain as vague as doctrine would allow in divulging the specific purpose of this design. Granted that God intended greater piety from the believer; it did not thereby follow that his spiritual improvement would once and for all defeat Satan. Nor did it follow that God's ultimate goals were realized. The minister would demand of the believer that, if through fear of Satan he might reach out to God, he must continue to reach out even if his peril were unabated.

Thus one notes a tendency in the Puritan literature on Satan toward a perfunctory acknowledgment of his specific part in the divine plan. Hence Willard could remark cryptically of Satan's activities in the world, "God hath some glorious design in it, else it should not be," whereas elsewhere he would write, "Let us expect that Satan will fall upon us again, and therefore take heed of growing secure."[15] And Cotton Mather, who embodied this tension between doctrine and piety as fully as any Puritan minister, would eventually be charged with having conceived of Satan as an independent being.[16] If, for the sake of doctrine, it were necessary to reject the idea of Satan's autonomy, as in fact Mather and other ministers were able to do in good faith, yet, for the sake of piety, it was important that the limits of this autonomy remain obscure and that the believer, even while accepting the fact of God's supremacy, never underestimate the power of Satan both in himself and in the world.

Now the doctrine of witchcraft and the implication of this doctrine for piety were almost a precise derivation from the theological rendering of Satan. As the most conspicuous manifestation of Satan's presence, witchcraft was both a proof of Satan's existence and a demonstration of his substantial powers. At the same time, witchcraft was possible only through God's allowance. The highly articulate Englishman William Perkins met these doctrinal requirements with perhaps the most adequate definition offered by a Puritan divine: "Witchcraft is a wicked Arte, serving for the working of wonders, by the assistance of the Devil, so farre forth as God shall in justice permit."[17] And although Cotton Mather omitted reference to divine intervention in one of his own formulations—"Witchcraft is the doing of strange (and for the most part ill) things by the helpe of evil Spirits, covenanting with (and usually representing of) the woeful Children of Men"[18]—he too later conceded in the course of a heated debate with his Boston critic, the merchant Robert Calef, "If any man will ask mee too Grant, that the Divels are in all the Efforts of their Power and Malice, limited to the God of Heaven, I do most readily grant it, and give thanks to God for it."[19]

When, however, the ministers moved from doctrine to piety, as in their writings on Satan, the emphasis shifted from the ultimate accountability of the witch to God to human vulnerability to witchcraft even though one might seek comfort from God. Indeed, Mather observed that the ravages of witchcraft spared no one, not even the most pious individual.

Consider the Multitudes of them, whom Witchcraft hath sometimes given trouble to. Persons of all sorts have been racked and ruined by it; and not a few of them neither. . . . Persons of great Honor have sometimes been cruelly bewitched. What lately befell a worthy Knight in Scotland is well known unto the world. Persons of Great Virtue too have been bewitched even unto their Graves. But four years are passed since a holy Man was killed in this doleful way, after the Joy as well as the Grace of God had been wonderfully filling of him.[20]

The holy man to whom Mather referred in this sermon of 1689 was Philip Smith, a prominent magistrate and member of the highest court in Massachusetts and a one-time deacon of the church in Hadley. The strange circumstances of Smith's death in 1685 following his quarrel with a reputed witch had been thoroughly investigated by a coroner's jury.[21] In view of the medical and judicial publicity that attended this case, Mather could hardly have chosen a better example with which to instruct his audience.

This is not to suggest, however, that the New England clergy offered their followers a despairing faith. The defense against witchcraft, as against all instruments of Satan, was spiritual reformation, both individual and collective. Thus Lawson recommended prayer as a solution to the problem of witchcraft:

Let us use this Weapon [prayer]; It hath a kind of Omnipotency, because it interests us, in the help of the Omnipotent: Satan, the worst of all our Enemies called in Scripture a DRAGON, to note his Malice; a SERPENT, to note his Subtlety, a LYON, to note his Strength. But none of all these can stand before prayer.[22]

Characteristically, Mather's counsel was more impassioned: "Let us pray much, and we need fear nothing. Particularly, Let Ejaculatory Prayers be almost continually in our minds, and so we shall never lie open to the fiery darts of the wicked one."[23] With these efforts at greater piety, the believer would have the promise, if not the certainty, of divine protection against witchcraft.

But if it were not a despairing faith, it was nonetheless demanding. The minister would offer the victim of witchcraft no easy solution to his distress and no guarantee of remedial action. God might listen to the prayers of his people, and a saving reply could be cautiously anticipated. But that he might not listen was always a possibility, and that he need not listen was to be accepted as a divine prerogative.

Thus the Puritan ministers in their sermons on witchcraft and on Satan sought to achieve a delicate balance of piety that moved the believer beyond complacency to a point close to but short of despair, a balance that was barely contained within their doctrinal framework. That this balance would prove too difficult to maintain for a people suffering the immediate effects of witchcraft will become clear in later discussion.

WITCHCRAFT AND NATURE

That witchcraft and witches existed as real occurrences was as thoroughly uncontroversial an assertion to the colonial of New England as it was to his contemporaries in western Europe. The proof consisted merely of pointing to the relevant biblical texts. How witchcraft occurred—whether in conformity with or in contravention of the laws of nature—was another matter altogether. Although the Bible, particularly the Old Testament, contained frequent and explicit reference to witchcraft, nowhere did it specify the manner of its operation. The problem of filling this void would challenge the skills of some of the ablest minds of post-Reformation Europe and America. Only in the framework of their general conception of the relationship between God and nature is it possible to appreciate the Puritans' concern with this problem, for it was in behalf of this conception that the reconciliation of witchcraft with nature would be undertaken.

In Puritan cosmology, all events in nature were believed to result from the intervention of a ubiquitous divine presence.[24] The regularities and patterns revealed in nature arose not from any inner necessity but rather from the ever-present enactment of God. Each instant of nature represented an act of divine will, and it lay within the power of God to alter or to bring to a halt the course of natural events at his pleasure.

Such a view of providence imbued the natural order with an ethical rather than a mechanical imperative. By means of nature, God communicated to humanity the purpose of his cosmic design. Sometimes, when he punished misdeeds or rewarded exemplary piety, his purpose was unmistakable. The eventual violent demise of Anne Hutchinson at the hands of Indians was an obvious judgment against her apostasy in the explosive Antinomian Controversy; and that one of her followers, Mary Dyer, should bear a hideously deformed child was simply an extension of that judgment.[25] At other times, God's intentions were less apparent as, for example, when he chose to take the life of a young child or visit suffering upon a devout believer. Thus, on the occasion of the impending death of his daughter, the Reverend Michael Wigglesworth could resolve in his diary to trust these intentions, however obscure: "And shall he not do with his own as he will, either to afflict it or take it to himself. His glory is better than the eas of the creature, and yet his glory shall be coincident with our good."[26] Whether in misfortune or deliverance, the natural order was perceived as the vehicle through which transcendent ethical realities were given tangible form.

Yet the Puritans united to this conception of a personal and arbitrary deity an unshakable belief that nature constituted a rational order. The reconciliation between these ideas required the utmost ingenuity in Scholastic reasoning. The central premise in the reconciliation consisted of positing that God voluntarily confined himself to work within the boundaries of the very same laws of nature that he had created. Thus, while God ruled the universe according to an arbitrary cosmic design, he nonetheless conveyed his design through the orderly and predictable sequences of nature.

The paradoxes latent in this position are ably expressed by Perry Miller: "Puritan thought . . . presupposed a natural framework in which arbitrary power was confined within inviolable order, yet in which the order was so marvelously contrived that all divinely avowed ends were swiftly accomplished."[27] The Puritans would endow the universe with the moral stamp of a willful and arbitrary ruler, and yet they would observe the consequences of this governance in the orderly and predictable arrangement of natural processes. Although they would attribute to this rule a direct personal involvement in human affairs, they would discover this involvement not in the working of divine miracles but in the ordinary laws of cause and effect.

This thesis, which maintained so careful a balance between God's control over nature and God's willing confinement within the limits of nature, formed one of the central lines of continuity in orthodox Puritan thought throughout the seventeenth century. In the shift in Puritan writings from emphasis upon one of these premises in the early decades to emphasis upon the other in the later decades, it is possible to discern the profound changes in intellectual climate that characterized the period.

To the earlier Puritan divines who wrote in England just prior to the New England migration, the primary danger to the scheme lay in a prevailing tendency to overestimate the violability of nature. The tradition of esoteric magic had gained a measure of intellectual respectability largely through the efforts of such hermeticists as Paracelsus and Ficino.[28] Accompanying this resurgent interest in speculative magic was the growing responsiveness of contemporaries to astrological prophecy, healing remedies derived from magical beliefs, and other occult practices.[29] Under these conditions, the response of the Puritan clergy was to stress the reasonableness of God and the immutability of the natural order. Thus John Preston, among the most influential of the Puritan ministers, flatly observed in 1629 that "God alters no Law of nature."[30] And William Ames, one of the leading Puritan theoreticians, argued that the power of God is better demonstrated in his control of natural processes than in his interruption of these processes.[31]

In the latter part of the seventeenth century, the strategy of disputation underwent a major shift to meet the now more pressing challenge of mechanical philosophy. As exemplified by such luminaries as Thomas Hobbes, the implications for Puritan cosmology were obvious. Nature was likened to a self-regulating mechanism that proceeded without reference to a first cause. That God created the universe was of course easily conceded by the proponents of this viewpoint, but the additional conclusion that God was now a passive spectator to his own creation clashed directly with the Puritan concept of a concerned and active deity.

It was partly in response to this challenge that the New England clergy came to give greater attention to events in which it was believed that God had revealed his presence directly before humanity. Although the recording of such events had been carried on informally since the inception of the colony,[32] the first attempt at systematization can be traced to a general meeting of prominent ministers on May 12, 1681. On this occasion, several proposals "concerning the Recording of Illustrious Providences" were submitted for general approval. Included among these proposals was this recommendation: "In order to the promoving of a design of this nature, so as shall be indeed for Gods glory, it is necessary that utmost care shall be taken that all and only Remarkable Providence be recorded and published."[33] Increase Mather's *Essay for the Recording of Illustrious Providences* of 1684 was one of the outcomes of this joint venture.

The specific types of events classified as special providences were given in another of the recommendations:

Such Divine judgments, tempests, floods, earthquakes, thunders, as are unusual, strange apparitions, or whatever else shall happen that is prodigious, witchcrafts, diabolical possessions, remarkable judgments upon noted sinners, eminent deliverances, and answers of prayer, are to be reckoned among illustrious providences.[34]

The unifying feature of such occurrences was that in each case God had manifested himself more directly than he did in the ordinary course of nature. Moreover, they were distinguishable from miracles in that they were effected not in contravention of the existing laws of nature but rather by the substitution of God for the usual agent in nature.[35] In effect, then, these events constituted a residual category of anomalous occurrences that could not be explained within the contemporary framework of scientific knowledge. Their importance as justifications for Puritan cosmology was that they demonstrated the existence of a proximate God, but not in violation of his rational order.

This happy reconciliation between theology and science had the distinct disadvantage, however, of placing the burden of proof on the clergy rather than upon their philosophical opponents. Before an event could serve as a nonmiraculous evidence of divine intercession, it was necessary to demonstrate both that its occurrence was not accounted for by ordinary laws of cause and effect and that at the same time its occurrence did not violate these laws. Unfortunately, such a paradox was more easily explicated in a sermon than demonstrated in nature.

It was in the framework of this onerous task that some of the ministers would undertake to transfer the grounds for belief in witchcraft from theology to natural philosophy. From one standpoint at least, witchcraft was an event that merited this concern, for, together with diabolical possessions, witchcraft involved one of the furthermost extensions of the invisible world into the lives of men and women. In both types of occurrences, Satan either directly or mediately through the witch made an open appearance before human witnesses. Such phenomena were usually referred to as preternatural occurrences and thereby formed a subdivision within the more general category of special providences.

Yet, with the exception of Cotton Mather, the ministers were in general reluctant to effect the epistemological changes that would have been necessary to accommodate their cosmology to a plausible contemporary scientific explanation of witchcraft. Among the clergy, Mather alone permitted himself to grapple with some of the far-reaching implications of such a reconciliation of witchcraft with nature. To account for the invisible powers of the witch without violating the laws of nature required the positing of a form of nonmaterial causation. The most concerted intellectual effort in this direction had been initiated by a group of English philosophers and scientists referred to by historians as the Cambridge Platonists. One of these men, Joseph Glanvill, had produced a powerful treatise in defense of belief in witchcraft entitled *Saducismus Triumphatus*,[36] and the New England ministers almost uniformly cited this work in their own discussions of the subject.[37] For the most part, however, they borrowed Glanvill's illustrations while neglecting the intellectual system that underlay them.

Among their other concerns, the Platonists endeavored to provide theology with a firm empirical foundation by eliminating from scientific thought the materialist view of the universe that later became identified with it. Against the assertion that natural processes were merely the result of matter in motion, the men of this school argued for the primacy of spiritual agency in nature. One of the Cambridge men, Ralph Cudworth, had referred to this spiritual agency immanent in the universe as the plastic spirit.[38] It is this concept that Mather introduced in his major work on witchcraft, *Wonders of the Invisible World*, when he wrote: "Witchcraft seems to be the skill of Applying the Plastic Spirit of the World, unto some unlawful purposes, by means of a Confederacy with Evil Spirits."[39]

Two years prior to this publication, a Harvard senior had taken the affirmative position in a debate over the question of "Whether the plastic force of the world can be applied to putting through a witchcraft job,"[40] but apart from these few occasions, the neo-Platonist vocabulary did not penetrate very far into the intellectual life of New England. Thus, in his correspondence with Calef in 1695, Mather remarked in the course of justifying his belief in witchcraft, "Briefly, I have not yett altered my Opinion, that there is a Plastic Spirit permeating of the World, which very powerfully operates upon the corporeal parts of it." In reply, Calef, although a man of considerable erudition himself, noted in the margin, "A plastic spirit. What foreign word is that."[41]

The efforts of the other clergy to confront the mechanical philosophies with the evidence of the preternatural were far less ambitious in scope. Both Increase Mather and Deodat Lawson accepted the fact of worldly intercessions by Satan on scriptural authority alone. From this apriorist position, Increase cleverly used the growing respectability of science to bolster his arguments in behalf of the invisible world. If humanity could produce wonders by means of its scientific knowledge, then could not the devil easily surpass these accomplishments with his greater understanding of natural laws? Thus Mather argued in defense of Satan's power to cause thunder:

an orthodox and rational man may be of the opinion, that when the devil has before him the vapors and materials out of which thunder and lightning are generated, his act is such that he can bring them into form. If chymists can make their Aurum fulminens, what strange things may this infernal chymist effect?[42]

Likewise, with respect to Satan's ability to create special illusions, he argued that the devil "has perfect skill in Opticks, and can therefore cause that to be invisible to one, which is not so to another, and things also to appear far otherwise than they are."[43] It followed then that the supernatural powers of the witch were made possible by the transfer of these diabolic skills at the time of the satanic pact or covenant.

The attempt to rescue Puritan cosmology from mechanistic philosophy and, eventually, from Newtonian physics continued well into the eighteenth century, and among the evidences to be offered in defense of theology, witchcraft would prove to be among the least reliable. Indeed, the sudden prominence of witchcraft in the writings of the New England ministers reflected less its actual importance to Puritan thought than the precariousness of the intellectual edifice within which it was rather indifferently maintained. Ultimately, the ministers would find in earthquakes and other cataclysmic events a more durable demonstration of the divine presence.

For one brief moment, however, the Puritan clergy came perilously close to anchoring the credibility of their grand vision of divine supremacy on the manifest operations of the witch. It was this moment of intellectual legitimation—however unfinished—that coincided with the Salem trials.

WITCHCRAFT AND HUMANITY

It was in the language of spiritual conversion that the clergy formulated the subtle dynamics of human complicity in witchcraft. The morphology of transformation from person to witch was conceived in terms that roughly corresponded to the stages of an individual's progress toward true faith in God. If, for the Puritans, the distance that a person must ascend to relate to God required the utmost of human effort, the spiritual access of humanity to Satan was that of moral proximity. Indeed, the real threat posed by witchcraft was not the damage it wrought upon its victims but the temptation it offered to an easily corruptible human nature.

From this vantage point, witchcraft was merely the endpoint of a continuum of iniquity along which all men and women could be situated; or, as Cotton Mather expressed it, witchcraft was "the furthest Effort of our Original Sin."[44] Likewise, the witches themselves were

only the extreme embodiments of a fundamentally human impulse toward evil.]As the English Puritan, Richard Bernard, attested, almost in
identification with the witch, "By nature are we the children of wrath,
and bemired with the filth of sin, as well as they [the witches]."[45]
Within such a framework, it was but a small and inevitable logical
progression from the assumption that witchcraft lay well within the
scope of human possibility to its corollary that much of human predisposition lay within the periphery of witchcraft.]

In the actual making of the witch, the clergy posited two sequences:
one from the standpoint of humanity and the other from the standpoint of Satan. In the first of these sequences, the volitional element of
witchcraft received primary emphasis. Here the initial step in establishing contact with Satan consisted of moral preparation. Bernard described this stage in the following terms: "Before the Divell can come
to solicitte for witchcraft, hee findeth some preparedness in such parties, to give him hope to prevaile."[46]

The form that this preparation might take included a wide variety
of sins of commission and omission. Usually, the clergy cited the basic
repertory of human vices such as greed, anger, malice, or lust as the
most frequent predisposition to witchcraft. Though it was recognized
that these iniquities might be rooted in poverty or misfortune, the Puritans refused to excuse such impiety on grounds of extenuating circumstances. Thus, during the Salem trials, Lawson counseled even the
person who might be falsely accused of witchcraft by his neighbors
not to surrender himself to malice or envy lest "the Great Accuser
(who loves to fish in troubled waters) should take advantage upon
you."[47] Similarly, Mather's remarks on discontent reveal an equal dis-
inclination to mitigate personal responsibility for witchcraft:

When persons through discontent at their poverty, or at their misery, shall
be always murmuring, and repining at the Providence of God, the Devils
do then invite them to an Agreement with, and a Reliance on them for help.
Downright Witchcraft is the upshot of it.[48]

The fact that preparatory vices could be extended to include sins of
omission as well as acts of unwitting complicity left the category potentially unbounded. Virtually any believer who failed to fully exert
himself in reaching toward God could be viewed as a candidate for
witchcraft. Such a premise may well have been overextended in the
admonition of the Reverend Samuel Parris to his votaries in the first
month of the Salem proceedings: "examine we ourselves well, what we
are—what we Church-members are; We are either Saints or Devils—

The Scripture gives us no medium."[49] But the advice, however incendiary, forcefully conveys the sense of spiritual precariousness that informed the Puritan lecture on witchcraft.

Following the stage of preparation, the prospective witch received a promise of general assistance from Satan. This promise might be delivered in the form of either an explicit or an implicit contract. In the explicit contract, Satan or a lesser demon made an appearance before the prepared party to give a more permanent seal to their alliance. The extreme simplicity of this ritual, as conceived by the ministers, well reflected the general absence of ecclesiastical ceremony in Puritan liturgy. There is no mention either of ritual profanation such as the drinking of murdered infant's blood or of any of the elaborate staging devices so frequently found in Continental versions of the pact.

In Perkins's rendering, the meeting is described more or less in the language of a business contract:

The express and manifest compact is so termed, because it is made by solemn words on both parties. For the satisfying hereof, he [the future witch] gives to the devil for the present, either his own handwriting, or some part of his blood, as a pledge and earnest penny to bind the bargain.[50]

In their comments on the subject, Lawson and Mather do not even provide this much elaboration, and in his exchange with Calef, Mather readily dispenses with ceremony altogether:

What will it now signify the Object, That all the Scriptures thus produced, say nothing of a Covenant written and signed with the Witches Blood, and some other Formalities in Witchcraft often spoken of? Those Formalities are neither essential to an Infernal Confederacy, nor have they the Lawes of Nations which have made such Confaederacy Capital, ever mentioned them.[51]

As a result of this covenant, however conceived, the full-fledged witch at last received the benefits of Satan's promise, which, according to Bernard, could consist variously of an offer "to helpe the poore to foode, the sicke to health, the irefull to be revenged . . . or the satisfying of lust to the lecherous."[52] In addition, the witch now enjoyed the ability to perform supernatural works with the devil's assistance. While the clergy tended not to be specific about the scope of these acquired powers, it was understood that they could never exceed those of Satan himself.

This human declension from original sin to preparation for further iniquity to the solemn pledge with the devil yielded a different sequence when charted from the standpoint of Satan. From this perspective, the initial phase of participation consisted of Satan's temptation of the prospective witch. Because of his subtle understanding of the weaknesses in human nature, he was frequently able to realize his goals. As Lawson observed, "indeed his [Satan's] Angelical Activity is such as doth render him capable to Operate far beyond Human Power of Resistance."[53]

After he had successfully tempted the candidate, Satan then exacted a pledge of loyalty in return for his favors. In this pledge, the future witch fully renounced his faith in God and offered his soul to the devil. The effect of this renunciation was to place the witch at the service of Satan in his unremitting war against God and true piety.

Now it was in the relationship between these two sequences rather than in the specific morphology of each sequence that the Puritan approach to witchcraft most distinguished itself from that of other Christian theologies. The crucial question consisted not in how a person became a witch but in whether the human categories for willing witchcraft corresponded to Satan's categories for imposing witchcraft. Human understanding was regarded at best as a fallible guide to the operations of the invisible world. Moreover, as the instrument of God, Satan partook of the character of divine inscrutability.

Thus, on the one hand, the believer could be provided only with the more noticeable signs of incipient witchcraft. The problem of evil in humanity and, by implication, human susceptibility to witchcraft was not so simple or obvious that it could be uncovered by superficial detection. The affinity between reprobate humanity and Satan might be sketched in rough outline, but its fine details were discernible only through a most rigorous self-examination. As Cotton Mather warned his congregation in 1689, no person could afford to dispense with such introspection: "They that are witches now, once little dreamed of ever becoming so. Let him that stands, take heed lest he fall."[54]

On the other hand, neither was the design of Satan so obvious that the identity of the witch could be easily detected by others. Unlike the Continental theologians, the Puritans provided no social or demographic profile of the likely witch. In the sermon literature on witchcraft, only William Perkins mentioned the preference of Satan for women over men and then more as an aside than as a point of emphasis.[55] Satan was far too canny to reveal himself in familiar social stereotypes or to guarantee visible social coordinates for his invisible operations.

Such lack of equivalence between human understanding and satanic design made the problem of identification an extremely complex theological issue. If human perceptions were unreliable in ascertaining one's own spiritual condition and if the clues offered by Satan to expose the witch were apt to be obscure or misleading, then a most frightful predicament resulted. Anyone—even the most pious of believers—could suspect himself and be suspected by others of witchcraft. Yet no one—no matter how obviously malevolent—could be demonstrated to be a witch.

Ultimately, the ministers were willing to allow for the possibility of visible signs of witchcraft that derived from the act of making a covenant with the devil. The translation of these signs into judicial procedure will be taken up in chapter 7, but it may be observed here that throughout the history of the crime in Massachusetts the clergy remained hesitant, if not unwilling, to issue the stamp of infallibility to any testimony short of the actual confession of the witch. Even this evidence, however, would be doubted in the aftermath of the Salem trials.

4

Witchcraft and Magic

A T THE VILLAGE level, popular concern with witchcraft was expressed
less often as anxiety about sin or iniquity and more often as fear
of direct personal harm. Even a cursory reading of depositions makes
clear that accusers and accused alike inhabited a world in which there
was almost boundless opportunity for the translation of malevolent intentions into effective action. An abstract of the specific misfortunes
linked to a single witch in one of the earlier Massachusetts trials may
serve to illustrate the scope of these attributions:

soreness around heart, breast, and shoulders
"lamentable torment [of] a Woman in Child Bed"
cattle unable to produce milk
disappearance of a knife
"Things he sould to Others did not prosper"
being pricked with pins and daggers
bewitchment of several children to death[1]

The beliefs from which these attributions arose rested upon a generalized acceptance of the efficacy of symbolic action. In this and
other respects, the assumptive framework underlying malefic practice
in New England closely resembled its European counterpart.[2] Conventional occult techniques involving the use of image magic, proper
application of amulets and incantations, and cursing constituted only
a few of the methods by which supernatural forces were believed to
be mediated.[3] More frequently, however, in seventeenth-century Massachusetts, the witch was believed to operate without the traditional
hardware or liturgy usually associated with occult practices. Even a
covert acknowledgment of enmity, unaccompanied by ritual behavior, was sufficient to arouse suspicion in a neighbor. The occasional
discovery of technical apparatus such as puppets, charms, witch bot-

tles, or, infrequently, texts on magic typically followed rather than
preceded allegations of malefic practice.

The extent and degree of popular apprehension over witchcraft becomes more comprehensible once it is appreciated that such fears arose
in a milieu where mystical forces were valued as at once serviceable
and awesome. In part because of unified ecclesiastical opposition to
magical practices but also because such practices were most likely to
be orally transmitted, only fragmentary records remain to document
the varied uses of mystical power in colonial Massachusetts. Nevertheless, from court records and narratives, together with the more
complete information available on contemporary English folk beliefs,
the general features of this supportive milieu may be reconstructed.

Legal actions against malefic witchcraft represented merely the final
point of defense against what were perceived as destructive magical
powers. Prior to entering his complaint into the legal domain, the colonial villager could draw upon a variety of protective magical formulas
to maintain some sort of equilibrium between good and evil mystical
forces. Several of these techniques—by no means an exhaustive list—
were mentioned in a sermon delivered by Deodat Lawson in the early
phases of the Salem trials: "The Sieve and Scyffers [Scissors]; the
Bible and Key; the white of an Egge in the Glass; the Horse-shoe
nailed on the threshold; a stone hung over the rack in the Stable."[4]
The first two items refer to elementary techniques of divination that
were used both in England and New England for prelegal criminal
identification.[5] The last two items refer to methods of defensive countermagic that could be applied both to the discovery and to the ward-
ing off of the malefic witch.[6] It is probable that official intervention
in cases of malefic witchcraft occurred only after these formulas had
been tried without success.

Equivalent procedures figured in the background of at least four of
the trials against witchcraft in colonial Massachusetts. The most often
mentioned procedure was to collect some hair or urine from the victim of maleficium and boil it in a skillet. When this was done, the
witch responsible for the injury would make an appearance before his
or her victim.[7] A variation on this use of image magic—the baking of
a witch cake containing the urine of afflicted victims—was one of the
folk methods contributed during the Salem trials.[8] In view of the
strong legal and ecclesiastical prohibitions against this usage, it is safe
to assume that such instances of countermagic were greatly underreported in the contemporary court records. Indeed, the church member who provided the recipe for the witch cake was publicly repri-
manded by her minister.[9]

Elements of folk magic played a positive as well as a preventative role in the village community, however. The malefic witch was only one among the several kinds of magical practitioners who inhabited the towns of seventeenth-century England and New England, and he or she may even be the one whose authenticity outside the context of legal action is most open to question. Of equal or greater importance to the villager were the skills of the good witch or wise woman or the wise man or wizard. These magical practitioners often gained enough local prominence in post-Reformation England to rival the clergy as consultants to persons in distress.[10]

Reference to the activities of these cunning folk are less frequent in Massachusetts than in contemporary England, but there is sufficient material to establish their continuing visibility in village life. In their writings on witchcraft, both Increase and Cotton Mather acknowledged the presence of "white witches" in the course of discouraging popular reliance upon them.[11] In at least two legal actions, there is specific mention of white witchcraft or wizardry as part of the formal testimony.[12] More important, it is clear that at least seven of the persons charged with witchcraft prior to the Salem trials engaged in healing activities that engendered both respect and apprehension in their neighbors.[13] A deposition against one of these accused witches even went so far as to cite her extraordinary competence as a healing witch as evidence against her.[14]

Despite continuing popular reliance upon such healing skills, it would be an exaggeration to suggest that the activities of these cunning folk were fully assimilated into the village routines. The unstable careers of these persons well reveal the hazards of engagement in an enterprise that functioned without institutional support. As one reputed white witch discovered in the course of attempting to rid a household of "praeternatural mischiefs," failure to effect a solution or cure could make the injury chargeable to the healer.[15] In addition, the need to conceal even the benevolent uses of folk magic from official surveillance might tempt a good witch to use his or her supernatural skills for other than curative purposes. One such healer was reported to have informed her client: "if shee would believe in her God, shee would cure her body and soule; But if she told of it, shee should be as a distracted body as long as she live."[16]

Nevertheless, there can be no doubt that folk magic functioned both as a defense against mystical attack and as a resource in the alleviation of suffering. The demand of the village peasantry for inexpensive medical care was sufficient in itself to guarantee the continued viability of magical healing practices throughout the seventeenth century.

Although there are no surviving records of financial transactions between white witches and their clients, it is probable that the cost for
such services compared favorably with the fees of contemporary physicians.[17] It is even possible that, as in England, such services might
occasionally be performed solely for reasons of social prestige and
without payment.[18]

It was in this village milieu, where mystical power operated both as
a resource and as a weapon, that allegations of malefic witchcraft
arose, and a contemporary gentleman—experientially removed from
the mainstream of folk magic by social class if not by geography—
might well dismiss such claims to victimization as contemptible and
malicious. Thus, the English clergyman, John Gaule, wrote of the
village accusers:

> Every poore and peevish olde Creature (such is their ignorance and unchari-
> tableness) cannot but fall under their [the villagers'] suspicion, nay their in-
> famous exprobations; every Accident (more than ordinary) every disease
> whereof they neither understand the Cause, nor are acquainted with the
> symptoms must be suspected for witchcraft. His Cow or his Hog, cannot be
> strangely taken, but straight it must bee reckoned and rumored for be-
> witcht.[19]

Similar reactions were recorded by prominent gentry during the
Salem trials.[20]

To interpret the link between witchcraft and misfortune in these
terms, however, is not merely to underestimate the degree to which
believers were in fact vulnerable to mystical harm but to render the
logic of attribution arbitrary and socially meaningless. In the rest of
this chapter, the concern will be to reconstruct this logic with greater
precision by describing how the victim made his or her allegation
comprehensible to an audience of believers and by demonstrating that
the variant expressions of suffering presented in these allegations can
be socially differentiated. To accomplish this objective, it will be
necessary to take the standpoint of the victim.

ACCOUNTS BY VICTIMS OF MALEFICIUM

For present purposes, it is assumed that those depositions that provide
accounts of misfortune caused by witchcraft constituted attempts by
victims to make their perceptions of maleficium comprehensible to
others. As shall be seen in chapter 7, it is unlikely that these depositions, when entered into the legal domain, were altered to comply with
legal conventions for other crimes. Indeed, the very unobservability of

supernatural causation made it difficult at best to apply any restrictive principles by which to unequivocally accept or reject incriminating testimony. Accordingly, it is plausible to hold that the believer's logic of association between witchcraft and maleficium was preserved in official court depositions.

In looking at these accounts, my concern is to make explicit the victim's perception of the witch. The statements contained in these documents regarding, first, the relationship between the victim and the suspected witch, second, the point at which suspicions became aggravated, and finally, the victim's perception of the intentions of the suspect form an action sequence from the standpoint of the victim. When the typical features of this sequence are abstracted, the victim's way of linking misfortune to the activities or person of the witch becomes understandable.

The analysis begins with a division of accounts in terms of two categories employed by seventeenth-century believers to distinguish among different types of malefic action.[21] Malefic actions that resulted in injury to the body of the victim or loss of or damage to property were referred to as ordinary witchcrafts. Malefic actions in which the thoughts and actions of the victim were altered and controlled by the witch were designated as bewitchments and will be treated separately. Important differences in the logic of attribution will be found to coincide with this division.

Ordinary witchcrafts. Two examples will serve as points of reference for the following discussion:[22]

I being set in a corner of the prison at Ipswich this night past between nine and ten of the clock at night, after the bell had rung . . . suddenly I heard a great noise as if many cats had been climbing up the prison walls and skipping into the house at the windows. . . . I seeing this, and considering what I knew by a young man at my house last Indian harvest, and, upon some difference with John Godfrey, he was presently several nights in a strange manner troubled, and complaining as he did, and upon consideration of this and other things that I knew by him, I was at present something affrighted. . . . I saw John Godfrey stand within the door and said "Jonathan, Jonathan." . . . "I come to see you; are you weary of your place yet?" I answered "I take no delight in being here, but I will be out as soon as I can." He said "If you will pay me in corn, you shall come out." [*Jonathan Singletarry* vs. *John Godfrey*, March 14, 1663, *EQCR*, 3:120–21]

Anthony Dorchester saith upon oath [that last September] four men had equal shares in a cow. Each had a quarter and the offal was to be divided also. Hugh Parsons desired to have the root of the tongue. But he had it not—it fell to my share. A certain time after I had salted it, I took the said root and another piece of meat and put it into the kettle as it was boiling over the fire at Hugh Parsons' house where I then lived. There was nobody there but he and his wife and I and my wife who was sick of consumption sitting on her bed and not able to get up without help. Neither were any of my children able to take such a thing out of the boiling kettle. This being the Sabbath Day, Hugh Parsons and his wife went to the church before me. Then I made myself ready and [arrived] after them and came home before them. I took up my meat before they came home. But the root which Hugh Parsons formerly desired was gone. Then I spoke of it to him and all that he said was that he thought I did not put it in. But I told him that I was sure that I put it into the boiling kettle. And I have even since believed that no hand of man did take it away but that it was taken away by witchcraft. [Deposition of Anthony Dorchester, *Dorchester* vs. *Hugh Parsons*, filed Feb. 25, Mar. 1, and Mar. 18, 1650/51, reprinted in appendix to Drake, *Annals*, pp. 230–31.]

Typically, in ordinary witchcrafts, the victim traced the source of malefic action to a transaction between himself and the suspect, the outcome of which was unsatisfactory to one or both of the parties. The substance of this transaction took various forms. In the case of Singletarry, it involved a suit initiated by John Godfrey to obtain payment for services he had performed for Singletarry. The outcome of this prior litigation had been that Singletarry, the defendant, was found guilty of withholding the requisite payment and, for lack of funds, was placed in jail.[23] Other types of transactions included property disputes over the use of land for grazing purposes, one neighbor's refusal to provide the goods or services asked for by another neighbor, or the exchange of goods and services in which one party perceived or was alleged to perceive a net loss. The common feature in all these dealings was the persistence of an unresolved grievance arising from a difference or disagreement over the terms of the settlement.[24]

The use of malefic witchcraft following upon these transactions was made comprehensible by the presumption of intent. Almost without exception, it was the suspected witch who was the more grievously injured party—whose offer of friendship was refused, whose property was trespassed, or whose call for help or services went unanswered. In 93 of the 103 accounts categorized as ordinary witchcrafts for purposes of this investigation, the alleged witch could readily be identified as the injured party. In the remaining ten instances, insufficient information was available to determine which party sustained the greater loss in the transaction. Under these conditions, the victim could establish a motive for the use of malefic witchcraft that closely resembled criminal intent for other illegal activities. As the aggrieved party, the witch acted to redress an injustice.

It was in the actual commission of the crime that the unique character of ordinary witchcraft was demonstrated. From the standpoint of the victim, it was not circumstance or opportunity that linked the suspect to the harmful act. Rather, it was the contextual relevance of the malefic action to the relationship he had formed with the suspect. The timing of the action and, frequently, the very form in which it was manifested demonstrated its supernatural origin. Thus it lent plausibility to Dorchester's account that the injury wrought by witchcraft achieved for Parsons an exact revenge for his loss. Similarly, other victims who were engaged in boundary disputes with a suspected witch might indicate maleficia by referring to the sickness or death of the very same cattle that had trespassed.

Within this logic of attribution, the link between witchcraft and misfortune was forged as a causal chain that subordinated natural processes to social processes. The mishaps and misfortunes experienced by the victim in his everyday life were conceived not as mere accidents devoid of meaning but rather as anticipated consequences of a problematic interpersonal relationship.

Bewitchments.   The following accounts provide examples of reports of bewitchment:

The deposition of Elizabeth Hubbard aged about 17 years who testifieth and saith that on May 11, 1692 I saw the apparition of John Willard of Salem Village who did immediately torment me and urged me to write in his book: but on the 18th of May being the day of his examination John Willard did most grievously torture me during the time of his examination for if he did but look upon me he would immediately strike me down or almost choke me and also during the time of his examination I saw the apparition of John Willard go from him and afflict the bodies of Mary Walcott, Mercy Lewis, Abigail Williams, and Ann Putnam, Jr. [*Elizabeth Hubbard* vs. *John Willard*, June 3, 1692, *RSW*, 2:1–2]

The deposition of Thomas Putnam aged 40 years and Edward Putnam aged 38 years who testify and say that we having been conversant with several of the afflicted persons, as namely Mary Walcott, Mercy Lewis, Elizabeth Hubbard, Abigail Williams, and Ann Putnam, Jr. and we have seen them most grievously tormented by pinching and pricking and being almost choked to death most grievously complaining of John Willard for hurting them. But on May 18, 1692 being the day of his examination the aforesaid afflicted persons were most grievously tormented during the time of his examination for if he did but cast his eyes upon them they were struck down or almost choked. [Thomas and Edward Putnam in behalf of Elizabeth Hubbard and others, *RSW* 2:6]

In the afternoon on the same day the child went to the meeting again and did not much complain at her return home, but about three hours in the night next following, the said child being in the bed with me, John Kelley, and asleep, did suddenly start up out of her sleep and holding up her hands cried, Father, Father, help me, help me, Goodwife Ayres is upon me, she chokes me, she kneels on my belly, she will break my bowels, she pinches me, she will make me black and blue. Oh father will you not help me, with some other expressions of like nature, to my great grief and astonishment. . . . We used what physical help we could obtain, and that without delay, but could neither conceive, nor others for us, that her malady was natural; in which sad condition she continued till Tuesday, on which day I, Bethia Kelley, being in the house . . . the child being in great misery, the aforesaid Ayres came in. Whereupon the child asked her, Goodwife Ayres why do you torment me and prick me. [Excerpt from deposition of John Kelley and his wife Bethiah in behalf of their daughter Elizabeth, *Elizabeth Kelley* vs. *Goodwife Ayres*, May 13, 1662, Colony of Connecticut, reprinted in Charles Hoadly, "Some Early Post-Mortem Examinations in New England," p. 212]

This type of account figures prominently in the history of witchcraft in Massachusetts, and there will be occasion in later chapters to examine the response of different groups, notably clergy and magistrates, to such reports within and outside the context of legal action. The very method of presentation indicates the importance of a third party both in verifying the malefic activity and in focusing the accusation upon particular persons. The influence of these reports upon witchcraft prosecutions varied considerably according to their interpretation by civil and ecclesiastical authorities, and the vast majority for which there are records were generated during the Salem trials of 1692. Yet there are enough instances of bewitchments prior to this event to warrant their analysis as part of the idiom of witchcraft and not merely as a historical idiosyncrasy.

A central characteristic of the bewitchment was that victim and witch were not presumed to have a preexisting relationship, although in fact the suspected witch was frequently known to the victim. No breach of norms preceded the act of witchcraft, and no dispute could be cited to relate the malevolent intentions of the witch to his or her victim. In this form of accusation, the victim bore no responsibility for the misfortunes that befell her.[25]

Given the absence of any prior relationship, the action of the witch manifested itself as arbitrary and unpredictable. The same witch might torment other victims for no apparent cause, and the same victim might be tormented by other witches with whom she shared no apparent relationship.[26] To the victim of bewitchment, the activities of the malefic witch occurred without intelligible motive and were independent of any interpersonal context. At most, it could be predicted that such a witch would act with impersonal malice toward all who were vulnerable. As might be anticipated, the effects of bewitchment were standardized rather than personalized as in the case of ordinary witchcrafts. Typically, the victim reported or was observed to experience fits and convulsions accompanied variously by choking, pinching, or pricking sensations. Frequently, she would be visited by the specter of the suspected witch, the presence of which was visible only to the victim and was made manifest to others by the victim's agitation. Beyond these basic uniformities, the effects might vary according to the selective or more intense probing of a concerned party.

In contrast to ordinary witchcrafts, it is not possible to interpret the meaning of these malefic actions from the standpoint of the victim because the interpretation was invariably supplied by a third party. The subsequent elaboration of such rudimentary signs as fits and convulsions into disease or alternative categories of preternatural affliction will be discussed in the following chapter. But the very susceptibility to variable interpretation is itself a revealing feature of this form of victimization.

Ordinary witchcrafts versus bewitchments. It may be observed that reports of ordinary witchcraft and reports of bewitchment reflect two different approaches to the linking of misfortune to witchcraft. Table 3 serves to clarify these differences. Obviously, in comparison to victims of ordinary witchcraft, victims of bewitchment displayed the greater vulnerability to mystical harm. Vicious and painful assaults upon their bodies occurred without any provocation and continued unimpeded by their attempts at self-defense. In a narrative published in 1704, one of the witnesses to the Salem trials provided a particularly graphic description of the helplessness of such victims before the wrath of their tormenters:

Sometimes in their fits, they have had their tongues drawn out of their Mouth to a fearful length, their heads turned very much their Shoulders;

Table 3   Comparison between Reports of Ordinary Witchcraft and Reports of Bewitchments

	Reports of ordinary witchcraft	Reports of bewitchment
Relationship of victim to witch	Victim and witch share a history of problematic relationships	Possible familiarity between victim and witch not relevant to malefic action
Source of malefic action	Action follows from problematic transaction; typically victim is implicated in breach of norms.[a]	Action is arbitrary and unpredictable
Assignment of motives[b]	Intentions of witch are relevant to account; motives of witch are situated within framework of retributive justice	Intentions of witch are not relevant; motives of witch are nonspecific and reflect undifferentiated malice
Type of malefic action	Misfortune is personalized and contextually appropriate	Misfortune is impersonal and standardized

[a] This feature of ordinary witchcrafts is also found in witchcraft allegations in African contexts; see, for example, Max Marwick, *Sorcery and Its Social Setting*, p. 11. Marwick refers to these components of the accuser's account as "moral overtones."

[b] To state the distinction in other terms, only the reasons why the witch acted were available to the bewitched, whereas the goals and objectives of the witch were available to the victim of ordinary witchcrafts.

and while they have been so strained in their Fits, and had their Arms and Legs wrested, as they were quite dislocated, the Blood hath gushed plentifully out of their mouths, for a considerable time together; which some, that they might be satisfied that it was red Blood, took upon their Finger and rubbed their other Hand. I saw several together thus violently strained and bleeding in their fits, to my very great astonishment, that my fellow-Mortals should be so grievously distressed by the invisible Powers of Darkness.[27]

Victims of bewitchment manifested their powerlessness not only through their vulnerability to malefic assaults but also through their response to these assaults. Frequently it was a third party—often a close relation or a patron of the bewitched—who made public the suffering of the victim and who directed accusations to particular suspects.[28] The potentially strategic use of the victim by the patron to designate political and economic rivals as witches will be considered later.[29] But for present purposes it is sufficient to note that the participation of the bewitched both in worldly and otherworldly engagement with the malefic witch was marked by extreme passivity.

The victim of ordinary witchcraft was likely to offer a far more active response to the malefic assault. It was he who transacted with the witch in the course of village routines, and it was by virtue of his normative violations that the occasion for mystical attack arose. For such victims, the response of the witch appeared not as an arbitrary or unanticipated assault but rather as the expected outcome of conflictual relations. Far from revealing helplessness in the face of malefic assault, the more frequent response of such victims was one of active and even effective confrontation. Thus Jacob Knight, upon the visitation of a specter, was able to drive it away after successive reappearances.[30] Similarly, James Carr could report the successful repulsion of a specter following a confused encounter with a suspected witch.[31]

In the ordinary witchcraft and the bewitchment, the several different kinds of participants in the dynamics of malefic witchcraft expressed different degrees of vulnerability to attack from the invisible world. What remains to be demonstrated is that these expressed relationships to the invisible world had visible social coordinates and that the spiritual resources that the two sorts of victims could mobilize against mystical attack corresponded to the political resources that such persons commanded in their more worldly engagements.

THE SOCIAL CORRELATES OF VICTIMIZATION

In Table 4, it is shown that the overwhelming majority of victims of ordinary witchcraft were men, whereas women comprised the greater proportion of the bewitched. In part, the large percentage of men shown as victims of ordinary witchcraft may merely reflect a general tendency for male heads of households to initiate legal action when their families were threatened.[32] On the other hand, this greater proclivity to exercise legal rights must also be understood in the context of the considerably greater political power accorded to men in colonial Massachusetts. Only men were permitted to vote in elections, to serve on juries, or to hold political office.[33]

Yet, at least within marriage, it may be argued that the position of women in New England was not one of complete subjugation. Although the husband was uniformly acknowledged in Puritan society as the supreme authority in the family,[34] certain legal precautions were introduced into colonial judicial practice to protect women against the absolute exercise of such authority. Courts were willing to uphold the complaints of wives against neglectful husbands and, as authorized

Table 4 Characteristics by Sex and Marital Status of Victims of Malefic Witchcraft

Marital status	Victims of ordinary witchcraft		Victims of bewitchment[a]	
	Male	Female	Male	Female
Single	8% (6)	(0)	(4)	79% (30)
Married	78 (57)	94% (28)	(1)	16 (6)
Widowed	2 (1)	3 (1)	(0)	3 (1)
Unknown	12 (9)	3 (1)	(0)	3 (1)
Totals	100% (73)	100% (30)	(5)	101% (38)

Note: In compiling this table, the following criteria were used to categorize victims' accounts of malefic witchcraft. Victims of ordinary witchcraft: This category includes only those victims who reported a transaction between themselves and the suspect prior to the malefic action. Victims of bewitchment: This category includes only those persons whose accounts were formally recorded as legal actions. This restriction to formal legal actions is intended to provide greater comparability between the two types of victims. See App. E and F for data on which this chart was based.

a It should be noted that the tables presented by John Demos in a paper on New England witchcraft employ data that overlap in part with these data. Demos has confined his analysis to the Salem trials, and he distinguishes only between victims of bewitchment—whom he refers to as accusers—and other witnesses, including all persons who presented testimony at the Salem trials, whether as victims, as supporting witnesses, or in other capacities. Needless to say, these differences in the organization of material merely reflect the divergent but not unrelated analytic objectives of the two studies.

in the "Body of Liberties" in 1641, to apply penalties to husbands who physically abused their wives.[35]

It was in the area of property rights, however, that colonial women gained most from entry into marriage. Widows were allowed "a competent portion of [their husband's] estate"[36] and could file suit if this condition were not met. And, in further recognition of women's rights of ownership in marriage, courts in both Massachusetts and Plymouth allowed prenuptial contracts between widows and their prospective husbands with respect to property allocations.[37] Such protections afforded the dutiful colonial wife an economic security not generally available to her English counterpart.[38]

Perhaps, then, the more relevant comparison in tables 4 and 5 is between women who were victims of ordinary witchcraft and women who were victims of bewitchment. In table 4 it is found that in the former category of victimization, 94 percent of the women were married, whereas in the latter category fully 79 percent were single. In addition, it is observed in table 5 that among the female victims of ordinary witchcrafts 53 percent were twenty years of age or older as compared to only 21 percent of the women among the bewitched who were over twenty years of age.

Thus it is possible to specify with greater precision the social categories from which those victims most vulnerable to malefic witchcraft were drawn. The modal age groups of such victims as well as their marital status are significant in this context. The years between ten and nineteen in the life cycle of Puritan children frequently coincided with a major shift in their relationship to their families of origin. During this period, the child was often removed from the parental home to another household to serve as apprentice if male or as maidservant if female.[39] Six of the most frequent accusers during the Salem trials lived under these domestic conditions.[40] This finding suggests that the social group whose members were most susceptible to the arbitrary action of witchcraft consisted of young women who were no longer under the protective care of their parents and had not yet settled within the relatively secure framework of marriage.

The exceptions to the modal type of bewitched victim further reveal the close affinity between social subordination and this expression of victimization. The one married man among these victims was the West Indian servant of a minister; and, of the six married women who

Table 5 Characteristics by Sex and Age of Victims of Malefic Witchcraft

Age	Victims of ordinary witchcraft		Victims of bewitchment	
	Male	Female	Male	Female
19 or under	5% (4)	3% (1)	(4)	63% (24)
20–29	18 (13)	13 (4)	(0)	8 (3)
30–39	14 (10)	10 (3)	(0)	5 (2)
40–49	25 (18)	13 (4)	(0)	8 (3)
50–59	12 (9)	7 (2)	(0)	0
60–69	4 (3)	3 (1)	(0)	0
70 or over	3 (2)	7 (2)	(0)	0
Unknown	19 (14)	43 (13)	(1)	16 (6)
Totals	100% (73)	99% (30)	(5)	100% (38)

Note: See App. E and F for data on which this chart is based.

are classified within this group, one was a servant to the same minister and another the wife of an impoverished laborer.[41] Two of the remaining four wives, both of whom were accusers during the Salem proceedings, participated only briefly as victims of witchcraft.[42]

In light of these considerations, the variant expressions of victimization by witchcraft can be socially situated. The men and women whose responses were contained in reports of ordinary witchcraft came from among the active members of village society. For the most part, this group consisted of husbandmen and their wives who were established as heads of household within their respective families of procreation and who could therefore enter into independent transactions with their neighbors. Such persons could meet the effects of malefic witchcraft on the same equal terms that they related to their village peers. On the other hand, the victims of bewitchment consisted of persons whose activities were under the formal supervision of others and for whom these others made decisions affecting their livelihood and their daily routines. Such persons were as unable to negotiate the terms of their encounters with the malefic witch as they were unable to set the terms of their transactions with their adult superiors.

5

The Interrelationship between Popular and Theological Meanings of Witchcraft

F ROM PRECEDING discussion, it is apparent that the category of witchcraft entered the public domain in seventeenth-century New England through two clearly separable channels. On the one hand, popular belief in folk magic made the malefic power of witchcraft a practical and immediate concern of the colonial villager. On the other
hand, the profound theological investment in the existence of a super-
ordinate invisible world provided witchcraft with its epistemological
foundations. The overlap between these two sources produced a category whose reality could be taken for granted by members of this
society.

This minimal agreement that witchcraft must be reckoned as an
empirical fact only barely concealed the enormous discrepancies between the two perspectives, however, for beneath this apparent consensus lay the ever-widening gap between magical beliefs and religion.
Such a rift between magic and religion well antedated the Protestant
Reformation. Indeed, as modern social theorists have argued, it may
well be that the exclusion of at least some elements of magic constitutes a defining characteristic of religion.[1] Within the framework
of early and medieval Christianity, however, the considerable degree
of interpenetration between the two belief systems imposed definite
limits on this exclusion. Magical techniques of conjuration, divination,
and healing did not differ in principle from ecclesiastical reliance upon
charms or benedictions to perform church-related works. Thus it did
not escape the attention of the authors of the *Malleus* that the sacraments of the church could be applied to the casting of spells as well
as to the exorcism of evil spirits or that ecclesiastical prayers for re-
lieving a victim of his maladies might be subtly altered into a magical
summons for the infliction of pain.[2] Ultimately, the pre-Reformation
conflict between magic and religion was more a jurisdictional dispute
than a direct confrontation between antithetical beliefs. The primary

stress in official ecclesiastical injunctions against magic, from the *Canon Episcopi* of the tenth century to the *Malleus*, was upon its illegality rather than its lack of efficacy.[3] The interdependence between the two systems was such that to question the credibility of one would have undermined the authority of the other.

One of the important consequences of the Protestant Reformation was to polarize the conflict between magic and religion. The Protestants extended the attack on magic to include its ecclesiastical as well as its popular applications. In England, the polemic took many forms. Rituals of exorcism and consecration were equated with acts of conjuration and magical incantation. The doctrine of transubstantiation, which formed so crucial a part of the Roman Catholic mass, was itself denounced as popish necromancy.[4] The use of holy water in benedictions and in the sacraments was likewise dismissed as an impious superstition.[5]

All this was merely the polemical expression of a central tendency in Protestant theology to emphasize piety rather than worship as the means and measure of salvation. Nonetheless, in their devaluation of the role of ritual and liturgy in the life of the believer, Protestant writers subverted the magical world view to a degree not possible for the medieval church. The conflict between magic and religion became substantive. By asserting that God turned a deaf ear to ritual manipulations of the supernatural, the Protestants challenged magical beliefs at their core. Magic was not merely unlawful; it was ineffective as well.

But this massive Protestant assault on magic was not merely part of a theological offensive against outmoded ecclesiastical forms. Nor was magic deplored because it failed to produce workable solutions to practical problems. To the seventeenth-century Englishman, such deficiencies—if perceived at all—did not distinguish magic from medical technology or, indeed, from much of scientific learning.

The more Protestants elevated divine will beyond the range of human manipulation, the more desperate and urgent their struggle against any resurgence of interest in magical practices became. Magic sapped the new piety of its strength and energy. Magical practitioners assumed that the awesome powers of the invisible world were available to humanity for the most petty and trivial of secular pursuits. They presumed to command God's protection with the recitation of simple incantations. They sought to reveal the mystery of the divine plan by the mere plotting of constellations on an astrological chart. Where the Protestant clergy attempted to draw from the believer an active and sustaining commitment to God, the proponents of magic fostered passivity by promising the user immediate results with a minimum of effort. Magic absolved its practitioners of responsibility for their actions and of responsibility to God.

It is not surprising, then, that the most vocal and persevering critics of magical practices among the English Protestants were the Puritans and their later derivatives in New England. Perkins had gone so far as to denounce the use of "exorcisms over holy bread, holy water and salt (and the casting out or driving away of devils by the sign of the cross)" as downright sorcery and witchcraft.[6] Indeed, the early Puritans had approached the remnants of ecclesiastical ceremony in the Anglican church with much the same contempt that the Anglicans viewed such practices among the Roman Catholics.[7]

Perhaps the most revealing record of Puritan attitudes toward magic is contained in the Puritan response to astrology. With regard to the English response, Keith Thomas has observed that although "clergymen of all brands were suspicious of astrology, there can be no doubt that in Post-Reformation England, the most sustained opposition to it came from the Puritans."[8] These suspicions were given forceful expression in 1652 when a coalition of Presbyterian and Independent clergy petitioned Parliament to suppress the practice of judicial astrology altogether.[9] In New England, such militant opposition was hardly necessary in view of the dearth of astrological publications. A 1956 survey of early writings on the subject has disclosed only three publications in the seventeenth century despite the proliferation of astrological treatises in contemporary England.[10] At Harvard, only four theses were presented on astrology between 1653 and 1717, when discussion was finally closed with the proposition "that Astrological conjectures are intolerable and must be utterly rejected."[11]

What made astrology so intolerable had little to do with its unscientific premises. The Puritans fully incorporated natural astrology— the investigation into the causal relationship of heavenly bodies to natural phenomena—into their curriculum in astronomy.[12] It was judicial astrology—the branch that dealt with general predictions in establishing nativities, in deciding the appropriate moment to act, and in resolving personal dilemmas—that the Puritans uniformly opposed. Likewise, Perkins's repudiation of astrology as a form of idolatry in a work published in 1585 cannot account for the special intensity of the Puritan rejection.[13] Other Protestant clergy had advanced the same objection.

The real threat posed by astrology was that it departed from assumptions similar to those held by Puritans but arrived at thoroughly incompatible conclusions. Thus vulgar astrological determinism overlapped with Puritan ideas on predestination in that both conceived of human destiny, including the prospects for salvation, as fixed in advance by divine will. But to apply such a premise toward the casting of nativities or the prediction of divine election was to casually surrender one of the essential mysteries in Puritan dogma, for it was the very uncertainty of the believer's relationship to God that safeguarded the divine prerogative from human manipulation.[14]

Similarly, the doctrine of special providences converged with astrology on the matter of construing the movements of heavenly bodies as portentous occasions. Again, however, it was not the intention of the Puritan ministers to use celestial events to predict the future or to make prophecies. The special providence was a revelation of divine will, the meaning of which would become clear after the fact. To extrapolate future events from the study of planetary conjunctions was to place men and women on a par with God by presuming that God's will could be foretold by the working of humanly conceived formulas.

Accordingly, in his investigation into the providential meaning of comets in *Kometographia*, published in 1683, Increase Mather was at great pains to distinguish his concerns from those of astrological prediction. He conceded that comets may be portentous signs of evil events, but he also stipulated that if "any man should now positively affirm that within this twelve month another Blazing Star will appear, it would be presumptuous, although it is possible and probable that it may so come to pass."[15] That astrological prophecies were nonetheless frequently inaccurate was a failing in which Mather could take great comfort: "Thus God delights to baffle Judicial Astrologers, when they will presume to know the times and the seasons which he hath kept in his own power."[16]

The fact that the Puritans, in defense of their theology, perceived in magic rather than in science the more serious challenge to their beliefs may strike the modern reader as a colossal historical miscalculation. But such a conclusion fails to consider that the important innovations of puritanism related to piety and not to epistemology. The orthodox Protestants of the seventeenth cenutry operated within a symbolic framework they shared with the Roman Catholic and, to a significant degree, with the believer in magic. Their contribution to theology consisted in recasting the meaning of these symbols rather than in discrediting them. As Robert Merton and others have argued, the Puritan of post-Reformation England and New England had good reason to believe that scientific activity could be incorporated within the new piety without challenging its epistemological foundations.[17]

On the other hand, magical beliefs undermined Puritan piety from within a shared symbolic universe. The fortune-teller, the astrologer, the alchemist, and, indeed, the witch all coexisted with the Puritan in a reality shaped by accessible and intrusive invisible forces. The possibility that common acceptance of this shared reality could be used to legitimate profoundly antithetical values made such a coexistence intolerable for both types of believers.

Now it was at just such a precarious intersection between magic and religion that the category of witchcraft arose in colonial New England. In the following discussion, it is suggested that this point of convergence between the orthodox Puritan and the magical practitioner in mutual acknowledgment of a potent invisible world formed a most inconvenient alliance for each.

THE CONFLICTING USES OF WITCHCRAFT

The conflict between magic and religion extended directly into the realm of witchcraft beliefs. At the popular level, emphasis upon the malefic aspects of witchcraft proceeded from a thorough involvement with the uses and potentialities of magic. At the ecclesiastical level, emphasis upon the volitional element in witchcraft derived from the general theological concern with the extreme moral options open to men and women.

The two approaches were incompatible in terms of both defining the problem of witchcraft and prescribing the course of action to meet this problem. From the popular standpoint, the primary threat posed by witchcraft centered upon its harmful effects. Moral considerations such as whether or not the malefic witch had repudiated God were extraneous to this concern, although not necessarily in conflict with it. In contrast, from the theological perspective, it was the possibility of humanity's open defiance of God that made the offense of witchcraft so serious. Here the problem of witchcraft consisted not in the exercise of malefic powers but in the means by which these powers had been obtained. A policy that focused exclusively on one of these formulations would not meet the requirements of the other. To punish witches for their malefic practices was to acknowledge their extraordinary magical powers while ignoring the fact of their extreme impiety. By the same token, to condemn witches only on theological grounds was to overlook the devastation of the lives of their victims.

The conflict between the popular and theological approaches involved far more, however, than a dispute over competing definitional claims. At stake was a choice between rival systems for dealing with the problem of suffering.

At the village level, malefic witchcraft formed the central point of reference within a milieu where folk magic was believed to both cause and deter personal misfortune. Indeed, the accounts of some accusers and victims reveal that an entire life history of suffering could be explained in these terms. Thus John and Mary Pressy, the impoverished neighbors of Susanna Martin, attributed their failure to prosper and to expand their cattle holdings to a curse that Susanna had delivered about twenty years prior to their accusation.[18] Similarly, Caleb Moody, among the more prominent of the accusers, attributed to his neighbor, Elizabeth Morse, responsibility for the death of his cattle over a period of sixteen years.[19]

Against these malefic assaults, the usual defense was retaliatory countermagic. The malefic witch confronted the victim not as the embodiment of divine wrath but in the more mundane posture of a personal adversary. Within this framework, the victims were able to disavow personal responsibility for their misfortune even though, as previously indicated, their own unethical conduct was frequently believed to have precipitated the attack. Only if they had perceived themselves as culpable would it have been appropriate to seek protection by acknowledging their sins before God.

This recourse to witchcraft as an explanation for suffering contrasts markedly with the response of the Puritan gentry to adversity in their own lives. Only on one occasion did Cotton Mather suspect that witchcraft was the source of his personal misfortune. This suspicion arose in the immediate aftermath of the Salem trials when his newborn son had just died under peculiar circumstances.[20] Likewise, during the Salem trials, Lawson gave some weight to the reports of accusers that his deceased wife and daughter had been murdered by witchcraft in 1689.[21] But neither Mather nor Lawson made these suspicions the basis for a formal accusation.

The more characteristic response of civil and ecclesiastical leaders was to refer suffering to the agency of providence. In this form of interpretation, the sufferers virtually invited upon themselves responsibility for their personal misfortunes. That God should visit the catastrophe rather than the witch made the punishment somehow deserved, no matter how obscure its relationship to the sin. Thus, for example, the pious judge and merchant Samuel Sewall consoled himself over the death of his aborted son not by fixing blame upon others but in a prayer of humiliation.[22] Similar demonstrations of piety are also recorded in the diaries of John Hull, Michael Wigglesworth, and Cotton Mather during periods of familial and personal crisis.

The main thrust of ecclesiastical policy toward witchcraft was to impose theological priorities on the preexistent popular interpretations and to insist that popular remedies against malefic practice be replaced by the theological preservatives of piety and moral reformation. The earlier Puritan treatises gave more emphasis to the former point of contention, and, indeed, some historians have credited these writings with effecting a change in English law from a secular statement to a theological statement of the crime of witchcraft.[23]

Foremost among these writers was Perkins, who argued forcefully that the volitional element alone should define the seriousness of the offense of witchcraft:

But why should the witch be so sharply censured? . . . Even if no harm arises . . . the cause (then) of this sharpe punishment, is the very making of a league with the Devill, either secret, or open, whereby they covenant to use his helpe for the working of wonders.[24]

Similarly, Bernard devoted substantial portions of his work to disentangling the witch as apostate from the witch as doer of harm. From his standpoint, the latter attribution was most often the result of a simple misunderstanding between neighbors.[25]

One of the more radical attempts to extricate theological from popular interpretations was undertaken by the English Puritan, George Gifford. In his *Dialogue Concerning Witches and Witchcraftes*, published in 1593, Gifford wrote in the contemporary vernacular in an effort to convey to a popular audience the difference between witchcraft as derived from Scripture and witchcraft as it arose from folk understandings of maleficium. At one point in the dialogue, Daniell, the spokesman for the theological understanding, replies to a defender of popular beliefs:

The holy scriptures doe command that witches should be put to death; therein you say right: but if you did take it, that the work of God commandeth they shall not be suffered to life, because they kill men and beasts, or because they send spirits which possesse men, and torment their bodies, you are much deceived; for you shal never finde, of all that have bene tormented and plagued by evil spirits, that the holy Ghoste layeth it upon witches.[26]

By the time the dialogue is concluded, virtually none of the popular associations between witchcraft and magic has gone unchallenged.

The greater emphasis in Puritan writings, however, was upon the

popular remedies to the problem of witchcraft, for the clergy were
well aware that a rise in popular suspicions of malefic witchcraft invariably increased the demand for countermagic to combat this danger. No major ecclesiastical treatise on witchcraft by Puritan ministers
in the seventeenth century failed to expound at length on the utter
unacceptability of these remedies.

From the theological standpoint, there was no justification for any
distinction between malefic practice and protective countermagic. All
supernatural effects that did not derive directly from God were assumed to have their origins in Satan. Thus Increase Mather wrote of
those who used words or charms to dispel witchcraft or to heal dis-
eases: "Such persons do . . . fence themselves with devils shield
against the devils sword."[27] Cotton Mather found reason to make a
more direct appeal against such usage in 1692:

> They say, that in some Towns it has been an usual thing for people to cure
> Hurts with Spells, or to use detestable Conjurations, with Sieves, Keys, and
> Pease, and Nails, and Horeshoes, and I know not what other Implements,
> to learn the things for which they have a forbidden, and an impious Curios-
> ity. 'Tis in the Devils Name, that such things are done; and in Gods Name I
> do this day charge them, as vile Impieties.[28]

Equally vehement warnings would be repeated by the clergy well
after the Salem trials.

Such stern strictures against the practice of countermagic left the
user open to public censure or, in some instances, to more formal
sanctions, such as church discipline or legal reprisal. That Thomas
Wells, an Ipswich resident, was alleged to have boasted that he could
raise spells was enough for a formal charge even though no witnesses
were available to testify to his ability.[29] Cotton Mather records in his
diary that two young women were disciplined by their church for
consulting a fortune-teller.[30] And at least two of the pre-Salem trials
against witchcraft stressed the defendant's knowledge of magic as the
grounds for prosecution.[31]

An account by an accuser in 1680 provides an illustration of a more
informal exercise of ecclesiastical sanctions.[32] The complainant, a resident of Newbury, applied the familiar recipe of mounting a horseshoe
above her door to prevent the entrance of a suspected witch. It worked,
she claimed, until a neighbor, who called the device a "Piece of Witchery," took it upon himself to knock the horeshoe down. Thereupon,
she remounted the horseshoe with similar success; the alleged witch
was inhibited from entering her home. The neighbor persevered in his
original course of action, however, and returned this time to remove

the horseshoe and carry it away. The accuser reports that after this removal the suspect was able to enter her house unimpeded and that, as a result, her mother's illness rapidly worsened.

The folk dichotomy of magical practitioners into healing versus cursing witches or good versus bad witches was also repudiated by the clergy. With some justification, Perkins perceived that the good witch posed the greater threat to piety. The superstitious persons among the populace, he argued, would fail to see that the harmful and the beneficial uses of witchcraft were morally equivalent:

It is their nature to abhor hurtful persons such as bad witches be and to count them execrable, but those that do them good they honour and reverence as wise men and women, yea, seek and sue unto them in times of extremity, though of all persons in the world they be most odious.[33]

Bernard opposed the popular distinctions with equal force:

There ought no distinctions of Witches too be made into good and bad, blessing and cursing, white and black Witches, as thereby either sort should escape death. They may differ in name, but all are abominations to the Lord and ought to dye.[34]

The milder tone in Cotton Mather's remarks on the subject probably reflects the fact that white witchcraft was never as firmly established in New England as in England:

There is mention of Creatures that they call White Witches, which do only Good-turns for their Neighbors. I suspect that there are none of that sort; but rather think, There is none that doeth good no, not one. If they do good, it is only that they may do hurt.[35]

In their appropriation of the category of witchcraft, the clergy intruded themselves into the core of a system of magical beliefs. The effect of this intrusion was to alter the meaning of witchcraft in such a way as to frustrate the popular usage. By means of this redefinition, the clergy outlawed both the harmful uses of magic and the defenses that arose to combat this harm. At the popular level, witchcraft became less a problem that could be solved than a predicament for which no lawful remedy was available.

THE PUBLIC RESPONSE TO AFFLICTIONS:
A FOCUS OF CONFLICT

Because the empirical references of the popular and the theological conceptions of witchcraft were usually widely divergent, proponents of the two belief systems were often able to coexist without direct acknowledgment of their fundamental disagreements. To be sure, the tendency among the common folk to give exclusive emphasis to the malefic component of witchcraft was viewed with apprehension by the clergy. And, undoubtedly, the theological insistence that witchcraft was, above all, an intentional betrayal of God must have struck the beleaguered villager as a most unnecessary addition to the original grievance. Yet insofar as the reasons for these different concerns were not probed too deeply, the believer in magic and the Puritan minister could afford at least a semblance of tolerance toward the other's response to witchcraft.

In the case of afflictions, however, such mutual disregard became untenable. For the seventeenth-century colonial, *afflictions* referred to the condition of a victim whose thoughts and actions were either partially or fully controlled through the agency of an evil spirit. If this control originated directly from the invisible world—that is, directly, from Satan or his representatives—it was designated as *possession*. The mediation of this control by witchcraft—referred to as *bewitchment*— was discussed in the preceding chapter from the standpoint of the victim. But, whether as a major theological event or as a powerful malefic assault, the affliction marked a crisis that could capture the attention of the entire community. It was during these critical episodes that the latent contradictions between the two belief systems surfaced as open controversy.

To appreciate its impact in historical context, the affliction must be understood within the framework of seventeenth-century diagnostic categories,[36] for while the behavioral signs of the affliction might suggest a variety of psychiatric syndromes to the contemporary observer, it was their resemblance to the core religious experience of Protestant pietism—the experience of conversion—that most impressed the ecclesiastical leadership of colonial New England.[37] That Increase Mather recognized this behavioral proximity is clear in his warning to the community after the Salem bewitchments:

We in New England have lately seen not only miserable Creatures Pinched, Burnt, Wounded . . . but some Ecstatical Persons, who have strongly imagined that they have been attended with Celestial Visitants revealing secret and future things to them which if it should appear to be a Diabolical Imposture . . . be of dangerous consequence.[38]

Likewise, it was only half in jest that he and his son described as diabolic possessions the "shakings" and "tremblings" that were viewed by the Quakers as the outward signs of conversion.[39] It was not by mere chance that the sudden appearance of mass bewitchments in 1692 was accompanied by a less spectacular but nonetheless striking increase in the incidence of reports of divine visitation.[40]

In both the "devil's trance" and the "divine trance," as Perkins called them,[41] the subject would be seized with extreme pain and suffering. Typically, in the affliction, the victim displayed what witnesses described as fits and convulsions. These usually consisted of sudden and unexpected movements of the body accompanied by cries of pain. As exemplified in the autobiographical account of Thomas Shepard, a prominent New England minister, the throes of divine possession could be equally distressing: "And now the terrors of God began to break in like floods of fire into my soul. . . . For three quarters of a year this temptation did last, and I had some strong temptations to run my head against walls and brain and kill myself."[42]

Moreover, the parallels ran deeper. In a later phase of the affliction, the victim would begin to display talents or exhibit attitudes that were totally inexplicable to persons familiar with his or her biography. Thus, unaccountably, in 1662, Ann Cole of Hartford began to speak in fluent Dutch, to the amazement of both her family and her neighbors.[43] And Mercy Short, during her affliction in the summer of 1692, came to demonstrate a facility with biblical passages that Cotton Mather claimed even he could not equal: "I do affirm that no man living could have singled out Psalms more expressive of, and suitable to, her circumstances than those she pitched upon."[44] Although less frequent, similarly extensive personal transformations were not unusual concomitants of conversion.

Ultimately, however, the most revealing moment in the progress of the affliction consisted of direct communication between the victim and the invisible world. Only a few of the afflicted ever obtained this degree of immediacy with a demonic presence. On these occasions, the victim would appear to resist either verbally or physically the assaults of the evil spirit. Even more infrequently, the demon would actually seem to take possession of his victim by, among other indications, transmitting his deep, bass voice through the unlikely medium of a young girl's lips.[45] Such moments provided the opportunity for a face-to-face encounter between the forces of good as represented by the Puritan minister and the forces of evil as embodied in the person of the afflicted.

In a religious community almost devoid of liturgical devices, the affliction emerged as one of the most dramatic expressions of the cosmic struggle between God and Satan. That most of the victims were young and female was particularly appropriate in view of the theological

meanings attached to the experience.[46] In the working out of the affliction, the pathetic convulsions of a young girl formed a fitting portrait of the human condition in direct combat with Satan. Only with
the intervention of divine will could human effort—otherwise feeble
and gratuitous—contribute to deliverance from evil. In the affliction,
the Puritan clergy and the believing Puritan rediscovered the true measure of humanity.

For all its promise as a focus for unified communal action, the affliction was more often the source of deep divisions between popular and
theological audiences. The sheer abundance of reported afflictions at
the village level was as much an embarrassment as a point of proof to
the theological doctrines that lent them substance. And the tendency
of the village laity to view the affliction as the outcome of local witchcraft intruded upon its theological meaning as a communication of
providential design. Perhaps most critically, the readiness of the common folk to treat the affliction by means of countermagic posed a direct challenge to the healing methods of the clergy. In each phase of
public response to the affliction—its verification, its signification, and
its treatment—the two audiences waged a battle on two fronts: against
Satan and against each other.

The division that arose during the process of verification prefigured
the disputes that would erupt in the later phases of public reaction. For
the clergy, the chief problem was how to define the conditions under
which theological support for suspected afflictions would be offered.
To offer this support too freely was to yield to the popular predilec-
tion for capriciousness and disorder in the invisible world. It was this
overzealousness among the village laity that had preoccupied the English gentry and clerics just prior to the Puritan migration. So frequent
were the reports of possession and bewitchment at this time that even
King James—earlier an active publicist of the dangers of witchcraft—
began to redirect his energies away from polemics against skeptics toward the detection of frauds and impostors.[47]

Other, less conspicuous figures in England had supplied a more systematic solution to this problem of containment. Among the most
influential of these men was John Cotta, a Northamptonshire physician, whose several texts on the discovery and trial of witchcraft were
standard references in both England and New England. It is significant
that Cotta distinguished between the "vulgar view" and the "learned
view" of bewitchment. The vulgar and unlearned observer, he argued,
was competent only to detect the more flamboyant signs of bewitchment, such as the vomiting of iron, coals, and the like or the speaking
in languages unknown to the victim. The assessment of earlier signs

such as fits and fevers required the expert judgment of a skilled physician.[48] Still more cautious were the writings of Meric Casaubon, an
erudite Anglican clergyman, who suggested that even acts of divination or feats requiring extraordinary strength might proceed from natural causes.[49] These and similar treatises reflected the growing reluctance among English authorities to confer validity upon popular
perceptions.

Yet an excess of caution in the verification of afflictions was almost
as subversive as the lack of it. The procedures used to curb popular
enthusiasm could also be employed to encourage doubt and disbelief.
To disqualify popular claims by substituting natural for supernatural
causes was to risk surrendering to the skeptics and mechanists one of
the most striking events in the lexicon of special providences. As mentioned above, the embattled New England clergy of the late seventeenth century promoted the affliction as one of the few remaining
demonstrations of an immediate divine presence. Thus the diagnostic
refinements proposed by Casaubon and other diligent examiners ultimately threatened to undermine the very doctrines they were designed
to protect.[50]

Given these cross-pressures, the variable strategies of colonial ministers for meeting the problem of verification become comprehensible
less as expressions of personal idiosyncrasy than as responses to a common dilemma. The caution exercised by Samuel Willard during the affliction of Elizabeth Knapp in 1671–72 was no more permanent a solution to this dilemma than the relative credulousness exhibited by
Cotton Mather some two decades later. Under Willard's supervision,
Elizabeth was subjected to the full measure of contemporary checks
against fraud and disease. Two weeks after she had experienced violent fits and convulsions, Willard nonetheless deferred to the judgment
of a physician that her condition arose from natural causes.[51] Only
upon the resumption of symptoms, after medication had been tried
without success, did Willard accept a rediagnosis from the same doc-
tor that the distemper was preternatural in origin.[52] The later, more
spectacular signs of the affliction were observed with similar restraint.
Indeed, on several occasions, Willard went so far as to confront Elizabeth with contradictions in her own testimony.[53]

Mather's approach to verification differed less in procedure than in
emphasis. If, for Willard, the audience of reference was the village
laity, for Mather it was the growing number of clerics and educated
gentry who doubted the possibility of supernatural visitations altogether. This polemical concern is evident from Mather's earliest published account of an affliction in 1689. Here four prominent ministers

introduced the narrative with a statement denouncing the doctrinal errors of those who questioned the existence of good and evil spirits.[54]
Likewise, it was this audience of unbelievers whom Mather addressed
after describing the suffering endured by Margaret Rule in 1693:

> It were a most Unchristian and uncivil, yea a most unreasonable thing to
> imagine that the Fitt's of the young Woman were but mere Impostures.
> And, I believe, scarce any, but People of a particular Dirtiness, will harbor
> such an Uncharitable Censure.[55]

Under Mather's sponsorship, the participation of physicians and other
expert witnesses was enlisted not so much to moderate popular zeal as
to shake the convictions of the skeptic.

The two approaches well exemplify the problematic relationship between popular and theological audiences. Underlying the verification
of afflictions was a choice between competing cosmologies. Against
the popular view of a world inhabited by ubiquitous occult forces lay
the theological conception of a natural order that was in theory arbitrary but in practice almost inviolable. The effect of Willard's restraint was to sustain this boundary between theological rationality
and popular occultism even in the midst of an acknowledged violation
of natural law. In contrast, Mather's greater receptivity to popular discoveries tended to collapse this boundary. Not unexpectedly, it was to
Mather, perhaps more than to any other colonial minister, that the villagers turned for advice on questions of malefic practice.[56]

Now if, in fact, it were accepted by both the clergy and the village
laity that the affliction was genuine, then what did it signify? Here
was another crucial difference between the popular and the theological
response. For the villager, the affliction was almost invariably linked to
witchcraft. Typically, the suspected agent of this witchcraft was a
woman of questionable reputation who, in any case, had had problematic dealings with the family of the afflicted. Thus it came as no surprise to the spectators in Hartford when Ann Cole singled out Rebecca
Greensmith, her next-door neighbor, as the source of her distress. According to contemporary description, Rebecca was a "lewd, ignorant,
considerably aged woman."[57] Similarly, Mary Glover, an old Irish
washerwoman, was called out by the Goodwin children during their
lengthy affliction of 1688. For every recorded affliction in seventeenth-
century New England, there was at least an attempt by the victim or
the victim's family to attribute responsibility to witchcraft.[58]

For the Puritan minister, however, the affliction signified something
far different and far more important than a quarrel between neighbors.
God did not permit such a rare manifestation from the invisible world

merely to serve the caprice of a local malcontent. The affliction was a message to the entire community, even though its immediate effects might be suffered by only one member. On the subject of Elizabeth Knapp's affliction, Willard addressed his votaries in Groton:

There is a voice in it to the whole land, but in a more especial manner to poor Groton; it is not a Judgment afar off, but is near us, yea among us, God hath in his wisdom singled out this poor Town out of all others in this Wilderness, to dispense such an amazing Providence in.[59]

Even more grandly portentous meanings would be applied to the Salem afflictions.

With this judgment came moral imperatives that were at best poorly served by the popular interest in witchcraft. To seek public reprisal against a few malefactors was to divert the community from its collective responsibility. Thus it was less as fellow victims than as fellow accomplices that Willard exhorted his congregation:

Let us make a more near and special use of it [the affliction]: Let us look upon our selves to be set up as a Beacon upon a Hill by this Providence, and let those that hear what hath been done among us, hear also of the good effects, and the reformation it hath wrought among us.[60]

Just prior to the Salem trials, Lawson would urge a similar awakening of conscience in the face of a more massive preternatural assault.[61]

In the signification of afflictions, the two audiences circumscribed the same phenomenon within vastly different parameters. At the popular level, the affliction was viewed as an instrument of vengeance with a field of action that included only several warring parties. For the clergy, however, the scale of operation was immeasurably greater. The dozen or so prominent ministers who had witnessed the afflictions of Ann Cole, Elizabeth Knapp, and the Goodwin children did not attend these sessions to discover witchcraft.[62] For these men, the affliction was important because it permitted a precious, although fleeting, glimpse of providential design. It was this use, above all, that Increase Mather had intended when he recommended that such events be recorded.

Once again, the different responses of Willard and Mather to allegations of bewitchment reflected their general relationship to the popular audience. When Elizabeth cried out against a woman in her neighborhood, Willard's sympathies were with the accused, whom he described as "a person of sincere uprightness before God."[63] He later cleared the woman from suspicion when Elizabeth made two mistakes in identification. Later, during the Salem trials, one critic who opposed the proceedings cited this case as a precedent for rejecting the accusations of afflicted persons.[64] Willard himself, writing under a pseudonym at this time, also reiterated his earlier stand against an interpretation of bewitchment.[65]

On the other hand, Mather took seriously the popular concern with witchcraft. Prior to the Salem trials, he had supported the claims of the Goodwin children against Mary Glover and actively contributed to her prosecution. Moreover, he maintained this openness to witchcraft accusations even in later involvements with afflicted persons. The allegations of Mercy Short were never carried as far as legal action; yet Mather's reaction to her charges could hardly have brought comfort to the accused: "But there is Cause to fear that some of the Persons thus Represented, are as Dangerous, and as Damnable Witches as ever were in the world."[66] He adopted a similarly equivocal posture during the affliction of Margaret Rule.[67]

In the final phase of public response—the actual treatment of the affliction—there was less room for such equivocation, for in seventeenth-century New England, the question of whether magic or religion would rescue the victim from diabolic assault became a choice between extremes. At one extreme lay the resources of countermagic. The charms, amulets, and incantations that were serviceable in combating witchcraft could also be applied to the more impersonal evil forces that tormented the afflicted; or the folk healers who, in other circumstances, might themselves come under suspicion could be commissioned to exercise their special skills. That such solutions were actively enlisted during the Salem afflictions drew the concern of several contemporaries, including both Mather and his critic, Calef.[68] Even so devout a believer as John Goodwin—who had been accepted into Mather's own Boston congregation—could admit that he was sorely tempted to use these "tricks" during the affliction of his children.[69]

These temptations seem less reprehensible when the theological alternatives are considered, for while the Puritan clergy were willing to acknowledge human vulnerability to mystical harm, they were reluctant to concede that the individual could do very much about it. This powerlessness before the invisible world was, in large measure, the legacy of the Reformation.[70] For the believing Puritan, as for other English Protestants of the seventeenth century, the critique of ecclesiastical magic included a categorical rejection of the medieval exorcism. As Perkins expressed it,

The most learned Papists of this age doe teach and avouch, that there is in Gods Church an ordinarie gift and power, whereby some men may cast out devills, and help annoyances that come by Witchcraft. The Protestant is of a contraire judgment, and holdeth according to truth, that there is noe such ordinarie gift left to the church of God, since the daies of the Apostles.[71]

It was not that the New England ministry lacked a prescription to meet the ravages of the devil. Indeed, both Mather and Willard, in the company of their colleagues, urged upon their charges a strenuous regimen of prayer and fasting. It was simply that the God from whom they sought protection offered no guarantee that such human efforts would be effective. In contrast to the near-infallible Catholic exorcism, the Puritan method of expulsion was intended as an act of pure propitiation with no certainty of outcome.

That Willard adhered to these norms of supplication is strongly implied by his own candid testimony. After months of careful ministration to Elizabeth's affliction, he nonetheless concluded his involvement with clear misgivings about the success of his treatment: "her condition is such that administers many doubts . . . , charity would hope the best, love would alsoe feare ye worst."[72] That Mather risked breaching these norms is equally probable for, unlike Willard, he sought both to uphold doctrine and to provide an effective cure. Thus Mather's use of the methods of prayer and fasting met with consistent success. Indeed, by the time of Mercy Short's affliction, he had begun to develop a formula for treatment that he called "A Beseeching of the Lord Thrice."[73] This involved massing together the church members in the vicinity to engage in three days of prayer and fasting three times in rapid succession.

Mather was not unaware of the dangerous implications of this procedure, however. His comments on the method of Margaret Rule's deliverance contained a warning that as much acknowledged as excused his use of a formula:

Yet I must earnestly Entreat all my Readers to beware of any superstitious conceits upon the Number Three; if our God will hear us upon once Praying and Fasting before him 'tis well, and if he will not vouchsafe his mercy upon our thrice doing so, yet we must not be so discouraged as to throw by our Devotion.[74]

This caveat notwithstanding, Margaret recovered on schedule.

In the treatment and cure of the affliction, the community faced a crisis of inaction. On the one hand, the clergy uniformly prohibited the popular reliance upon magical palliatives. On the other hand, they were unable to substitute an effective alternative without a serious compromise in their form of piety. And yet an admission of helplessness by the Puritan divines could only intensify the popular demand for protection against mystical harm. For the New England clergy, there was no satisfactory resolution. To introduce certainty into their treatment was to risk the surrender of a basic precept; to deny certainty altogether was to yield spiritual leadership to a more confident healer.

The colonial encounter with afflictions reveals in microcosm the increasingly precarious basis for unified communal action against mystical assault. To the urgent problem of how the believer should conduct himself during these crises the normative guidelines were at best ambiguous. The solution of countermagic involved the use of illicit recipes, the effectiveness of which had been seriously called into question by Protestant polemics. The orthodox solution provided even fewer guidelines for action, for here it was understood that human effort neither brought the affliction nor guaranteed its removal. The mysterious and arbitrary will that moved these events could be reached, if at all, only by further exertions of piety.

Eventually, the community would effect a compromise between these mutually unacceptable solutions in the form of decisive legal action. But for some of the clergy who momentarily supported this compromise, such an alliance between human effort and providential design would later be viewed as an unforgivable presumption.

THE DILEMMA OF WITCHCRAFT

The effects of the Protestant Reformation on magical beliefs, in general, and on witchcraft beliefs, in particular, have been brilliantly analyzed by Keith Thomas in his *Religion and the Decline of Magic*. In brief, Thomas argues that the Protestant movement maintained with full force the potency of the medieval symbols of good and evil but devalued the ecclesiastical liturgy that had served to mediate between these symbols and humanity. The consequence for believers was that they remained at the mercy of invisible forces but could no longer confide in ecclesiastical magic or its folk counterparts to regulate their influence.

By itself, this disequilibrium in mystical forces may help to account for the increase in demands for witchcraft prosecutions in England during the late sixteenth and early seventeenth centuries. The effect of Protestant deritualization was to deny the victims of witchcraft the very ecclesiastical guarantees that had previously fortified them against malefic practice. As a result, they began to transfer their demands for protection from the church to the courts.

Yet at least in New England, it is clear that witchcraft posed a problem for its theological as well as its popular proponents. It was not merely the predicament of the believer whose defenses against malefic practice had been weakened by ecclesiastical reform. It was also the predicament of a clergy whose recommendations for dealing with evil and misfortune often failed to meet the expectations of their congregations.

The adjudication of witchcraft allegations within the framework of the law was at best a stopgap measure to contain popular apprehensions. The court might act to punish the offending witch, but it did not necessarily reduce the vulnerability of the victim. Indeed, it is evident that accusers perceived themselves under great peril when entering formal complaints against malefic practice. Throughout the witchcraft prosecutions in Massachusetts, victims would claim that the very act of offering negative testimony had resulted in serious personal adversity.[75] From the popular standpoint, retaliatory countermagic continued to constitute the best solution to the problem of witchcraft.

The event of witchcraft thus presented the clergy with a considerable risk, for there was always the possibility that ecclesiastical involvement would reinforce popular anxieties without channeling these anxieties into theologically acceptable responses. The period of most active prosecution in Connecticut in 1662 had been accompanied by a reversion to divinatory techniques in the detection of witchcraft.[76] Similarly, the Salem trials were the occasion for the surfacing of magical practices on an unprecedented scale.

The anticipation of such a normative breakdown may help to explain the ecclesiastical emphasis upon the regulation of means for the discovery and prosecution of witchcraft, for it is apparent that the clergy were as concerned with the propriety of the procedures for controlling witchcraft as with the control of witchcraft itself. No matter how immediate or serious the problem, Puritan publicists insisted that methods for the detection and prevention of witchcraft be rigidly circumscribed within divine law. From the treatises of Perkins and Bernard to Increase Mather's *Cases of Conscience* of 1692, this stipulation precluded the use of an ever-expanding list of magical countermeasures. In chapter 7, it will be shown that judicial compliance with these regulations made the proof of witchcraft a task of great difficulty.

Thus, in seventeenth-century New England, the coexistence of popular and theological beliefs within the symbolic framework of witchcraft yielded a dilemma for both those who feared witchcraft and those who legitimated these fears. To assert the priorities of one belief system was to create a crisis for the other. To insist on the enforcement of theological directives was to upset the balance of mystical forces that helped to stabilize the popular usage. On the other hand, to reinforce the popular understanding of witchcraft was to stimulate a demand for services that could not be performed within the framework of Puritan doctrine.

The resolution to this dilemma was an awkward truce between popular and theological audiences. The clergy paused just short of outright repudiation of witchcraft belief to effectively contain its popular expression, and the common folk only barely escaped ecclesiastical censure in their search for protection against mystical harm.

It is in the framework of this dilemma that the curiously divided and unstable New England policy toward witchcraft becomes comprehensible. The more immediate sources of this policy will be analyzed in the following chapters.

Witchcraft and Community

6

The Identification of the Malefic Witch

BEFORE 1692, it was from the communities rather than from official directives by the state that the impetus for legal action against witchcraft arose. Here, as already observed, the culpability of the witch consisted neither in complicity with Satan nor in conspiracy against the state but in the willingness to make use of malefic magic. Thus, in the pre-Salem litigations, it was in the form of testimony alleging specific damage or injury that the courts of New England received evidence of witchcraft from the villages of New England.

Yet, if the initial identification of the witch came from below, the response of officials was nonetheless crucial in establishing this identification as a legal fact, for while the accusation embodied the popular emphasis upon the witch as doer of harm, the prosecution provided the vehicle for the expression of theological concerns. In the actual production of witches, the conflict between popular and theological audiences over the definition of witchcraft resolved itself into a dispute between the terms of accusation and the terms of prosecution.

For purposes of analysis, then, it is useful to conceive of the production of witches in pre-Salem New England as an outcome of the articulation of two distinct sequences of imputation. The first of these sequences consisted in the stages by which members of the community organized their perceptions of malefic harm into formal accusations against particular persons. The second sequence entailed the validation or invalidation of popular testimony according to criteria that carried the authority of the state. In this chapter, it is the first of these sequences leading to the identification of the malefic witch that will constitute the focus for discussion.

In the following sections, an attempt is made to demonstrate that the selection of witches constituted both a response and a creative adaptation to a specific social and political context. Recent contributions to the investigation of European witchcraft beliefs have established that the structural analysis applied by social anthropologists to the study of witchcraft allegations in simple societies may be fruitfully extended to the rural communities of post-Reformation Europe.[1] Accordingly, one of the analytic objectives of the present chapter is to define the social position of the witch in relation to the community and to formulate in structural terms the reasons why occupants of this position were particularly open to suspicion by other members of the community.

To define the context of suspicion, however, is not to explain how or why these suspicions were organized into allegations of malefic witchcraft. Ultimately, the identification of the witch must be understood not just as a response to given structural conditions but also as a creative redefining of these conditions. The preexistence of structural conflicts within the New England community may have provided the occasion for remedial collective action, but the formulation of these conflicts as a problem of witchcraft required the interpretive efforts of members. It is the other analytic objective of this chapter to describe how members accomplished through this interpretive work the transformation of the suspect into the witch.

A DEMOGRAPHIC PROFILE OF THE MALEFIC WITCH

To describe collectively the accused witches of pre-Salem Massachusetts is to catalog the dimensions of social and political disaffiliation in the New England town. Although twenty-five of the thirty-four suspects were women, they had far more in common than their sex. A few, such as Eunice Cole of Hampton and Mary Webster of Hadley, were poor to the point of destitution and required public assistance for their support.[2] Others, like Mary Hale and Ann Hibbins of Boston— both of whom possessed at least modest financial resources—were widows who were distinguished by their domestic isolation.[3] Still others, who were neither extremely poor nor widowed, such as Elizabeth Morse and Jane Walford, were either approaching old age or were well beyond sixty at the time of their arrest.[4] It was these attributes of poverty, old age, and widowhood, taken singly or in combination, that characterized the overwhelming majority, or nineteen of the twenty-five accused female witches.

It may be argued that these attributes would be interrelated whether or not the population consisted of suspected witches. Obviously, widowhood was more likely to occur in old age than in youth, and the prospects for remarriage among widows were far less promising for paupers than for women of means.[5] Nevertheless, there is evidence to suggest that this interrelationship may have been more than incidental, for the accusation tended to coincide with that point in the biography of the suspect when the combined effects of poverty, old age, and widowhood were most visible.

Thus Mrs. J. Parsons, who was the plaintiff in a defamation suit involving witchcraft in 1656, found herself the defendant in a witchcraft trial some twenty years later.[6] Similarly, Susanna Martin, who had been a plaintiff in 1669 while she was married, was later, during her old age and widowhood, among the first of the accused witches of 1692.[7] But the most dramatic instance of downward mobility culminating in a charge of witchcraft is exemplified by the case of Ann Hibbins.

Ann was connected by marriage to one of the most prominent members of the colony. Her husband served in the highly prestigious capacity of magistrate from 1643 to 1654 and functioned for at least two years as the colonial agent in England.[8] Furthermore, his brother-in-law, who may also have been Ann's brother, was variously treasurer, deputy governor, and even governor of the colony in 1641.[9]

Prior to his election to magistrate, however, Hibbins had experienced a serious financial reversal involving the loss of 500 pounds. Whether or not this substantial loss "discomposed his wife's spirit," as one seventeenth-century chronicler has alleged, is difficult to assess.[10] What it most certainly occasioned was the removal of Hibbins and his wife from the ranks of the wealthy, if not from the ranks of the socially reputable.

Shortly thereafter, in 1640, Ann became involved in a bitter dispute with a fellow member of the Boston church. Unwilling to accept the terms of mediation proposed by the church elders, she was excommunicated in 1641 despite her husband's prestige both in the church and in the community.[11] No further sanctions were imposed until after her husband's death in 1654. With his death, Ann had become merely an elderly widow with diminishing financial resources. It was in 1656 when Ann had met these conditions of old age, widowhood, and relative poverty that she was accused of witchcraft.

The male suspects, like their female counterparts, were also drawn from the fringes of the community, but their disaffiliation was more closely linked to their position in the labor force than to their relationship to a family. Four of the nine accused men were designated as hired laborers, and two were referred to as seamen. Both forms of occupation were characteristic of men without property and without residential stability. Indeed, John Godfrey, one of the hired laborers, was so unattached to any community that in one deposition he was described by the court as a "resident at Andover or elsewhere at his pleasure."[12] Only one of the men, Hugh Parsons, a sawyer and brick-layer, can be placed roughly within the middle ranks of colonial soci-ety. That one of his chief accusers was his wife, who was herself sus-pected of witchcraft, may help explain the discrepancy.[13]

Thus, at least for the pre-Salem suspects, the demographic attributes of the malefic witch yield a remarkably uniform distribution. Why these aggregate social characteristics should reflect so well-defined a pattern will become evident in the following discussion.

THE MAKING OF THE MALEFIC WITCH:
THE STRUCTURE OF ACCUSATIONS

Because charges of witchcraft in New England were almost invariably initiated by the complaint of the accuser rather than by the confession of the defendant, the question of how the accuser determined his choice of suspect becomes the crucial consideration in the identifica-tion of the malefic witch. Yet, if taken at face value, the accuser's own testimony provides at best a most cryptic account of the basis for his selection. That the accusation often referred to disputes that occurred years and even decades prior to the formal laying of charges appears on first inspection to reflect among colonial villagers an astonishing ca-pacity for bearing silent grudges. That in addition the injury sustained by the accuser was frequently as negligible as a momentary cramp or the disappearance and eventual recovery of a cooking utensil makes the charge of a capital crime seem absurdly out of proportion to the offense. Indeed, it is only when the accusation is conceived in terms quite different from those in which it was presented that its plausibil-ity as well as its structural basis become accessible to the historical observer.

The accusation was less a response to any particular dispute or trans-action than a comment on the relationship within which this transac-tion had occurred. In themselves, the objects of dispute would hardly have warranted the vehement response expressed by a formal accusa-tion. The first stage in the career of the witch began not with a dis-agreement over the disposition of land or property but rather with a relationship that had deteriorated to a point beyond reconciliation.

The effects of this rupture in the relationship between the witch and other members of the community are well conveyed in the letter of William Morse in behalf of his accused wife, Elizabeth. Challenging Caleb Moody's allegation a decade after an altercation with Elizabeth, Morse complained that "he being in Church communion with us should have spoken it like a Christian and then proceeded so wee might give an answer in less time than ten Years." And in response to another accusation with even older origins, Morse remarked: "This being twelve years ago did amaze us now to hear of it."[14] It was this withdrawal of neighbors from usual forms of mediation, such as arbitration by church elders or public discussion in a town meeting or even open exchange, that prepared the groundwork for the eventual identification of the witch.

What stabilized the relationship in the period between these initial suspicions and the formal accusation can be only roughly inferred from historical materials. It is apparent, however, that villagers were inhibited from disclosing their suspicions by the fear of witchcraft itself. John Chase deposed that shortly after giving testimony against Elizabeth Morse he was "taken with bloody Flux and his wife troubled with sore breasts." William Fanning was similarly troubled by the attack of a cat and the agitation of his mare upon charging Elizabeth with malefic witchcraft. For at least six of the pre-Salem cases, accusers claimed to have suffered a personal injury or direct threat from the invisible world by virtue of their public opposition to the suspect.[15] It is not unlikely that through fear of such retaliation neighbors may have preferred to avoid all actions that would antagonize the witch, including formal legal reprisal.

From this vantage point, the formal accusation constituted merely the final dissolution of an already untenable relationship. The fears of witchcraft that prolonged an otherwise tense and hostile relationship could only aggravate the suspicions from which they were generated.

Eventually, the same neighbors who had refrained from action through fear of retaliation would begin to perceive danger in the mere presence of the witch. No charge more fully reveals the intensity of suspicion that prevailed between the witch and her accusers than that of overinquisitiveness. By the time of the formal accusation, even the unexpected solicitousness of the suspect during the sickness of a neighbor was sufficient to arouse grave apprehensions. For John Godfrey, it was enough that Rachel Fuller visited his sick child and took the child's hands in her own to convince him that she was the chief instrument of the sickness.[16] Likewise, Nicholas Rowe attributed his own worsening condition to the moment when Jane Walford visited him in sickness and placed her hands upon him.[17] It is no exaggeration to suggest that the formal accusation coincided with that moment when the tangible offense of the witch had become one of simple proximity to the victim.

The predicament of the economic dependent. The concentration of village tensions into this vicious cycle of suspicions reflected a more basic predicament in the form of association between the prospective witch and other members of the New England community. Even before suspicions were generated, relations between the witches of pre-Salem Massachusetts and their neighbors were likely to be problematic, if only because of the witches' economic dependency.

Like their English contemporaries, the colonists distinguished between the worthy poor, those who could not earn enough to live on, and the unworthy poor, those who were able to work but chose not to.[18] While members of the former class of pauper were entitled to public support, those such as idlers and beggars, who comprised the latter class, were subject to prosecution under criminal law. The third category of pauper as defined by English law consisted of those who were able-bodied but could not find work. Because of a chronic labor shortage in seventeenth-century New England, virtually none of the colonists fell into this category.

Accordingly, it may be noted that the social characteristics of those who were both eligible and available for poor relief in colonial Massachusetts overlapped considerably with the social characteristics of the malefic witch. The class of paupers who did not work because they were unable to work included such groups as orphans, widows, unwed mothers, and men and women incapacitated by age, sickness, or other infirmities.[19] It is from this population of the "impotent poor"—as well as from the population of those who risked inclusion in this category— that the overwhelming majority of pre-Salem witches were drawn. And it is in terms of the policies and practices affecting the disposition of this group that it becomes possible to formulate the structural sources of conflict between witch and accuser.

The colonial system of poor relief entailed an important modification of contemporary English welfare policy.[20] Where the English relied primarily on private charity and bequests to the church for support of the poor, the colonists ruled that the final responsibility for support rested upon the individual townsmen of the place in which the pauper resided. Such a policy required a form of public taxation or ratepaying, which had been tried in England without success. There the various attempts to replace voluntary charity with collective responsibility had met strenuous and effective opposition from groups of ratepayers. In New England, on the other hand, the ratepayers endorsed the innovation in principle while, in practice, they engaged in more subtle forms of obstruction.

The predicament of the colonial pauper was to be placed within a system that deemphasized the contribution of private charity before the values embodied in public taxation had been fully institutionalized. That rates for the benefit of the poor were exceedingly low throughout most of the seventeenth century testifies less to the absence of poverty in New England than to the ingenuity of colonial villagers in diverting responsibility for the poor away from themselves. In an economy in which ten to twelve pounds a year were required for the maintenance of a poor person, Watertown paid only twenty-six pounds for its poor in 1671, Salem less than twenty-five pounds in 1657, and Charlestown as little as ten pounds in 1655.[21] Even Boston, the most populous of the colonial towns, was contributing only fifty-three pounds for welfare in 1654.

Central among the villagers' strategies for limiting their liability was the stringent application of the New England settlement law or right of inhabitancy. Within their own boundaries, the New England townships maintained absolute sovereignty regarding the admission of new inhabitants into their jurisdiction.[22] In practice, this right of inhabitancy or right to exclude undesirable strangers was directed primarily against persons who held incompatible religious beliefs and, more particularly, against persons who were likely to become public dependents.[23] Use of the New England settlement law transformed the moral consideration of who was to care for the poor into the legal consideration of who were the town's poor.

So wary were the colonists of assuming support for the indigent and the incompetent that even the presence of near kin in a town did not guarantee rights of inhabitancy. Often, fathers were required to give bond against the possible dependency of sons or daughters by marriage on penalty of having the offending stranger evicted from the town. The selectmen of Dorchester went so far as to fine Henry Merrifield ten shillings for receiving his daughter in midwinter unless he could present proof that the townsmen from her previous residence were chargeable for her support.[24] In Springfield, even the sons of the first settlers were not admitted to inhabitancy without security of bond.[25] But the finest interpretation of the law seems to have been reserved for widows; not infrequently, they were refused inhabitancy even if their husbands had been members of the town.[26] More general safeguards against the introduction of dependents by the inhabitants themselves included the passage of ordinances forbidding both the entertainment of strangers and the sale of land to strangers without the permission of selectmen or the giving of a bond in case the newcomer should require support.[27]

The passage of a law in 1659 by the General Court, which entitled persons to poor relief after three months of residence, gave rise to another set of practices to reduce public liability. Because the town could avoid liability if notice were given to the stranger prior to the time limit, the practice of taking exception to or "warning out" undesirables became widespread throughout the colony.[28] Before 1692, such warrants were likely to be executed by actually forcing the offending party to leave the town.[29]

Even in those instances when the towns did acknowledge responsibility for their poor, the blessings to the pauper were not unmixed. To forestall total dependency, the colonists sometimes relied upon drastic preventative measures. Occasionally, townsmen might be authorized to advise a neighbor on how to live a more orderly existence. In more extreme cases, an entire household would be restructured by indenturing the children to various members of the town or by putting the parents out to service.[30] That parents who were on public relief should employ their children to help defray the expenses was a routine expectation; if they did not, the town could order that the children be put to work.

If, at last, responsibility for support could be neither diverted nor mitigated, town policy toward the destitute inhabitant was apt to be quite pragmatic, if not actually punitive. The mode of administering relief to Eunice Cole, among the pre-Salem witches, was not untypical of the method of support for paupers in general. When, in 1659, her aged husband, William, petitioned for relief from the town of Hampton, the General Court ruled that the town take possession of his estate and use its earnings to supply the Coles with food and other necessities. In compliance with this order, the town then became responsible for the maintenance of William and his wife, even though she was imprisoned for witchcraft at the time. Indeed, when the town failed to meet payments for Eunice in 1664, the jailkeeper of Boston arrested one of the selectmen from Hampton pending receipt of the debt.[31]

Upon release from prison in 1670, Eunice, now a widow, went "on the town." In this method of relief, each of the inhabitants would take turns providing the pauper with food, lodging, or other necessities. In Eunice's case, her neighbors were ordered to support her by the week in the order in which they dwelt. In other towns, the poor person might be transferred between lodgings at regular intervals. In 1687 in Hadley, one widow was moved from house to house at two-week intervals. Another pauper from Hadley was boarded with a total of thirty-two households over a sixty-five-week period.[32]

Undoubtedly, the general reluctance of hard-pressed New England

towns to bear additional financial burdens together with the severity
of their remedies rendered precarious the position of the impoverished
villager. But the problem of the poor was not merely the product of
an ambiguous and frugal welfare policy. Even if the economically vulnerable inhabitant were able to avoid poor relief, he may still have required some form of cooperation or charity from neighbors to survive
the harsh conditions of the colonial frontier. Yet, because of the evolv-
ing social and economic relations among members of the town, this resource of neighborliness also became progressively unreliable with the
passage of generations.

The aggravation of the predicament.   If members of the first generation of settlers organized themselves into communities that encouraged
close cooperation between neighbors, by the third generation this relationship of mutual interdependence had been transformed into one
of intense political and economic rivalry. The pronounced social cohesion of the first settlements was as much a consequence of favorable
circumstances as of intentional planning. The moral directive of political leaders such as John Winthrop, the first governor of the Massachusetts Bay, that the colonists place service to the community above personal interests was all the more easily implemented because of their
extreme social and religious homogeneity.[33] The early communities
were likely to consist of members who were similar in terms of wealth,
occupation, age, and religious commitment. For the most part, they
were white males between the ages of twenty and forty who were
drawn from the middle ranks of English society, from those categories
designated as yeoman and husbandman. The majority either were engaged in agricultural pursuits or held skills that could be readily transferred to an agrarian economy.[34]

The high degree of political consensus and stability of leadership in
the early settlements indicates that the colonial design for social unity
was secure for at least the first generation. In villages such as Dedham,
Hingham, and Andover, this consensus meant that local leaders could
execute decisions affecting the financial and administrative organization
of the town with little or no opposition from the other inhabitants.[35]
But the lengthy careers of these first- and second-generation leaders
also testify to the political harmony that prevailed among the founding colonists. The forty-three men who served as selectmen in Dedham
from 1639 to 1687 averaged eight terms of office each.[36] Similarly, in
the 1660s, the typical board of three selectmen in Watertown had a
cumulative total of over fifty years of experience as selectmen.[37] The

initiative with which this substantial political mandate was executed presupposed broad areas of agreement among the villagers over the ordering of social and economic relations.

Contributing further to the social cohesion of the early communities was the actual physical plant of the town. It was not unusual for the villages to retain corporate control over sizable proportions of their landholdings and to distribute the remainder according to the open-field system.[38] The employment of this system insured that members would be in close proximity while in the village and while working on their land. The retention of corporate ownership of the land favored close cooperation between town members in decisions regarding its use.

Whether it is perceived as progress or as moral declension, there is little question that the reality of the New England community came to depart increasingly over the first sixty years from the blueprint for the New England community. Gradually, villagers began to redefine their priorities in favor of personal acquisition over the fulfillment of self through community. In the more heavily populated towns of Boston and Salem, the emergence of bitterly competing factions belied the spirit of village harmony. By 1650, Boston townsmen had already begun to identify themselves less in terms of common political or religious goals than in terms of special economic and geographic interests.[39] Even in smaller communities such as Watertown and Dedham, a similar trend toward political fragmentation was visible by the final decades of the seventeenth century.[40] Groups of villagers who had previously subordinated their sectional interests to the welfare of the community increasingly became more willing to separate themselves from the community if their demands were not met.[41]

The collapse of village cohesion was manifest as well in the altered physical plant of the town. Within the first two generations, property owners had begun to consolidate their scattered landholdings into larger single estates and to move their dwellings from the village center to the outlying areas where their farms were located. By the end of the colonial period, the disintegration of the open-field system had become widespread throughout Massachusetts.[42] The families that had earlier been concentrated within a small section of the community had become dispersed and isolated from each other on independent farms.

Perhaps the most direct indication, however, of a decline in communitarian values is registered in the increasing use of litigation of the inhabitants of the colony. In the first generation, town residents tended to rely on informal mechanisms of social control to resolve their disagreements. Indeed, during the first twenty years of settlement in such towns as Dedham and Sudbury, virtually all disputes between residents were settled by local arbitration and neighborly compromise.[43] Only three civil suits involving townsmen from Sudbury appear in the records of the Middlesex County Court between 1638 and 1656.[44]

In the changing communities of the late seventeenth century, however, efforts at local mediation were no longer sufficient to contain differences between neighbors. The decision of the residents of Dedham in 1687 to create the post of town treasurer, "to demand, sue, . . . and to receive money from the inhabitants to carry on such suits at law, or matters of trouble,"[45] expresses in microcosm a general trend toward the escalation of village conflict. It has been estimated that for Essex County 8 percent of the total population of adult males participated in civil suits for each year between 1671 and 1686. By 1720, there were more litigants in Suffolk County than there were adult males.[46]

Under these altered conditions in which villagers had begun to channel their energies into the accumulation of personal wealth and property, the predicament of the economically destitute and the economically vulnerable was further aggravated. In the shift from a subsistence economy to a surplus economy, neighborliness had become a commodity that one's fellows could no longer afford.

From predicament to open conflict. Nevertheless, it was not because of poverty alone that accusations were directed at the suspected witch. If relationships between economic dependents and their neighbors were frequently strained, they were not inevitably antagonistic. For some dependents, there remained open the possibility of leaving the community if their relationships to other villagers became unendurable. For still others, there may have been the buffer of an affluent relative or a charity-minded minister. Perhaps more typically, the dependent may simply have resigned herself to the policies of her reluctant benefactors.[47]

What distinguished the accused men and women from other economically depressed villagers was their mode of accommodation to their position. Whether or not they actually claimed to be witches, it is clear that several of the suspects actively sought a reputation for skill in magical arts. Thus Caleb Powell, a seaman, presented himself to William and Elizabeth Morse as someone who had "understanding in Astrology" and who "knew the working of spirits."[48] It was on this basis that he was commissioned by the Morses to rid them of the mischievous spirits who had suddenly visited their household. Similar claims to magical competence—including the ability to raise spells—

were made by the hired laborers John Bradstreet and Christopher Brown.[49] Another laborer, Thomas Wells, confessed to discussing witchcraft, Dr. Faustus, and other related matters with a neighbor, although he denied that he could raise spells.[50] Still others, such as Elizabeth Morse, Goodwife Burt, Margaret Jones, and Winifred Holman, were magical healers who supplemented their incomes with services to neighbors.[51] At least one third of the pre-Salem suspects either claimed or actually practiced magical skills.

More important, however, is that a reputation for such skills, no matter how passively pursued, was useful not only as a means of income but also as a means of retaliation or defense. Although direct warnings of revenge by witchcraft are rare, it is nonetheless evident that many of the accused men and women relied upon curses and veiled threats to safeguard their rights in dealings with neighbors. Thus, when Eunice Cole discovered that one of her sheep had died while under the care of Alexander Drake, she told him that "the right hand of God is upon your cattle."[52] And when John Remington announced his intention to trespass on John Godfrey's land, Godfrey informed Remington's wife that "if her husband drove cattle up to the woods in the winter he should have cause to repent."[53]

Equally adept in the use of veiled threat was Hugh Parsons, who warned a neighbor after she had interrupted a transaction, "Gammer, you need not have said anything, but I shall remember you when you little think on it."[54]

Curses, imprecations, and threats were not the only defenses of the accused witches. Also included among the ranks of the pre-Salem witches were the scolds and termagants of the community. Bridget Bishop, accused of witchcraft both before and during the Salem trials, had twice visited the county court because of violent public quarreling with her husband.[55] Susanna Martin faced two charges in 1669: one for witchcraft, the other for calling a neighbor a thief and a liar.[56] The rather ungracious response of Mary Webster to the selectman who arranged her poor relief was to threaten him with bodily harm.[57] Margaret Jones was similarly outspoken and combative in her public demeanor. From personal observation at her trial, Winthrop described her as "intemperate, lying notoriously, and railing upon jury and witnesses."[58] When coupled with a reputation as a witch, such displays of anger could transform an otherwise ill-tempered but helpless woman into an intimidating foe.

Such were the accommodations of the malefic witch to her vulnerable social position. She was not merely the potential ward of a community that had grown weary of its responsibilities; she was, in ad-

dition, willing to use unorthodox methods of self-defense if these
responsibilities were not fulfilled. While the more prominent members
of the community might use the church or the town meeting to assert
their demands, the weapons of the witch were necessarily the weapons
of the socially dispossessed.

For persons of low social standing, it is clear that reliance upon conventional forms of redress did not afford sufficient protection against
insult or injury. When Susanna Martin filed suit against William
Sargent for calling her son a bastard and for claiming that she had
assaulted another of her children, the court ruled in favor of the plaintiff but awarded her the embarrassing compensation of one-eighth part
of a penny in damages.[59] Likewise, when John Godfrey filed suit
against Daniel Ela for making the improbable claim that Godfrey was
in two places at once, enough witnesses were produced to obtain a
verdict against the plaintiff.[60] For an affluent member of the community like Mrs. J. Parsons, a successful defamation suit against a witchcraft accusation might yield a substantial award for damages in addition to a requisite public apology from the defendant;[61] but for an
impoverished widow like Jane James, a similarly successful suit might
bring an award of fifty shillings instead of ten pounds, with no provision for public acknowledgment.[62] For unsponsored women such as
Jane James, cursing, scolding, and, indeed, the invocation of evil spirits
constituted their few remaining defenses against public harassment.

Ultimately, the malefic witch became an object of communal hatred,
not only for her dependency but also for her lack of deference. Even
if the poor were not universally despised for their misfortune, they
were nonetheless enjoined by ministers such as Cotton Mather and
Thomas Hooker, among others, to judge themselves for their predicament rather than their neighbors.[63] Indeed, it was Mather who formulated an explicit link between the harboring of grievances among the
poor and the proclivity to witchcraft among the poor.[64] That Mary
Webster should publicly insult her village benefactor was all the more
outrageous in view of her already questionable claim to the goodwill
of the community. It was as much in response to this outrage as to her
supposed witchcraft that her neighbors, in order to alleviate the torment of Philip Smith, volunteered to drag her from her dwelling and
hang her until she was almost dead.[65] The disrespectful conduct of the
malefic witch only added to the provocation furnished by her circumstances; not only did she fail to contribute to the economic growth
of her community, but she dared to assert her demands upon the community in spite of this failure. It may well be this lack of deference
that the minister John Horton had in mind in his terse comment on

the execution of Ann Hibbins: "Mistress Hibbins was hanged for a witch only for having more wit than her neighbors."[66] If so, his words serve as a fitting epitaph for others among the ranks of the accused.

The focusing of the conflict.   On one level, it is hardly surprising that the principal opponents of the malefic witch should have so closely resembled her in terms of their own social position in the community. The accusers were drawn from among those villagers who were most likely to have contact with the suspect. The clients who would later accuse midwives and folk healers like Elizabeth Morse and Goodwife Burt had availed themselves of these services because of their own relative poverty. Similarly, the villagers who engaged in modest business negotiations with John Godfrey and Hugh Parsons were apt to be husbandmen whose resources were as slender as their disreputable associates. No magistrate, only one minister, and only two deputies figure among the 112 pre-Salem accusers for whom there are surviving records. On the other hand, included among the accusers are four of the accused suspects themselves.

Even if other poor persons were most likely to have contact with the suspect, however, this greater opportunity for conflict cannot account for the actual occurrence of conflict. What helped to canalize these associations into open antagonisms rather than into cooperative relationships was the tacit acceptance by both parties—suspect and accuser—of the moral premises of economic individualism. If the more privileged members of the community had begun to divide themselves into competing interest groups according to their special occupational or geographic needs, so too had the less privileged come to incorporate even fewer of their neighbors in their own efforts to maximize resources. The antagonism between accuser and witch belied a deeper tension between those who were barely self-sufficient and those who were unable to subsist, between those who enjoyed a modicum of respectability and those who were held in disrepute. In the new logic of economic individualism, those who were most likely to need charity or support from other villagers were least willing to give charity when they were subjected to reciprocal demands. And those who were most apprehensive over the uses of retaliatory witchcraft were those most likely to require similar defenses when their own interests were threatened.

The resolution of the conflict.   It is in the context of this antagonism between the suspect and her accuser that the interpretive work embodied in the witchcraft accusation becomes comprehensible. It has already been pointed out that it was the accuser rather than the suspect whose breach of norms triggered the dispute that preceded the accusation. These breaches covered a wide variety of transgressions ranging from the abuse of property to mere rudeness. Thus, when David Wheeler refused to perform a service for Elizabeth Morse, he found that he could not hunt successfully until he eventually completed the task. Similarly, when Zachery Davis failed to keep his promise to Elizabeth to bring quills (for writing) even after being reminded, his calves began to act strangely.[67]

Sometimes the accuser demonstrated a simple lack of generosity. On two separate occasions, Symon Beman displayed such attitudes toward Hugh Parsons. Once he refused to give Parsons material for a cap because he was too busy. Another time he turned down Parsons's request for some food for his horse. The outcome of this second transaction was that Beman fell off his own horse several times.[68] An even more revealing example is the interaction between Rachel Clinton and a neighbor just before the Salem trials.[69] After Rachel had been reduced to destitution, she asked to board at the home of Mary Edwards. She was told without explanation that she could not be accommodated. Mary then offered her some pudding, which Rachel received very scornfully. Some months later, according to Rachel's accuser, assorted livestock on the Edwards farm were suddenly taken ill.

In effect, the bulk of the accusations had their common point of reference in the misconduct of the accuser and the anticipation of justifiable anger from the witch. The accuser operated not only in defiance of the supposed retaliatory power of witchcraft but in clear violation of traditional village morality. That the accuser-victim was aware of his misconduct is highly probable since it is on this basis that he established the link between his misfortune and the witch. On a number of occasions, however, it appears that a guilty conscience alone could provoke an accusation, even without benefit of an actual dispute. Thus William Branch wished to refuse Hugh Parsons his services as a neighbor but in fact did not deny these services.[70] For these unneighborly misgivings he was punished with a burning distemper whenever he passed Parsons's door.

The efforts of Thomas and Macfarlane to describe in relation to sixteenth- and seventeenth-century England how the accusation accomplished for the accuser a resolution of his conflict with the suspect are clearly applicable to New England as well.[71] While the accuser-victim recognized that his transaction was instrumental in generating the malefic response, he chose to acknowledge only one of two equally obvious implications. The one implication—that the witch would re-

taliate against the accuser with the resources of her malefic power—
formed the thesis of the accusation. The other implication—that if he
had observed the norms of neighborliness the dispute would not have
occurred—completely escaped the accuser's attention. By means of the
accusation, the conflict over the disposition of the poor achieved its
final resolution. The accusation conferred upon the villager a near-
infallible warrant for uncharitable conduct toward his dependent
neighbor. The frequently contemptuous response of the malefic witch
provided the occasion for the exercise of this warrant.

Nevertheless, it should be noted that not all the pre-Salem cases
fully conform to the model presented in the foregoing analysis. In two
of the cases—those of Anna Edmunds and Mrs. Lake—it would appear
that the accuser quite blatantly exploited the suspect to avert legal
reprisal for a serious crime.[72] In both cases, the principal accusers
charged the suspect with the murder of a child by witchcraft and
were themselves later held accountable for the deaths on the nonmys-
terious grounds of child neglect. In three other cases involving male
suspects, accusers are conspicuously absent from the proceedings. Here
it is possible that the very eagerness of John Bradstreet, Christopher
Brown, and James Fuller to publicize self-proclaimed magical skills
brought them to the attention of the courts before their neighbors
could.[73] Perhaps the one genuinely anomalous case is that of Mrs. J.
Parsons, whose wealthy husband was alive at the time of her indictment.[74] It is clear, however, that her wealth did allow her to exercise
an option that was unavailable to others among the accused. Upon her
acquittal in 1675, she and her husband moved to another community.

Yet, in spite of these few and partial deviations, the dynamics of
witchcraft accusations were surprisingly consistent for a majority of
the cases. The accusation represented a resolution to a tension that had
its structural origins in the relationship between the colonial dependent and other members of the community. Fully twenty-five of the
thirty-four suspects were either impoverished, over sixty, and/or widowed. What catalyzed this tension into open conflict was the accommodation of the suspect to her precarious circumstances. At least
eleven of the pre-Salem accused claimed proficiency in magical skills
or actually practiced magical healing. Another ten of the suspects, not
including those directly engaged in magical practices, had histories of
aggressive confrontation with neighbors. The use of such unorthodox
means of self-defense was, in part, a consequence of the unavailability
of conventional forms of mediation for persons of degraded status.
Finally, the witchcraft accusation offered a solution to the conflict
both because it legitimated unneighborly conduct toward the un-

wanted dependent and because it promised to release the villagers from a responsibility that was otherwise inescapable.

One question, however, remains disturbingly unresolved: Why were women so overrepresented among the ranks of the accused? It is, of course, possible that this overrepresentation merely reflects a corresponding disproportion of women in the population of colonial dependents. Unfortunately, the problem of obtaining valid estimates on the distribution of the poor by sex in seventeenth-century Massachusetts renders it unfeasible to test this hypothesis.

Certainly, it is conceivable that even if men and women were equally represented among colonial dependents, there may have been fewer opportunities for impoverished women to supplement their inadequate incomes by legitimate means. Such constraints might have induced more women than men to engage in the subterranean and hazardous enterprise of magical healing. Somewhat more intriguing, though, is the possibility that the angry and defiant responses of economically vulnerable women produced a stronger reaction from the community than would have been the case had they been expressed by similarly distressed men. Perhaps these displays of contempt were all the more terrifying to neighbors because of their unexpected source. At the very least, these two hypotheses, when considered together, suggest an alternative framework for accounting for the unequal sex distribution of pre-Salem witches.

THE MAKING OF THE MALEFIC WITCH: THE PROCESS OF SIGNIFICATION[75]

The focusing of witchcraft accusations on particular suspects by no means constituted the final phase in the making of the malefic witch. Far more was involved in the identification of the witch than the discovery of who was responsible for the malefic act. By the time of the formal accusation, the suspect who allegedly made use of malefic magic had been transformed into the witch whose use of malefic magic was integral to her identity. In the making of the pre-Salem witch, the final proof of guilt consisted in establishing an intrinsic relationship between the act and the person. To the villagers who presented their evidence before the court, the witch was not merely the doer of evil deeds, she was the perfect physical and moral embodiment of these deeds. It is by describing the process by which this transformation from suspect into witch was accomplished that the meaning of the label for contemporaries becomes comprehensible.

Some preliminary distinctions are necessary in order to better un-

derstand how this process operated. In addition to allegations specify-
ing malefic harm, several other kinds of evidences were introduced by
witnesses to confirm or disconfirm the identity of the witch. For analytic convenience, it is useful to distinguish these evidences, first, in
terms of how they associated the suspect with the malefic act and,
second, in terms of whether they supported or challenged this association. The evidences used to establish this association consisted of
two types which, for present purposes, will be designated as *primary
signs* and *secondary signs*. The former type of evidence consisted of
behaviors, gestures, and other physical signs that were alleged to distinguish the witch from other persons. These signs might include, for
example, unusual bodily features or demonstrations of preternatural
skills. Secondary signs, on the other hand, referred to the moral character of the suspect. In this type of evidence, the witness indicated
that the suspect belonged to a moral category of persons who were
likely to be witches.

Correspondingly, evidences initiated in behalf of the suspect will be
designated as *primary countersigns* and *secondary countersigns*. The
former type of evidence consisted of attempts to disclaim the presence
of primary signs, as, for example, the allegation that an unusual bodily
feature was the result of natural rather than supernatural causes. Similarly, secondary countersigns included allegations that the suspect deviated from the moral category of persons who were likely to be
witches.

The signification of the malefic witch may be conceived in process-
ual terms as the product of the collective negotiation of these evidences. If the witnesses against the suspect sought to establish that the
act of witchcraft was committed by someone who bore the primary
and secondary signs of the witch, the defenders of the suspect could
meet these claims by pointing to countersigns. The general thrust of
the negative testimony was to establish that the vicious character of
the crime coincided with the moral character of the perpetrator.
Ideally, the final version of the witch would yield no contradictions;
the blatant obviousness of the doer would dispel any doubts about the
improbability of her deed. In turn, the intended effect of the counter-
sign was to deprive this version of its internal coherence. Typically,
the central premise of the defense was that the visible and invisible
coordinates of the crime were profoundly incongruent, that what was
inferred about the suspect in her invisible malefic activities was not
reconcilable with what was known about her in her everyday activities. It was in these terms that the community negotiated not just the

guilt or innocence of the suspect but also the survival or loss of her reputation.

At stake in this collective bartering over identity was the credibility of the accuser as well as that of the suspect, and of her opponents as well as of her defenders. In the pre-Salem cases, however, this risk to the accuser was most often mitigated by the timing of the accusation. For the majority of pre-Salem suspects, communal agreement on their culpability was a foregone conclusion. It was not until the Salem proceedings that differences in judgment about the suspect would generate intense and prolonged conflict between villagers.

The case of Hugh Parsons in 1651 provides an example in which the process of signification occurred with hardly any contest at all to the accusers.[76] In addition to allegations of acts of witchcraft from nine witnesses, Parsons was further charged by his neighbors with behaving like a witch and with displaying the moral character of a witch. With regard to primary signs, one witness testified that the suspect had been able to make a lost implement appear by merely pointing in a certain direction. But the most incriminating of these signs was supplied by Parsons's own wife. Among other indications, she alleged that her husband was often outside until midnight, that he made strange noises in his sleep, and that, on one occasion, he had transformed himself into a "great, nasty dog." Furthermore, according to witnesses, the moral conduct of the suspect was equally unambiguous. That he treated his wife poorly, that he failed to attend church lectures, and that he did not show grief at the sickness of his son were all taken as additional proofs of his culpability; as many as six witnesses testified to his indifference to his son's suffering. In the testimony of twenty-three witnesses against Parsons, the accumulated evidences yield a unified portrait of someone whose covert acts of malefic witchcraft cohered nicely with his unsavory moral character.

Nevertheless, even during the pre-Salem litigations, only rarely was a suspect selected who completely lacked social support. Even Hugh Parsons received some consolation when his Boston jailer swore that he could detect no witch's marks on the suspect. The cases of Mrs. J. Parsons in 1656 and Winifred Holman in 1662 provide examples of suspects who not only attracted a measure of village support but who also were able to organize this support into an effective defense against their accusers.[77] In both cases, the suspects gained legal initiative over their accusers by filing defamation suits. The advantage of this legal device was that it enabled the suspect to challenge her accusers before the community had become mobilized against her. The defamation suit was available, however, only to suspects with sufficient financial resources to pay court expenses.

The evidence against Mrs. Parsons consisted of allegations of witchcraft and primary signs. To meet these claims, she was able to produce witnesses who advanced alternative explanations for her alleged malefic acts. In response to the charge that she had killed a neighbor's ox by means of witchcraft, for example, two witnesses to the event testified that the animal had been bitten by a snake and that accordingly they "saw nothing but what might come to passe in ye ordinary way." Similarly, with regard to a complaint from her seamstress that her yarn was unaccountably thinner whenever she did work for Mrs. Parsons, two other employers of the seamstress testified that her yarn was threadbare for them as well. On the other hand, the defense of Winifred Holman consisted of testimonials to her character. In response to the allegation that she and her daughter were responsible for the affliction of a neighbor and the sickness of her child, the suspect presented two petitions, both of which were signed by her neighbors. In the second petition, which included two deacons from her church among the signatories, her neighbors specifically cited her moral conduct as grounds for challenging the validity of the accusations: "we have not in the least measure perceived, either by words, or deeds, anything whereby we could have any grounds or reason to suspect her for witchery or any thing thereunto tending."[78]

Together, the two cases further reveal the terms of negotiation in the popular identification of the witch. The weighing of evidence for and against the suspect was far less likely to consist of formal tests for the validation of these claims than of a simple matching of reputations between her advocates and her adversaries. For suspects such as Mrs. J. Parsons and Winifred Holman, whose credit in the community equaled or exceeded that of their accusers, the invoking of status considerations constituted the most effective line of defense. It was ultimately in these mundane terms that the villagers resolved for particular cases the lofty questions of whether priority should be given to natural or supernatural causes or whether the worldly activities of the suspect would more accurately define her character than her presumed otherworldly activities.

In the process of signification, the members of the community decided whether and in what terms the suspect would be transformed into the witch. The negotiation of evidences insured that, for those suspects who retained a measure of public confidence, the transformation would never be quite completed. But if the members accomplished this transformation, the very qualities of unneighborliness that they had exhibited toward the suspect would become the essential attributes of the suspect's own identity as malefic witch. The ungrateful and contemptuous termagant whose pleasure it was to torment her neighors by means of malefic magic was in her final unveiling the creation of the entire community.

7

The Official Response to Popular Demands

I F THE CRIME of witchcraft in pre-Salem New England were prosecuted at the instigation of the village laity, the terms in which this
prosecution was conducted were nonetheless strongly influenced by
the clergy. The authority of the church both in the constitution and
in the prosecution of the crime was necessarily more direct in Continental Europe, where clergymen formed the vanguard of inquisitorial
activity, but despite the fact that the New England clergy voluntarily
excluded themselves from political or legislative office, the authority
of the colonial minister in matters of criminal law closely rivaled that
of his Continental counterparts.[1] Especially in the handling of capital
crimes such as witchcraft and idolatry, which had their basis in scriptural injunctions, the New England magistrate was inclined not merely
to seek counsel from prominent members of the clergy but to invest
this counsel with binding authority. Under these conditions, the most
pressing task of the magistrate in the adjudication of cases of witchcraft was to reconcile this weighty theological presence with the popular demand for legal redress.

In the theological version of the crime, it was the intentional component of the act rather than the destructive consequences of the act
that established it as a capital offense. From this standpoint, the critical validation of the crime consisted not in the complaints of victims,
however numerous, but in the confession of the suspect. Without some
form of acknowledgment or proof of this volitional complicity, the
prosecution of the witch became morally irrelevant both with regard
to her personal salvation and with regard to her usefulness as an example for the religious community.

Indeed, the clergy sought confessions from all capital offenders, and
not just as a perfunctory exercise of ministerial duties. The "execution
sermon," during which a prominent minister would seek to elicit a
confession from the offender on the very scaffold where he was to be

hung, formed an integral part of judicial ceremony in seventeenth-century New England.

Ideally, the ceremony would be conducted before a large public gathering.[2] The clergyman would denounce the offender as the moral exemplar of violations of divine law. In turn, the convicted murderer or rapist or pirate would provide a biography in which he recounted the gradual progression of sins that had culminated in the commission of a capital crime. Thus the young servant who murdered his master in Boston in 1674 berated himself for the sin of pride.[3] It was, he confessed, this surrender to pride, manifested by his unwillingness to defer to his master, that hastened his moral degeneration. Similarly, the unwed Boston mother who murdered her infant in 1646 acknowledged that it was her early disobedience to her parents that prefigured her eventual atrocious crime.[4]

The execution sermon, with its dialogue between reprobate and visible saint, provided a forceful vehicle for the dramatization of communal norms, but the potential impact of this ceremony was even greater for witchcraft than for other capital crimes. No wrongdoer could more completely affirm the value of piety than the penitent witch who reached beyond the outermost limit of impiety to renounce her alliance with the devil. In the confession of the witch, the members of the community would be reminded of their own lesser and more subtle complicity with Satan and of the terrible price to be exacted if they maintained this complicity.

It was to be the misfortune of the clergy that the occasions for these ceremonies were exceedingly rare and that even their momentary abundance during the Salem trials would later be proved counterfeit. Thus, in his review in 1689 of the history of witchcraft in New England, Cotton Mather gave special emphasis to one of the few cases that conformed to the ecclesiastical typology of sin and moral regeneration:

There was one Mary Johnson Tryed at Hartford, in this countrey, upon an Indictment of Familiarity with the Devil. She was found Guilty of the same, cheefly upon her own Confession, and condemned. . . .

She was by most Observers judged very penitent, both before and at her Execution. . . . And she died in a Frame extremely to the Satisfaction of them that were spectators to it.[5]

Unhappily, Mary Johnson may have been the only convicted witch in New England whose legal career and whose execution brought this satisfaction to the clergy as well as to the village laity.

THE PROBLEM OF PROOF

If it is appreciated that the gap between the accusation and the conviction frequently traversed not merely the boundaries of class in the
differentiated societies of seventeenth-century England and New England but also two divergent responses to the problem of witchcraft,
we can then see why, even in the context of belief, the task of validat-
ing the identity of the witch posed a judicial predicament of considerable complexity. The primary obstacle to any easy solution lay with
the very legal traditions within which the colonial magistrate and his
English counterpart functioned. The solidly entrenched English norms
against the use of torture to obtain evidence precluded any automatic
translation of village suspicions into terms compatible with doctrinal
formulations.[6] And the absence of any obvious financial incentive such
as rights of confiscation of the property of accused witches further
inhibited the development of unrestrained discovery methods similar
to those employed on the Continent. In short, the sure methods of the
Inquisition could not be applied in the Anglo-American context without a radical restructuring of existing legal institutions.

Given these conditions, the trials of witchcraft became a continuing
source of judicial embarrassment. On the one hand, the evidence from
confessions that could establish guilt according to the theological expectations of the crime was only rarely forthcoming either in England
or in New England. Macfarlane reports that only a small proportion of
prosecutions in Essex, England, were founded upon confessions, and
Thomas indicates from pamphlet literature that contemporaries were
aware of special difficulties in eliciting such testimony.[7] Of the pre-
Salem prosecutions in New England, combined evidence from published court records and contemporary accounts reveals at most five
confessions from the seventy persons indicted.[8] That there were voluntary confessions at all was undoubtedly an important buttress to the
continued legitimation of witchcraft prosecutions, but that there were
so few in proportion to the demand for legal action only added to the
dilemma faced by deliberating bodies.

On the other hand, decisions based upon the kind of evidence that
was forthcoming were apt to generate controversy, no matter what
the verdict. To acquit the suspect because the popular testimony fit
poorly with the theological requirements for the crime was to risk
the outrage of an entire village. Not infrequently, the popular demand
for legal redress was forcefully communicated right in the courtroom.
The official who presided in cases of witchcraft was likely to encounter a sizable delegation from the village where the suspect resided. In-

deed, fully eighteen witnesses against Elizabeth Morse were willing to
bear the expense of two days' journey from Newbury to offer their
testimony before the Court of Assistants in Boston. So militant were
these popular demands on one occasion that a lord chief justice in
England subsequently admitted to having approved the conviction of
three women in 1682 for fear that clemency would precipitate a village uprising.[9]

At the same time, to yield to village pressures was not merely to
surrender the judicial prerogative to mob action. Even more importantly, the official validation of allegations of maleficia placed the
court in potential conflict with the church. A conviction based on such
testimony gave official encouragement to the very magical beliefs that
the Protestant clergy had sought to officially proscribe.

The substantial corpus of legal guides published in England throughout the seventeenth century testifies to the persistence of this dilemma.
The problem of reconciling the popular testimony with the theological definition of the crime posed a challenge equal to the most subtle
logicians of the age. To give satisfaction to both constituencies—the
village laity and the clergy—necessitated the discovery of some point
of agreement between two mutually conflicting directives. To grant
official legitimation to evidence founded upon magical beliefs was to
risk ecclesiastical censure. To withhold official legitimation from all
evidences except confessions was to deny the village laity any form of
redress other than extralegal action.

Among the many treatises that attempted to resolve this predicament, the contributions of the English Puritans William Perkins and
Richard Bernard merit special consideration. In addition to serving as
prototypes for later formulations, the recommendations of these two
men were consulted by members of the New England clergy both before and during the Salem proceedings. Though several of the later
texts modified the rules for interpretation presented in these works,
such widely used manuals as Michael Dalton's *Countrey Justice*, in its
fourth edition by 1630, borrowed explicitly from Bernard. In turn,
Joseph Keble's authoritative text, *An Assistance to Justices of the
Peace*, was indebted to Dalton for the sections on witchcraft.[10]

The principal recommendation of Perkins and Bernard was to advise
that evidences be sorted into two broad classifications according to
their conformity to theological definitions. The more weighty testimony, referred to as convictive or sufficient proofs, established a direct link between the accused witch and the devil. In the event that
confessions might be unobtainable, Perkins allowed as equally sufficient the testimony of two witnesses of good repute that the suspect

had invoked the devil or entertained a familiar "in likeness of mouse, cat, or other visible creature."[11] To these evidences, Bernard added as sure identifications the presence of witch's marks (physical marks on the suspect's body believed to be produced by the devil) and the witness of God himself revealing the identity of the witch through some form of providential sign.[12]

The less weighty testimony, accorded the subordinate status of presumptions, incorporated those evidences based more exclusively upon the witch as doer of harm. Within this classification, magical beliefs were granted legal expression in terms of criteria adapted to the popular usage. Thus evidence of malicious intent as displayed by cursing, by threatening, or even by subtle violations of propriety such as over-inquisitiveness could be introduced as testimony against the suspect.[13] A stronger case could be made—although still not convictive—if the voicing of such malevolent feelings were accompanied by the sudden misfortune of the intended victim.[14] In the absence of any specific indications at all, neighborly consensus on the notoriety of the suspect would be sufficient in itself to at least initiate formal proceedings.[15]

The intricate specifications of Perkins and Bernard assume coherence if they are recognized not as merely an aggregate of disparate criteria but rather as part of an overriding strategy to elicit a theological proof from the myriad allegations of maleficia. Popular beliefs were accorded legal weight only at the initial phases of the discovery process. The role of presumptive evidence was merely to bring the suspect to the point of prosecution. Indeed, Bernard makes clear that such testimony, no matter how strong, should not be used to justify the imposition of the death penalty.[16] The indispensable convictive proof was to be obtained by alert and vigorous judicial cross-examinations. Perkins even went so far as to recommend torture if the presumptions were strong enough, while Bernard's proposal that judges note errors and inconsistencies in the responses of the suspect conformed more closely to legal conventions for other crimes.[17] In the course of successful prosecution, the accused witch as doer-of-harm would be transformed into the convicted witch as doer-of-harm-by-means-of-covenant-with-the-devil.

Yet, for all their ingenuity, the legal guides of Perkins and Bernard and their later exponents were able to resolve only one part of the judicial predicament. By granting priority to the theological version of witchcraft without entirely negating the popular version, a workable, if tenuous, compromise between the conflicting objectives of clergy and laity was achieved. The more forbidding problem, however, was to define a source of evidence more easily secured than the confession, which nonetheless conformed to the increasingly stringent theological requirements for sufficient proof.

The type of evidence most likely to satisfy these conditions was the witch's mark. Dalton's *Countrey Justice* includes a fairly precise description of this sign:

some big or little teat upon their [the witches'] body, and in some secret place where he [the devil] sucketh them. And besides their sucking, the Devil leaveth other marks upon their body, sometimes like a blew spot or red spot, like a flea-biting; sometimes the flesh sunk in and hollow; (all which for a time may be covered, yea taken away, but will come again to their old form.) And these the Devil's marks be insensible, and being pricked will not bleed, and be often in their secretest parts, and therefore require diligent and careful search.[18]

The use of the witch's mark as a means of identification had two distinct advantages. Most importantly, the search for these marks had the full sanction of ecclesiastical authorities, and the establishing of guilt through an expert search of the suspect's body promised to greatly simplify the task of judicial investigation.

Not surprisingly, this method of identification became a routine and integral component of Anglo-American prosecution. Indeed, in England—largely through the zeal of Matthew Hopkins during the witch-finding movement of 1645—an incipient technology of pins and pricking devices was developed to facilitate detection. In New England, examinations for devil's marks were conducted in Connecticut and Massachusetts both before and during the Salem trials.[19] In one pre-Salem case, the findings of this examination were even included as part of the indictment:

[Mary Webster] hath entered into covenant and had Familiarity with him in the shape of a Warraneage [Indian name for a black cat] and had his Imp sucking her, and Teats of Marks found on her, as in and by several testimonies may appear.[20]

Nevertheless, despite its several advantages, the use of this technique was far from uncontroversial. Official reliance upon the witch's mark exposed the court to a form of criticism it was ill equipped to oppose, for the task of systematically distinguishing natural from supernatural excrescences placed the trial of witchcraft within the hostile jurisdiction of medical authority. Although it is difficult to assess the precise impact of contemporary medical discoveries upon the detection of witch's marks, the legal guides of medically informed clergymen such as Meric Casaubon and Thomas Ady urged increasing caution in the interpretation of such evidence.[21] Also, it may be noted that when competent physicians were directly involved in the search, the results were generally exculpatory. The inclusion of the eminent William Harvey and six surgeons in the examination of the Lancashire witches in England in 1634 eventuated in the exoneration of all four of the accused.[22]

Whether or not qualified physicians participated in the search, the medical competence of the examiner remained a potential source of embarrassment to the court. Matthew Hopkins himself was hard-pressed by challenges from critics that reliable identification of witch's marks was impossible.[23] Nor did it escape the attention of his oppo-nents that the persons most likely to acquire the physical deformities that could be confounded with witch's marks were drawn from the ranks of the poor and aged. Hopkins's own formulation of this com-plaint and his response to it give some indication of the terms in which debates over the validity of the test were conducted:

Querie 5. Many poore people are condemned for having a Pap, or Teat about them, wereas many people (especially ancient People) are, and have been a long time, troubled with natural wretts on severall parts of their bodies, and other naturall excrescencies as Hemerodes, Piles, Childbear-ing, &c. . . .

Answer. The parties so judging can justifie their skill to any, and shew good reasons why such markes are not meerly naturall, neither that they can happen by any such naturall cause as is before expressed.[24]

Opposition to the use of witch's marks appears to have surfaced later in New England than in England. That examinations were con-ducted almost entirely by matrons and midwives may in part account for this relative lack of controversy. The position of the female practi-tioner in colonial society made it unlikely that she would challenge the test on formal medical grounds. Not only were women in general excluded from medical education in English universities, but their op-portunities for nonmedical education were drastically limited as well.[25] The illiteracy of seven of the eight women who comprised one panel of female examiners during the Salem trials may well have been repre-sentative.[26] In light of these obstacles, the probability that such women could draw upon recent medical discoveries in female sexual anatomy to make fine distinctions between natural and supernatural excres-cences is extremely low.

There were more profound reasons for silence than mere lack of technical expertise, however. Even more unfavorable for the female critic was that the positions of examiner and suspect were so easily reversible. The susceptibility of female practitioners to witchcraft accusations has been discussed in the preceding chapter. The folk healer or midwife who protested too strongly against an affirmative finding might soon discover herself transposed from the investigator in a search to the subject of a search.

An incident in an early Connecticut witchcraft case well illustrates this hazard, although the woman in jeopardy had not been involved in the inquest. Following the execution of a convicted witch in 1654, one of the female bystanders was alleged to have stepped up to the gallows to inspect the corpse. After "tumbling the body up and down," according to one testimony, she declared that "if these be the markes of a witch, then she was one," and that "other women might have the same [marks]."[27] The inference among several of her fellow spectators that this was a tacit confession of her own culpability formed the basis for a later witchcraft litigation.

In spite of these obstacles, by the time of the Salem trials, judicial reliance upon the witch's mark had become a subject of open debate. In fact, one of the earliest of the accused witches, Rebecca Nurse, petitioned the court that she be examined by a different panel of midwives and matrons after the first search yielded positive findings.[28] Her request was granted, and the second search produced negative findings. But the advice of a group of Connecticut ministers in 1692 was even more damaging to proponents of the test. In opposing the conviction of several Hartford women, they cited as one of their four objections "That ye unusuall excrescencies found upon their bodies ought not to be allowed as evidence against them without ye approbation of some able physitians."[29] The close communication among the New England ministers insured that the General Court of Massachusetts as well as the Particular Court of Connecticut would have to respect this opinion.

If the search for witch's marks could provoke controversy, the use of other forms of evidence proved even less viable as solutions to the judicial predicament. The belief that Satan rewarded his allies with the service of a familiar provided the rationale for the method of "watching." In this method, as developed by the inventive Hopkins, the investigators would keep the suspect awake and ambulatory for several days and nights "in order to catch their imps in open view."[30] While this method did generate confessions, the rather thinly disguised element of torture made it unpopular in England and New England. The only recorded instance of colonial application occurred during the trial of Margaret Jones in 1648.[31]

More controversial than either the search for witch's marks or watching was the method of proof referred to as "spectral evidence." In brief, this form of evidence was founded on the belief that demons could assume the identity of a person, and, as a specter, inflict harm on the body of another person or simply perform general mischiefs. If this evidence were admitted, the accused would be left with virtually no means of challenge. If she were miles away from the crime or even in a large public gathering at the time of the assault, the accuser could claim that it was her specter rather than her person that established her guilt.

The validity of spectral evidence was questionable on strict theological grounds, for it entailed the assumption that the devil would use spectral representations to betray only the guilty. To hold that the activities and intentions of Satan were so easily discernible by humanity was to affect a compromise in Puritan dogma that many New England ministers were unwilling to make. The reinstatement of this evidence in spite of these theological misgivings will be discussed in chapter 9.

Apart from these several tentative evidences, there were few other opportunities for the court to simplify procedure. Among its many far-reaching consequences, the relentless Protestant campaign against ecclesiastical magic penetrated to the very core of the law. The scant vestiges of magic in English common law and its colonial variant became ever more peripheral under the hostile scrutiny of Protestant polemicists. The method of "swimming" the witch—based on the assumption that the pure element, water, would expel so corrupt a substance as the witch's body—was roundly condemned by Increase Mather in 1684 as lacking any scriptural foundation.[32] The deputy governor of Connecticut, William Jones, went even further by describing the test as "supstitious [superstitious] and unwarrantable and worse."[33]

So, also, were the various other occult formulas that presumed that God would perform miracles at the request of the court repudiated. The ordeal by touch, in which the suspect was asked to touch the corpse of her alleged victim in anticipation of a telling sign, was dismissed as mere paganism. Other tests, such as the scratching of the suspect's body or the use of wizards to show the face of the witch in a magical glass, were characterized by Jones, and by other Puritan critics, as "dangerous and diabolical."[34] That such methods were used at all should not suggest that the Protestant campaign was unsuccessful, for the water test, which was applied in Connecticut in 1662, was discontinued after that date.[35] And the ordeal by touch, which was used to indict Rachel Fuller in 1680, disappeared from judicial procedure after only a few exposures.[36] Such backsliding testifies more to the desperation of the court than to the ineffectiveness of the clergy.

In the adjudication of the pre-Salem witchcraft cases, the conflict between the clergy and the village laity over the constitution of the crime yielded a judicial predicament. The legal expression of this predicament was an irreconcilable gap between the terms of accusation and the terms of prosecution. To accept the terms of accusation was to reintroduce magical beliefs into the very operation of the law; yet for the court to confine itself to a strict theological interpretation of the law was to turn a deaf ear to the frequently militant popular demand for legal redress.

Efforts to rescue the court from this dilemma through the introduction of objective tests were ultimately unsuccessful. No feasible means could be devised for translating the popular testimony into theologically acceptable terms. Each attempted solution exposed the court to fierce opposition, whether from the clergy or from other influential quarters. The cross-pressures engendered by the coexistent popular and theological versions of the crime proved inescapable. It is in the context of these cross-pressures that the equivocal response of the courts to popular demands becomes comprehensible.

THE TRIAL OF WITCHCRAFT: FROM JUDICIAL
STALEMATE TO THE PRAGMATIC SOLUTION

No single moment in the making of the malefic witch more directly reflects the deep divisions within the colonial response to the problem of witchcraft than does the rendering of the final verdict. It is at this point that the delicate truce effected by the clergy and the laity was most vulnerable to dissolution. If the court should acquiesce to the popular demand, it would place in jeopardy the vital alliance between the magistrates and the clergy. If the court should oppose the popular demand, it risked inciting a village riot. Given these grim options, one may better understand the curious inability of the court to commit itself to any decisive action at all, for the history of judgments in the pre-Salem litigations is a history of delay, hesitation, and uncertainty. It is a history of appeals, reprieves, and equivocal verdicts. That such lack of resolve was not characteristic of the courts in other legal undertakings will become clear later when their role in the Salem trials is discussed.

The earliest four recorded cases reveal little dissension within the court. The trial of Margaret Jones appears to have progressed to her conviction and execution without any legal interruptions. The approving presence of Governor Winthrop during these proceedings may help account for the lack of complications. Two of the other cases— those of Mrs. Lake in 1650 and Mrs. Kendal in 1651—also eventuated in convictions and executions. The loss of original court records precludes any further assessment of these deliberations. In the remaining case, the suspect was arrested but was not brought to trial.[37]

Not until the cases of Mary Parsons, Hugh Parsons, and Ann Hibbins did the forces in contention over the verdict express themselves in open legal disputation. The juries, acting in behalf of the popular interest, decided on a guilty verdict in at least two of the cases, and possibly in all three. The magistrates, acting under the pressure of theological constraints, voted for acquittal in each of the cases. The disposition of Mary Parsons in 1651 was the easiest to resolve, in spite of these conflicting judgments. After her indictment by the grand jury following her examination in Springfield, she was cleared by the General Court from charges of witchcraft, the court ruling that the testimonies "were not sufficient to prove her a witch."[38] She had also been indicted for the murder of her child, however. On this charge she was found guilty by her own confession and was presumably executed on May 29, 1651.

The dispute surrounding her husband's case was more overt. Parsons was not formally indicted until a year after his arrest. When he was finally brought to trial on May 12, 1652, the jury found him guilty, but the magistrates did not consent to the verdict.[39] The case was then referred to the final court of appeal, the General Court. On May 31, 1652, this body ruled that Parsons was not legally guilty of witchcraft and released him from jail.

The same pattern of disagreement emerged in the trial of Ann Hibbins, but with a less favorable outcome for the prisoner. In her appearance before the Court of Assistants in 1655, Ann was tried and condemned by the jury.[40] The magistrates again refused to accept the verdict, and she was brought before the General Court on May 14, 1656. Here, it was decided by vote that she was guilty, and, accordingly, she was executed on June 19. As the eighteenth-century historian Thomas Hutchinson aptly summarized the verdict, "the popular clamor prevailed against her."[41] More significantly, however, in the execution of Ann Hibbins, this popular clamor overcame magisterial caution for the last time.

In later cases, where the suspect was not acquitted outright, the conflicting predilections of magistrate and jury yielded a judicial policy that was both equivocal and ambiguous. The legal careers of John Godfrey and Eunice Cole well illustrate the discomfort of the court.

Between 1658 and 1669, the immensely unpopular Godfrey was implicated in five separate legal actions relating to witchcraft.[42] Three of these causes were defamation suits in which he participated as plaintiff; in the other two actions, he was the defendant on charges of witchcraft.

The outcome of the first of these two actions is unclear. It is known only that he was imprisoned some time in 1659 and that he was eventually released after appearing before the Court of Assistants. It is the outcome of the second trial in 1665 that reveals the awkward position of the court. On this occasion, Godfrey pleaded guilty to performing acts of malefic witchcraft upon his accusers. Nevertheless, the evidences were deemed insufficient for conviction. The court found Godfrey "susptiously Guilty of witchcraft, but not legally guilty according to the lawe and evidence . . . received."[43] The verdict was accepted, and the defendant was discharged without being either condemned for witchcraft or cleared from suspicion of witchcraft.

Such judicial uncertainty is evident as well in the legal disposition of the case of Eunice Cole. Eunice's involvement with the courts on charges of witchcraft extends over an even greater time period than that of Godfrey.[44] Between 1656 and 1680, she was tried as a witch on three separate occasions and spent a considerable portion of these twenty-five years in prison. In the first of these cases, in 1656, Eunice was found guilty as charged but, in contrast to judicial policy for other capital convictions, she was not sentenced to be executed. Instead, she was placed in jail for an indeterminate length of time or until the court should decide to release her. The length of her imprisonment on this charge is not recorded. In 1665, having been imprisoned on another charge not related to witchcraft, she petitioned the General Court for an early release. In response, the court ordered that she might have her liberty on payment of security and if she departed out of their jurisdiction. Eunice refused the offer, in part because she could not afford the payment but also because travel through the wilderness was hardly a tenable option for an old and impoverished widow.

That she was released in either 1671 or 1672 is known only because, shortly after this time, she was brought before the court on a second round of charges. The decision in this trial of August 1673 was almost identical to the verdict rendered in the case of John Godfrey: "In ye case of Unis Cole now prisoner att ye Bar not legally guilty according to Inditement but just ground of vehement suspissyon of her haveing had familiaryty with the devill."[45] Finally, in September 1680, she was again prosecuted for witchcraft, but this time the case progressed only as far as the quarterly court. Here it was decided in accord with the previous verdict that "no full Proof" of her witchcraft could be established, although "from Examination of Testimonies the court vehemently suspects her so to be."[46] She was nonetheless imprisoned until her eventual return to Hampton.

The disposition of the cases of Godfrey and Cole reveal the court at considerable pains to reconcile the popular demand for legal redress with the theological insistence upon strict interpretation of the law. The reluctance to convict the suspect on the basis of popular testimonies, no matter how abundant, was designed to satisfy the theological requirement. At the same time, the tendency of the court to qualify its judgments by including reference to suspicious practice may have in part appeased the popular demand.

The weakness in the policy was demonstrated by its very consequences. The equivocal verdict did not resolve the dilemma of the court; it merely postponed the dilemma until a future date. Godfrey, Cole, and others underwent the full cycle of prosecution only to reappear again and again as a continuing source of judicial embarrassment. Another case in which this policy was applied—that of Caleb Powell in 1680—was less prolonged, but presumably only because the suspect chose to leave the colony.[47]

The development of a more stable solution to the legal problem of witchcraft can be traced in the handling of two other cases. One of these cases, that of Elizabeth Morse in 1680–81, is particularly crucial to this investigation, but not just because it defines a shift in judicial policy. Even more importantly, enough original records have survived from this case to permit a fairly complete reconstruction of the actual terms in which the magistrates and the jury negotiated the verdict. The other case, that of Katherine Harrison in 1669, is included for consideration because, although it was decided in the colony of Connecticut, it was most likely the legal precedent for the case of Elizabeth Morse.

The intense legal conflicts generated during the trial of Katherine Harrison culminated in the formulation of explicit criteria for the rejection of popular testimony. Katherine deviated in one important respect from the usual demographic profile for the malefic witch; although old and recently widowed, her husband had left her a substantial estate valued at around 930 pounds.[48] In spite of this wealth, a considerable number of witnesses filed depositions against her, and she was indicted by the Court of Assistants at Hartford on May 25, 1669.[49]

Shortly after this date, a partial trial was held at the May session of the court, but the case was adjourned until the next session because the jury could not agree on a verdict. On this occasion, in October 1669, the jury passed a verdict of guilty, which the Connecticut magistrates, following the practice of their colleagues in Massachusetts, refused. Moreover, to help resolve their differences with the jury, the magistrates sought the advice of a panel of prominent ministers on how to evaluate the popular testimony. The advice was solicited in the form of several questions, to which the clergymen responded with precise opinions a week after the request.

The first of these exchanges gave legal expression to the most critical issue in the dispute:

To ye 1st Quest whether a plurality of witnesses be necessary, legally to evidence one and ye same individual fact? Wee answer:

That if the proofe of the fact do depend wholly upon testimony, there is than a necessity of a plurality of witnesses, to testify to one and ye same individual fact: and without such a plurality there can be no legal evidence of it.[50]

Ostensibly, the purpose of this exchange was to establish whether the evidentiary requirements for witchcraft should be made consistent with the requirements for other capital crimes, for the rule requiring two witnesses for a capital conviction survived in New England as a remnant from ecclesiastical law. When, in 1641, Gov. William Bradford of Plymouth asked for ecclesiastical opinion on whether "one witness with other circumstances shall be sufficient to convince," the ministers based their defense of the two-witness rule on biblical precedents.[51] The advice of the Plymouth authorities was, in turn, noted by John Winthrop in 1641, and the rule was enacted by the General Court of Massachusetts in the same year: "no man shall be put to death without the testimonie of two or three witnesses, or that which is equivalent thereunto."[52]

The reinvoking of the two-witness rule had a special bearing on the trial of witchcraft, however. At stake was the question of whether the village accusation would continue to carry any legal force at all. By definition, acts of malefic witchcraft made sense only in the context of the victim's personal relationship to the suspect. The bursting of Joan Francis's barrel following her refusal to offer Katherine Harrison's daughter any emptyings and the death of John Graves's cattle after his trespass upon Katherine's land formed connected events within a particular history of problematic transactions.[53] Indeed, the peculiar and essential horror of the malefic act derived from its thoroughly appropriate exaction of vengeance for the grievance that preceded it.

No two testimonies were alike—nor could they be alike if the malefic act were to be distinguished from the more impersonal damage wrought by a natural catastrophe or a divine judgment or some other less focused disaster. The effect of theological insistence on the two-witness rule was to reinforce the very evidentiary standard that the village accusation could not meet. By these means, the magistrate was furnished with an impeccably legal basis for repudiating the popular understanding of witchcraft.

The other two exchanges between the magistrates and the ministers added little to the first. Spectral evidence, like allegations of maleficia, was to be allowed as convictive testimony if and only if the same apparition was sworn to by a plurality of witnesses. To the final question of whether the ability to foretell the future or to reveal a secret constituted a demonstration of familiarity with the devil, the ministers replied affirmatively but with considerable qualification. Only if such knowledge had not been gained "by human skill in art" or "by strength of reason" or "by divine revelation either mediate or immediate" could it be taken as evidence of a pact with the devil.[54] The ministers made clear that other explanations would have to be fully exhausted before such testimony would be allowed convictive weight.

The more immediate consequence of the ecclesiastical advice was to place the case of Katherine Harrison in temporary legal abeyance. When, at length, a new trial was held on May 20, 1670, the verdict was delivered by a special court composed exclusively of magistrates. The decision of this body represented a departure from the previous policy of equivocation:

Having considered the verdict of the Jury respecting K. Harrison, [we] cannot concur with them so as to sentence her to death or to a longer continuance in restraint, but doe dismiss her from her imprisonment, her pay her just fees: willing her to minde the fulfillment of removeing from Wethersfield which is that will tend most to her safety and the contentment of the people who are her neighbors.[55]

On the one hand, the judges acknowledged the incompatibility between the terms of accusation and the terms of prosecution. The popular testimony was not sufficient to justify official validation of the charge of witchcraft. On the other hand, the judges also acknowledged the intensity of the village antagonism toward the suspect. The attempt to meet both the theological guidelines for the crime and the popular expectations for legal redress yielded a pragmatic solution to the problem of witchcraft. The overt village demand for punishment of the suspect was rejected on grounds that her guilt had not been demonstrated. The underlying but unstated village demand for release from further contact with the suspect was granted by decreeing that she leave the jurisdiction.

An appreciation of the legal career of Katherine Harrison makes comprehensible the equally subtle judicial deliberations in the case of Elizabeth Morse. Like her Connecticut predecessor, Elizabeth was strongly disliked by the members of her community. Information on her social background and reputation as a magical healer has been presented above. By the time of her initial examination, the village consensus had already crystallized. Members of at least nineteen families representing twenty-five neighbors were willing to come forth either as victims or as corroborators of the effectiveness of her diabolical skills. The expense willingly incurred by these witnesses while submitting their testimony provides tangible evidence of their determination to gain legal satisfaction.[56]

The ensuing legal contest over the disposition of Elizabeth Morse was more prolonged and intense than that of any other pre-Salem litigation. The case came before the Court of Assistants on May 20, 1680, some five months after Elizabeth's initial examination in Newbury. The inclination of the jury at this trial may be inferred from their passage of a special ruling on May 22:

Whether severall distinct single testimonies of preternatural and diabolicall actions by the prisoner at the bar, though not any two concurring to prove the same individual act, is to be accounted legall evidence to Convict of Witchcraft. This was resolved in ye affirmative by ye Court.[57]

Having thus disposed of the major legal obstacle to conviction, the jury reconvened on May 27 and decided upon a verdict of guilty. Elizabeth was sentenced to death by hanging, as required for all capital crimes.

The intervention of the magistrates was almost immediate. On June 1, they granted a reprieve of the sentence and postponed a final review of the case until the next session of the Court of Assistants. In the interim, Elizabeth was placed in a Boston jail, where she would remain for a year while her case was negotiated between the jury and the bench. Approximately five months after the reprieve had been granted, some of the deputy members of the General Court addressed a complaint to the magistrates for not showing cause why the jury sentence was overruled: "The Deputies . . . relating to the woman condemned for witchcraft do not understand the reason why operation of the sentence given against her by this court is not executed."[58] Although the response to the complaint is not recorded, the minister John Hale, in his discussion of the case about twenty years after the trial, mentions two of the grounds upon which the magistrates based their decision for reprieval:

They were not satisfyed that a Specter doing mischief in her likeness, should be imputed to her person, as a ground of guilt.

They did not esteem one single witness to one fact, for two witnesses, against the person in a capital crime.[59]

At length, possibly at the urging of William Morse, who submitted three petitions to the General Court in behalf of his wife, the case was reopened. Elizabeth was brought before the Court of Assistants on June 1, 1681. Like the decision of the Connecticut magistrates, the final verdict also represented a pragmatic solution to the problem of witchcraft. An almost precise compromise was effected between the village demand for judicial protection and the demand of the clergy and magistrates for strict adherence to evidentiary requirements. Because the later demand was not met, Elizabeth was dismissed from the Boston jail and allowed to return to Newbury. Because she was nonetheless still perceived by the village inhabitants as a threat to their security, she was allowed to return to her home provided that "she not goe above sixteen Rods from hir Oune house and land at any time except to the meeting house in Newbury."[60]

The pre-Salem litigations gave direct legal expression to the conflicts between the popular and the theological versions of witchcraft. The popular demand for legal redress was represented by both the quarterly court juries and the grand juries, the latter composed of freemen selected from each of the towns. The theological insistence upon strict interpretation of the law was at first tentatively forwarded by the magistrates and later more forcefully asserted by the magistrates in coalition with the clergy. Early judicial attempts to reconcile the two approaches yielded equivocal decisions, which were framed roughly according to the recommendations of Perkins and Bernard. The effect of these decisions was to corroborate the suspicions of the villagers but to withhold the legal remedies for alleviating them. By 1680, the introduction of additional legal obstacles had made the task of translating popular testimony into a theologically acceptable proof insurmountable. The village accusation no longer retained validity as an imputation of deviance. Instead, it had become merely a communication to the court that tensions between the suspect and her neighbors had passed beyond the point of peaceful resolution.

THE VANISHING MALEFIC WITCH

That witchcraft prosecutions should have gradually declined throughout the later half of the seventeenth century only to rise dramatically
during the Salem trials of 1692 has constituted one of the central
enigmas for later generations of historians in their attempts to reconstruct the legal history of the crime. Indeed, the problem of how to
reconcile the judicial restraint of the pre-Salem prosecutions with the
judicial zeal of the Salem prosecutions has led some historical observers
to seek refuge in psychoanalytic explanations. Only by positing a
generalized cultural hysteria or by entertaining doubts about the sanity
of the magistrates has it been possible to account for the apparent inconsistency in judicial conduct.[61]

It is only when the complex interrelationships between the popular
and the theological versions of the crime are fully appreciated that the
dramatic reorientation of the court may be more precisely described.
The temporary disappearance of witchcraft from the legal records of
New England before 1692 represented neither a victory of skepticism
over credulity nor the triumph of judicial compassion over judicial
severity. It was not out of disbelief in witchcraft that the magistrates
deprived the village accusation of its legal force. If the popular version
of witchcraft were successfully contained by judicial fiat, it is because, by this same exercise of judicial prerogative, the theological version of the crime was thereby affirmed. The abrupt rise in witchcraft
prosecutions after decades of steady decline marks not a reversal in
this policy but rather the endorsement of one version of the crime following upon the repudiation of the other.

After the controversial conviction of Ann Hibbins in 1656, only one
other person was executed for witchcraft prior to the Salem trials. But
the case of Mary Glover in 1688 figures less as a return to earlier policy
than as a precursor of the policy to come, for at last, in this trial, the
clergy and the magistrates could unite not in opposition to the popular
preoccupation with magic but in defense of church and state against
the conspiracy of witchcraft.

Mary was charged with the affliction of four children of a respected
member of Cotton Mather's own Boston congregation.[62] Four
ministers and several physicians testified to the validity of the afflictions. The investigation of the suspect was far more thorough than any
conducted for previous trials. Mary's house was searched for puppets
and images, and her body was examined for witch's marks. She was
also requested by the magistrates to recite the Lord's Prayer, a task
she could not complete without blaspheming. Finally, she confessed.

But judicial rigor was applied even to this testimony. Five doctors decided that she was compos mentis and that her confession could be
accepted by the court.

Mary Glover was hanged in Boston on November 16, 1688. Just
before her death, she revealed the names of several confederates who
had assisted her in delivering the afflictions. This time, however, the
investigation was not pursued. Four years later, when the opportunity
arose once again, the magistrates were prepared to be more diligent.

Witchcraft and the State

The Salem Witchcraft Prosecutions:

The Framework for Official Initiative

IN EARLY FEBRUARY 1692, several members and friends of the household of Samuel Parris, minister for Salem Village since 1689, were taken with strange fits.[1] A local physician was summoned to examine Elizabeth, Parris's nine-year-old daughter; Abigail Williams, his eleven-year-old niece; and a few other girls and young women, all of whom complained of similar physical torments. Not unexpectedly, Dr. Griggs confirmed Parris's worst suspicions. The girls were victims of bewitchment.

Shortly thereafter, the youthful victims—or the afflicted, as they came to be designated by contemporaries—began to cry out the names of their tormentors. The first suspects were brought before local magistrates in Salem on February 29. Concurrent with these preliminary examinations, alternative nonlegal remedies were applied to the sufferings of the afflicted. A group of ministers congregated at Parris's residence for a solemn day of prayer on March 11. Also, one of the former ministers of Salem Village, Deodat Lawson, visited Parris a week later to offer his assistance. Neither of these attempts at intercession proved effective. The condition of the young women steadily deteriorated.

Eventually, a special court, the Court of Oyer and Terminer, was convened by the governor to sit in judgment over the alarming number of suspects now detained by the Salem magistrates. The Court of Oyer and Terminer was composed exclusively of prominent magistrates. When this body met for the first time on June 2, the ranks of the accused had swelled to over seventy men and women (see figure 1). The decision of the magistrates at their first formal session on June 10 defined the orientation of the court for the remainder of its existence. A verdict of guilty was turned in for the one suspect who was tried. In the next four meetings of the court, on June 30, August 5, September 9, and September 17, guilty verdicts were returned for all

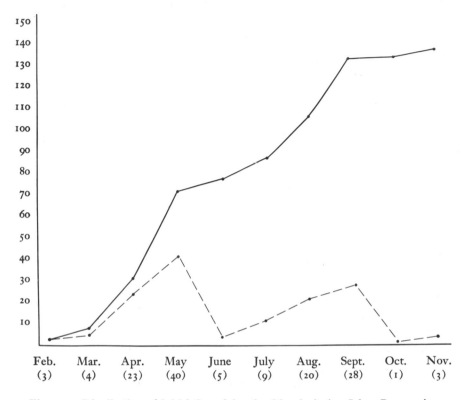

Feb.	Mar.	Apr.	May	June	July	Aug.	Sept.	Oct.	Nov.
(3)	(4)	(23)	(40)	(5)	(9)	(20)	(28)	(1)	(3)

Figure 1 Distribution of Initial Complaints by Month during Salem Prosecutions. *Note:* See App. C for data on which this chart is based.
[a] Total number of legal actions included in this chart is 136. In five cases, there is no record of the date.

———— Cumulative distribution of legal actions[a]

— — — Distribution of legal actions for each month

cases. By early October, fifty of the accused had confessed to the crime of witchcraft, another twenty-six had been convicted by the court, and, of these twenty-six condemned witches, nineteen had been executed.[2] Moreover, there was reason to believe that the work of the court of Oyer and Terminer had only just begun. The prisons of Boston, Salem, and Ipswich were filled to capacity with untried suspects. In addition, new allegations were filtering into the court each day.

Then, on October 12, in the midst of this apparently growing epidemic, Gov. William Phips, only recently appointed to his post, ordered a halt to the prosecutions. A new court was constituted on November 25 to replace the General Court—formerly the highest court in the colony—and to preside over the remaining witchcraft cases. In four sessions held on January 2, January 31, April 25, and May of 1693, this court—The Superior Court of Judicature—reversed the policy of its predecessor.[3] In the first session, held at Salem, the grand jury accepted indictments for only twenty-one of more than fifty persons awaiting trial. The magistrates returned verdicts of guilty for only three suspects, each of whom had offered a confession. Eleven other suspects were acquitted in the next three sessions of the court. At length, even the three convicted witches were reprieved by order of the governor and released from jail later in 1693. During the same year, all other pending actions issuing from the Salem trials were terminated by a general pardon. After 1693, there are no further records of legal action against witchcraft in Massachusetts Bay.

These, then, are the bare chronological outlines of perhaps the best-known episode in the history of witchcraft. The beginnings of a sizable American literature on the Salem trials extend back at least as far as the 1860s. Since that time, each succeeding generation has contributed to this corpus through both historical writings and creative literary efforts. Indeed, the Salem trials have formed the setting for at least three novels, about half a dozen plays, and even one opera.[4] The problem of how to reconcile the lofty images of Plymouth Rock and the American Revolution with the almost equally famous events of 1692 is a continuing national preoccupation.

In line with the general objectives of this investigation, this part of the study is concerned with describing changes in the legal and epistemological status of witchcraft as a category of deviance. In this chapter, an attempt is made to show how the colonists' formulation of the problem of witchcraft in 1692 constituted both a response and a solution to the political crises then besetting Massachusetts Bay. Here the goal is to situate public policy toward witchcraft during the Salem trials within its social and political context.

In the following two chapters, the emphasis is upon the production of witches. In chapter 9, the Salem trials are distinguished from the pre-Salem litigations both in terms of the social processes entailed in the identification of the witch and in terms of how the rules for the discovery of witchcraft were negotiated. In chapter 10, the concern is to explicate how and in what terms members renegotiated the rules for discovery in such a manner as to preclude the further production of witches.

At the same time, it should be noted that such an effort to bring or-

der and continuity to the events of the Salem trials entails a rather serious risk, for the Salem trials were an object of bafflement and consternation to the participants themselves. To overlook this consternation
for the sake of analytic clarity, to ignore the deep uncertainties of the
clergy in their attempt to formulate public policy or the desperation
of the magistrates in their search for judicial guidelines or the bewilderment of the convicted witches when held accountable for actions
of which they had no recollection, is to neglect a unique feature of
this occurrence.

What is significant about the Salem trials has less to do with their
success than with their failure. The scope of judicial activity during
the Salem trials can hardly be regarded as spectacular. In comparison
to Continental or even Scottish mass prosecutions, the scale of operation in 1692 was modest. It is the elements of normative ambiguity
that, above all, recommend the Salem trials for scholarly investigation.
The events of 1692 reveal how, in one society, the crime of witchcraft had become inoperational. No longer could members agree on
how to define the problem of witchcraft, how to interpret the rules of
evidence, or how to identify the malefactor. The experience of bewilderment expressed in the transcripts of the trials and in the narratives
of contemporaries is an important datum. Ultimately, it is this experience with which the historical observer must come to terms in order
to appreciate why the prosecutions of 1692 were among the final applications of the laws against witchcraft.

THE PLACE OF WITCHCRAFT IN PURITAN THEODICY

That the cries of the afflicted should be construed by some of the
clergy as an occasion for communal propitiation was hardly without
precedent in the brief history of New England. Examples of this usage
have been discussed in chapter 5. That others might attribute these
torments to the mediating activity of witchcraft was even less unlikely.
Even in 1692, a sizable proportion of villagers continued to regard
witchcraft as the most plausible explanation for the convulsions that
periodically seized their children. What is distinctive about the Salem
trials is how quickly and eagerly the community achieved a synthesis
of these two interpretations.

The Salem proceedings were premised upon the assumption that the
cries of the afflicted were indeed a collective responsibility, but this
time it was no vague and abstract failing of which the community was
culpable. This time the offense was as palpable as a conspiracy. In the

rapid unfolding of the Salem trials during the spring and summer of 1692, the inhabitants of Massachusetts were to discover that an organized plot to subvert the Puritan mission had successfully infiltrated the core of the church. The means by which this plot was uncovered will be considered later. The more immediate task is to appreciate how, in the 1690s in Massachusetts Bay, civil and ecclesiastical authorities were prepared for this catastrophe by both theology and circumstance.

The belief that afflictions were a collective responsibility had its roots in what Perry Miller has called "the master idea" of the New England Puritans—the doctrine of the national covenant.[5] Even before the actual habitation and settlement of the wilderness, the founders of New England conceived of the colony as bound by a special relationship to God. Winthrop articulated the terms of this relationship in midvoyage aboard the *Arbella:*

Thus stands the cause between God and us, wee are entered into Covenant with him for this worke, wee have taken out a Commission, the Lord hath given us lease to draw our owne Articles we have professed to enterprise these Accions upon these and these ends, we have hereupon besought him of favor and blessing.[6]

Within this covenantal framework, the Puritans accorded the colony a legitimacy that transcended royal prerogative. New England was not a mere commercial enterprise to be encouraged or discarded according to its material success. As the current repository of God's truth, the destiny of the settlement was linked to a far grander imperative. The measure of New England was the success with which the community fulfilled its covenantal obligation to God.

It was the idea of the national covenant that, more than any other theological conception, provided the framework within which seventeenth-century New England divines interpreted their collective experience in the wilderness. The subtle and intricate theological underpinnings of this idea have been well explicated in the works of Perry Miller. For present purposes, what is pertinent is that, in the context of this doctrine, the misfortunes that befell the New England community took on a special meaning.

For a chosen people, the judgments of Providence were sure and exact. Crop failures, epidemics, Indian raids, and sundry other disasters were perceived not as accidents or as the mere logical concomitants of wilderness living but rather as judgments rendered according to the moral failings of the community. As the national sins increased, so would the severity of divine afflictions. Insofar as God maintained his covenant with New England, the members would have clear and continuous guidelines regarding the extent of their progress toward or departure from the realization of communal goals.

Until the deeply troubled decade of the 1690s, there was little fear that these guidelines would disappear. No matter how grave the crisis and, by direct inference, no matter how far the community had degenerated, few civil and ecclesiastical leaders of the first two generations ever seriously doubted that the Puritan mission was salvageable.

For the first generation of ministers, the idea of the national covenant furnished not only a tool for diagnosing the ills of the society but a means for solving them as well. In response to the various judgments of war and calamity issued by an angry Providence, the General Court would order a day of humiliation in which members were enjoined to acknowledge their sins through prayer and fasting. Through such communal rituals, civil and ecclesiastical leaders sought not only to safeguard New England's covenantal status but to actively restore peace and prosperity.

The second generation of ministers broke with this formula. Gradually, the catalog of public misfortunes began to include not just external disasters but the sins and corruptions of the community itself. Miller gives October 19, 1652, as the date when the General Court included for the first time the moral failings of New England—"the worldlymindedness, oppression, and hard-heartedness to be feared among us"[7]—as well as the routine list of devastations as reasons for a public fast.

This emphasis upon spiritual corruption and moral deficiency reached its literary apotheosis between approximately 1660 and 1690 in a type of sermon that Miller has termed the jeremiad.[8] The jeremiad imparted a new meaning to the misfortunes that befell New England. The disasters visited upon the community were viewed less as the occasion for collective propitiation than as the punishment for collective sin.

Where the first generation of ministers had provided a means of deliverance from the problems that beset the colony, the second and third generations projected an implacable and limitless spiritual malaise. Typically, the jeremiad consisted of a denunciation of the community, followed not by a recommendation for remedial action but rather by a warning of further devastations if the members did not reform. Increasingly, as the ministers condemned the community for its spiritual corruptions, the expiatory rituals of prayer and fasting became ever less viable as solutions to public distress. As Miller has expressed it, "the day of humiliation became not a blood-letting and a cure, but an increase of appetite that grew by what it fed upon."[9]

By the early 1690s, ecclesiastical denunciation had escalated almost to the point where the success of a sermon could be measured by the vividness of its portrait of impending doom. It is in the context of this ever-expanding repertory of dire prophecies that the community was prepared for the most shocking demonstration of all. The judgment of witchcraft was the final realization of what ministers had been warning the members of for years. The spiritual declension of the community had brought New England to the brink of collapse, and the need for a redefinition of the goals of the Puritan mission had become urgent and immediate.

THE MASSACHUSETTS BAY IN 1692

This is not to suggest that the desperation of the 1690s was merely a product of literary artifice. To be sure, the woeful prophecies of the second and third generation were in some measure rhetorical devices designed to reinforce the members' commitment to the goals of the founders. Indeed, as Miller has pointed out, some of the most vocal denunciators found it expedient when seeking favor from the British government to concede that affairs in New England were not so bad after all.[10]

Nevertheless, in 1692, the threat of impending disaster could no longer be taken metaphorically. If the jeremiad provided a ready vehicle for the expression of gloomy predictions, the events of the previous decade endowed these predictions with plausibility. At the time of the Salem trials, the future of the Puritan mission in America was in real jeopardy. The prospect of political dislocation within the British Empire, combined with involvement in a fierce and costly war with the French and their Indian allies, more than fulfilled the dire expectations of the ministers.

Particularly disruptive were the relations between the colony and the English government. In 1684, after having allowed colonial political autonomy for over fifty years, English authorities decided to exercise stronger controls. The charter of 1629—the document that legitimated the colonial right of self-government—was revoked by order of King Charles II.[11] The immediate effect of this cancelation was to undermine the validity of colonial civil institutions.

Following Charles's death in 1685, his successor, King James II, appointed an official with authority to form his own advisory council in place of the General Court. The first of these appointees, Joseph Dudley, met with the General Court on May 17, 1686, to inform the members that their charter privileges had been terminated.[12] Dudley's tenure as "President of the Territory and Dominion of New England" lasted only seven months, however. His successor, Sir Edmond Andros, a devout Anglican, arrived in Boston on December 20, 1686.[13] Where Dudley had merely announced the dissolution of colonial institutions, the Andros regime proceeded as if the dissolution were already accomplished. Andros's refusal to recognize old land titles as well as his enactment of tax levies and other administrative changes without the consent of elected representatives incurred the opposition of the general public.

It may be that his insistence on holding Church of England services in one of the Boston meetinghouses produced the most provocative confrontation of all.[14] When several Boston ministers protested against this desecration of one of their buildings, Andros seized the South Meetinghouse by force. Eventually, this proprietary dispute was resolved when a new site was found for the exclusive use of an Anglican congregation. Even this gesture did little to alleviate the conflict between Andros and the Boston clergy. Indeed, when a military excursion into Canada failed in 1690, several ministers attributed the disaster to God's anger at the infiltration of Anglicans among his chosen people.[15]

Finally, encouraged by the English revolt against King James II in 1688, the members of the Massachusetts Bay successfully deposed Andros and held him captive while several members of his council were imprisoned. With the accession of William and Mary to the throne of England, indigenous civil and ecclesiastical institutions were revived, albeit only provisionally. A temporary governing authority, headed by Simon Bradstreet, presided over the Massachusetts Bay for the next three years.[16] During his administration, Bradstreet resurrected the General Court and petitioned the crown for the continuance of the original charter.

Not until October 1691 was political and institutional stability restored through the ratification of a new charter, which formally recognized Massachusetts Bay as a province within the British Empire. The price of this stability, however, was to place the Puritan mission in further jeopardy, for the charter of 1691 required that the political boundaries of Massachusetts be reconstituted to include previously disenfranchised religious groups.[17] The effect of this provision was to open the channels of political power to groups such as Quakers and Anglicans, for whom the New England experiment was anathema. The problem of how to maintain Puritan hegemony without contravening this provision for a dangerously enlarged franchise would plague civil and ecclesiastical authorities throughout the first half of the eighteenth century.

During the same period, Massachusetts Bay faced yet another challenge to its existence. In the intensification of the French and Indian War between 1689 and 1697, the colonists of New England learned to perceive the wilderness less as a force to be mastered in accordance with divine plan than as a menacing presence that threatened to encroach on their territories.[18] The God who had delivered the inhabitants through successful campaigns against the Indians in the 1670s now imposed upon his people a more alarming trial. In the unsuccessful invasion of Quebec in 1690, the members were warned that a wrathful and angry God might even permit his chosen people to fail.

In the early 1690s, virtually no colonial border was safe from attack.[19] In January 1691, one town on the northern periphery between New Hampshire and Maine was successfully attacked, and close to a hundred members of the community were killed. Later military excursions in July and August into Lancaster, Brookfield, and Billerica brought home to the settlers of Massachusetts the precariousness of their own borders. At a time when the Court of Oyer and Terminer was uncovering further plots of witchcraft against New England, Ebenezer Babson of Gloucester had a vision of ethereal Frenchmen and Indians haunting his community by night.[20] And when one of the afflicted, whose parents had been slain by Indians, reported to Cotton Mather on the activities of her spectral assailants, it came as no surprise that among their ranks were French-Canadian and Indian "Sagamores" and that the book that directed their diabolic mission was a Catholic devotional text written in French.[21]

The Salem trials coincided with a moment of grave uncertainty about the future of New England. The course charted by the first generation had become less a guide to the destiny of God's chosen people than a disturbing reminder of how far the later generations had fallen. It was not merely that the prospect of a community of saints had not yet been realized. Far more troubling was the suspicion that the whole framework of the national covenant no longer applied to the New England experience.

For some members, the political reversals of Massachusetts Bay could only be a source of comfort. For Quakers, Anglicans, and other dissident sects, the collapse of Puritan theocracy promised an end to religious persecution. For others, who viewed New England in terms of its economic possibilities, the weakening of ecclesiastical controls might even yield expanded opportunities for business and commerce.

For those civil and ecclesiastical leaders who identified with the goals of the founders, however, the abandonment of the national covenant signified nothing less than the loss of community. For ministers such as Cotton Mather and his father, a New England divested of its covenantal obligations to God was a New England beyond contemplation. For such men, the giving up of the Puritan mission yielded not social change but social extinction.

From an orthodox perspective, Massachusetts Bay, just before the Salem trials, presented the spectacle of a society at the point of dissolution. Already in 1689, Cotton Mather had remarked on the suicidal tendencies among his people: "'Tis almost unaccountable, that at some time in some places here, melancholy distempered Ragings towards Self-Murder, have been in a manner, Epidemical."[22] Early in 1692, large numbers of young persons had shocked the older generation by profaning the Sabbath.[23] During the same period, in response to an increase in urban crime, Boston had been obliged to provide for the nocturnal security of its inhabitants.[24] The aged merchant Joshua Scottow may well have articulated the ambience of the province when, in the early 1690s, he urged that a history be drawn up immediately because "how near New England now is to its breaking, the all-knowing One only knows."[25]

It is in the context of this profound social upheaval that members began to discern the conspiracy of Satan against God's chosen people. For at least some of the clergy and magistrates, the discovery of witchcraft would offer not only an explanation for the impending collapse of the old order but, even more importantly, a final vindication of the Puritan mission in New England.

THEOLOGICAL INTERPRETATIONS OF SALEM

Even if the Massachusetts clergy were by no means unanimous in their promotion of the Salem trials, several among their ranks were nonetheless indispensable in formulating a link between the crisis of New England and the discovery of witchcraft. In the sermons and writings of Deodat Lawson, Samuel Parris, and Cotton Mather in particular, the events in Salem Village and beyond were endowed with a meaning that both articulated and organized the contemporary response. It is in the light of these interpretations that the peculiar sense of urgency that gripped the magistrates of the Court of Oyer and Terminer becomes comprehensible.

The most predictable of the three formulations was the sermon delivered by Lawson to the congregation of Salem Village on March 24,

1692. Ostensibly, Lawson's early appearance at the scene of the witch-crafts may be attributed to his brief tenure as minister of the village between 1684 and 1688, but he may also have become involved for a somewhat more personal reason. Among the specters cried out upon by the afflicted were Lawson's wife and daughter, both deceased for three years.[26]

In *Christ's Fidelity*, Lawson situated the afflictions within a frame-work to which the inhabitants of Massachusetts Bay had become well accustomed. In Lawson's interpretation, New England's special rela-tionship to God was reaffirmed by the very intensity of the diabolic assaults: "The Covenant People of God, and those that would Devote themselves Intirely to his Service, are the Special Objects of SATAN's Rage and Fury."[27] The remedy to these assaults was, of course, the ref-ormation of the people and the repledging of members to the word of God.

This recommendation for prayer and moral exertion in no way pre-empted the role of the magistrates, however. It was to the officials of the Salem court that Lawson dedicated his sermon, and it was to these men that he offered these words of encouragement: To our HONORED MAGISTRATES, here present this day, to Enquire into these things; Give me leave much Honoured; to Offer One Word to your Consideration, Do all that in you lies, to Check and Rebuke Satan."[28] Yet Lawson's oration was far from incendiary. To be sure, it is clear from his de-scription of the sufferings of the afflicted—contained in his *Brief and True Narrative* of April 5—that he entertained no doubts about their authenticity. Nevertheless, he did introduce a note of caution. Among his recommendations to the congregation was the advice that villagers avoid "Sinful and unruly Passions, such as Envy, Malice, or Hatred of Neighbors and Brethren."[29] Thus, although he did not directly ques-tion the assumptions of the magistrates, he did express some reserva-tions about the evidence brought before them.

In *Christ's Fidelity*, the events at Salem were incorporated within the familiar typology of the jeremiad. The cries of the afflicted were viewed not as local disturbances confined to Salem Village but rather as a providential judgment that bore on the destiny of New England. The sufferings of the young women were themselves evidences of God's continued involvement with his chosen people. That six Boston ministers including Cotton Mather and Samuel Willard endorsed the publication of the sermon testifies to its general acceptability in ortho-dox circles.[30]

Far more provocative were the sermons Samuel Parris delivered to his votaries in Salem Village. It was Parris who translated the bitter

factional disputes within the community into a struggle of cosmic proportions. As Paul Boyer and Stephen Nissenbaum have indicated in
their investigation, *Salem Possessed: The Social Origins of Witchcraft*,
the residents of Salem Village had organized themselves into two rival
factions at the time of the trials.[31] The fundamental point of contention between the two groups centered upon the question of local autonomy. Those villagers who opposed the interventions of Salem Town
into the affairs of Salem Village were also disposed to support the ministry of Samuel Parris. On the other hand, those who sought to maintain close ties between the village and the town were more likely to
express dissatisfaction with Parris. The two factions differed correspondingly in their response to the Salem trials; members of the
pro-Parris faction were inclined to confirm the allegations of the afflicted whereas their opponents tended to challenge these allegations.[32]

Parris's accomplishment was to reformulate these conflicts within
the framework of biblical typology. During his weekly orations, the
villagers learned that support or opposition to the prosecutions was
not merely a choice of alignment in one of the two factions. At stake
was no less than a choice between God and the devil and between
heaven and hell.

That Parris was preoccupied with threats of internal subversion and
external interference even before the Salem trials is clear from his sermons of 1690 and 1691.[33] In these earlier writings, he had already begun to relate the betrayal of Christ by Judas to the betrayal of Salem
Village by some of its inhabitants. This typology of conspiracy was
further elaborated as the trials progressed. After a member of his
church had been cried out upon, Parris warned the congregation on
March 27, "Let none then build their hopes of salvation merely upon
this: that they are church members. This you and I may be, and yet
devils for all that." Later in the same sermon, he again expressed uncertainty about whether "God would not suffer devils in the guise of
saints to associate with us." The title of the sermon, "Christ knows
how many Devils there are," could not have reassured his audience.[34]

There is evidence that, by this time, Parris's biblical allegories had
become inflammatory. Lawson reported that, shortly after the lecture
began, Sarah Cloyce, a member of a neighboring church, "went immediately out of the Meeting-House, and flung the door after her violently, to the amazement of the congregation."[35] Calef speculates rea-
sonably enough that Sarah's dramatic exit was a protest against the
recent incarceration of her sister, Rebecca Nurse.[36] Some months later,
after Rebecca's execution on July 19, Parris recommended that disciplinary sanctions be imposed upon her husband, brother-in-law, and

son-in-law for not attending his weekly sermons.[37] It is no coincidence that the three offenders against whom this vindictive measure was directed had identified themselves with Parris's enemies well before the trials.

Toward the end of the Salem proceedings, Parris's imagery had become openly militaristic. In his sermon of September 11, the current witchcraft prosecutions were metamorphosed into a relentless war between Christ and Satan: "the devil and his instruments will be making war with the lamb and his followers as long as they can."[38] Within the context of this cosmic struggle, members were urged to consolidate against the enemy: "here are but two parties in the world: the lamb and his followers, and the dragon and his followers. . . . Here are no neuters. Everyone is on one side or the other."[39] Ultimately, for Parris, the rooting out of the conspiracy of witches was only a means toward the realization of a true community of saints. But in the interim the church would serve as an armed fortress against the growing corruptions of the external world. At a time when other clergymen of Massachusetts Bay were expressing doubts about the direction of the Salem trials, Parris continued to believe that the purging of the devil from his church by means of judicial intervention had yet to be completed.

There are intimations of apocalypse in Parris's sermon of September 11 that give the lecture a special sense of urgency. According to Parris, the struggle between God and Satan was only now approaching a resolution: "After this life the saints shall no more be troubled with war from devils and their instruments."[40] A quote from the English bishop Joseph Hall was included to indicate that the scale of diabolic operations had recently escalated: "the devil's prevalency in this age is most clear in the marvelous number of witches abounding in all places. . . . Heretofore only barbarous deserts had them, but now the civilest and religious parts are frequently pestered with them."[41] To an audience familiar with the Book of Revelations, the implications of this trend may well have been obvious.

It was left to Cotton Mather in *Wonders of the Invisible World* to state these implications openly, however. Conceived in the middle of September 1692 and published simultaneously in Boston and London during the later part of December, Mather's work was evidently a hasty production. Because of its late appearance, it is doubtful that it had much impact on the course of the trials. What is far more important is that the work was assisted in its planning stages by Stephen Sewall, the clerk of the Court of Oyer and Terminer, and enthusiastically endorsed in the opening pages by William Stoughton, the chief justice of the court. Whatever its literary or scholarly defects, *Wonders* is the most important of the contemporary narratives for the historical observer. Of all the narratives, only Mather's work articulates the official definition of the Salem trials.

To a considerable extent, Mather enlarged upon themes already developed in the writings of Lawson and Parris. His formulation of witchcraft as the latest judgment in a progression of catastrophes, including "wasting Sicknesses . . . desolating Fires . . . Losses by Sea,"[42] entailed no departure from the interpretation offered in *Christ's Fidelity*. His proposition that witchcraft demonstrated New England's privileged relationship to God—"Where will the Devil show most malice, but where he is hated, and hateth most"[43]—also fell well within the framework of the standard jeremiad. Similarly, his use of militaristic imagery to represent the forces in contention during the Salem trials in such phrases as "An Army of Devils" or "An Horrible Plot against the Country by Witchcraft" or "Military Government, among the Devils" merely applied to the federal level the same rhetorical devices Parris had applied to the village level.[44]

What distinguishes *Wonders* from the writings of Lawson and Parris is its vision of apocalypse. In Mather's rendering, the Salem witchcraft trials became the focal point of a grand cosmic drama. That multitudes of demons should suddenly appear in New England was no ordinary judgment against God's chosen people. The recent expansion of diabolic activities marked a decisive turning point in world history:

Good News to the Israel of God, and particularly for his New-English Israel. If the Devils Time were above a Thousand years, ago, pronounced short, what may we suppose it now in our time? No, the Devil was never more let loose than in Our Days; and it is very much that any should imagine otherwise; But the same thing that proves the Thousand Years of prosperity for the Church of God, under the whole Heaven to be not yet begun—does also prove, that it is not very far off.[45]

In *Wonders of the Invisible World*, a millennial view of history was superimposed upon the familiar framework of the jeremiad. New England was suffering for the sins of her people, but the Day of Judgment could no longer be situated in the indefinite future. The final confrontation between God and Satan was being enacted in the present: "The Wilderness thro' which we are passing to the Promised Land is all over fill'd with Fiery flying Serpents."[46]

From this historical perspective, Mather could contemplate the dissolution of New England with a certain equanimity—"There is little room for hope, that the great wrath of the Devil, will not prove the present ruine of our poor New-England in particular."[47]—for the same events that portended disaster promised deliverance as well. The unleashing of the devil in Massachusetts signified less the end of New England than the final salvation of the Puritan mission. New England would be destroyed—but God's chosen people would be saved.

Mather's interpretation of the Salem witchcraft casts the magistrates in an entirely different role from that ascribed to them by Samuel Parris. The Court of Oyer and Terminer became not just a bulwark against internal subversion but rather an instrument in the fulfillment of biblical prophecy. The object of judicial zeal became not so much the suppression of conspiracy as the preparation of the community for its final deliverance. That Mather's version provides a more complete understanding of the activities of the court will become apparent in chapter 9.

9

The Salem Witchcraft Prosecutions:

The Discovery of Conspiracy

THE SALEM PROSECUTIONS form a counterpoint to the legal proceedings prior to 1692. In the Salem trials, the court replaced the
community as the locus for legal initiative against witchcraft. The villagers who had earlier promoted the active prosecution of the malefic
witch were once again confounded by the policy of the magistrates.
The judicial caution that had thus far thwarted the popular demand
for legal protection was now succeeded by a new policy that was no
less disturbing in its indifference to the goals of village harmony. The
forces in contention over the constitution of the crime resurfaced
during the Salem trials, but this time it was the community that would
act in restraint of the court.

The transfer of legal initiative from the villagers to the courts had
profound consequences for the discovery and production of witches.
Because the magistrates controlled the legal machinery of the province, they were able to coordinate the different components of the
discovery process to a far greater extent than were the village laity
who had sought legal redress in the pre-Salem litigations. The active
involvement of the court in each phase of the discovery process—the
focusing of accusations, the formulation of rules of evidence, the gathering of incriminating testimony, the determination of appropriate legal sanctions, and the production of confessional accounts—yielded a
continuity in orientation that had been conspicuously lacking in the
earlier proceedings. The zeal and commitment of the magistrates guaranteed that the terms of prosecution would no longer conflict with
the terms of accusation. In the Salem trials, the transformation of the
suspect into the witch was accomplished without legal obstruction.

To be sure, the magistrates did not act without some measure of
popular and ecclesiastical support in their efforts to accelerate the discovery process. The most vocal encouragement for judicial intervention came from the afflicted themselves. Indeed, throughout the prose-

cutions, the afflicted maintained a demand for legal involvement that even the most eager members of the court were hard-pressed to satisfy. It was from these youthful victims of bewitchment that the court drew its most loyal and enthusiastic constituency.

Furthermore, there is evidence to suggest that, at least in Salem Village, the demand for legal initiative sprang from other, more influential sources within the community. That seventy-one persons presented themselves variously as sponsors of the afflicted or independent accusers or corroborators of negative testimony is sufficient in itself to indicate a substantial local mandate for official intervention. Moreover, Boyer and Nissenbaum have demonstrated that the alignment of villagers into sponsors and accusers, on the one hand, and suspects and their defenders, on the other hand, overlapped significantly with membership in the pro-Parris faction and in the anti-Parris faction, respectively. The clear implication of this finding is that the pro-Parris faction not only upheld the suspicions of the afflicted but may also have actively directed these suspicions toward their political rivals.

Additional support for the magistrates came from the ranks of the clergy. No minister was more ardent than Samuel Parris, who participated not only as a frequent sponsor of the afflicted but also as an outspoken advocate of prosecution at the preliminary hearings.[1] The Reverend John Hale of Beverly, although less closely associated with the afflicted, nevertheless volunteered testimony against three of the accused.[2] Nicholas Noyes, one of the two ministers of Salem Town, expressed his support with strong public endorsements of the findings of the court. After the executions on September 22, he is reported by Calef to have commented, "What a sad thing it is to see eight firebrands of hell hanging there!" On another occasion, his cooperation with the court was more direct; he informed a member of his church who had been convicted of witchcraft that he would withhold prayer on his behalf until he confessed.[3] The other two ecclesiastical advocates, Cotton Mather and Deodat Lawson, contributed to the promotion of the trials more as publicists than as active participants.[4]

To interpret the conduct of the Salem trials as merely a response to the demands of any of these constituencies, however, is to overlook important differences among the popular, theological, and official orientations to the problem of witchcraft. Ultimately, the objectives of the court transcended and even conflicted with the more limited concerns of each of the groups with which it was temporarily allied. Least of all can the afflicted be viewed as the locus of initiative for the prosecutions. That the magistrates concurred with most of their allegations should not be taken as an act of accommodation. Indeed, in the following sections it shall be demonstrated that the zeal of the afflicted becomes comprehensible less as an independent search for relief from witchcraft than as itself a by-product of judicial policy.

Nor can the trials be understood as an extension of the aspirations of the pro-Parris faction. Only during the early phases of judicial intervention did the pattern of accusations more or less coincide with the factional divisions in Salem Village. As will be shown below, later indictments were generated independently and even in defiance of local opinion.

Nor, finally, can it be demonstrated that the court acted merely as a vehicle for the advancement of vested interests within the Puritan church. The tendency among certain historians and other commentators to identify the prosecutions with the defense of an entrenched theological elite vastly oversimplifies the complex and problematic relationship that developed between clergy and magistrates as the trials progressed.[5] The related tendency to define the clergy as united in their sponsorship of the conduct of the trials is even more difficult to reconcile with the actual pattern of ecclesiastical participation.

Only in terms of their general orientation to the sufferings of the afflicted can it be suggested that the magistrates deferred to the judgments of the clergy. That the afflictions were events of preternatural significance, that they constituted a warning to the members of Massachusetts Bay, and that such manifestations called for some form of official intervention were premises that could be shared by civil and ecclesiastical authorities alike.[6] In terms of specific policy toward the afflicted and their alleged tormentors, however, it is clear that the magistrates did not feel bound by ecclesiastical controls. In the debate over the method of proof, the problem of selecting between two conflicting formulations of the rules of evidence resolved into a question of whether the magistrates or the clergy would define the terms of prosecution. It was the court that successfully asserted its authority in defiance of the recommendations of the church. If it is allowed that the magistrates acted in behalf of theological interests, it must be understood that it was they rather than the clergy who determined these interests.

The scope of judicial initiative during the Salem trials extended far beyond the prosecution of witches. That the magistrates generated convictions and executions from among the ranks of the accused was the least of their accomplishments. By directing the flow of accusations, the magistrates not only concentrated the energies of the entire community upon the threat of conspiracy but also helped to define the shape of the conspiracy. By manipulating the sanctions to be imposed upon malefactors, they transformed an ostensibly legal event into a ceremony of collective expiation. Under the management of the Court of Oyer and Terminer, the stages of the Salem trials came to conform less to the conventional sequence of a judicial prosecution than to the ecclesiastical typology of sin, confession, and moral regeneration.

It is the central objective of this chapter to show how this program of communal regeneration was essentially a product of judicial initiative.

DEFINING THE BOUNDARIES OF CONSPIRACY: THE SOCIAL DISTRIBUTION OF LEGAL ACTIONS

The transfer of initiative from the village laity to the courts resulted not only in an increase in the scale of legal actions but, even more importantly, in a profound change in the social distribution of legal actions. That females composed approximately three quarters of the total number of arrested suspects—107 of 141 persons arrested—may well constitute the only point of demographic continuity between the pre Salem and the Salem prosecutions. In terms of other social characteristics, such as age, wealth, marital status, occupation, and geographic proximity to the accuser, many of the suspects of 1692 bore little or no resemblance to their pre-Salem predecessors.

Perhaps no single feature of the Salem proceedings generated more concern among contemporaries than this utter incongruity between the traditional parameters of suspicion and the parameters of 1692. Even during the first month of prosecutions, the magistrates demonstrated a willingness to disregard the status considerations that had figured so prominently in the earlier litigations. Suspects were imprisoned whose social position in the community grandly contradicted the popular expectations for the malefic witch. As the trials progressed, the afflicted in collaboration with the magistrates began to define new and more inclusive boundaries of suspicion, only to traverse these limits shortly after they had been established. That a minister as eminent as Samuel Willard felt constrained to publish his rather mild objections to the court under a pseudonym or that the highly respected Thomas Brattle, an affluent merchant and a fellow of the Royal Society of London, chose to circulate his criticisms only among trusted friends indicates how widely experienced was the fear of judicial retaliation.

By the summer of 1692, the social limits of candidacy for witchcraft had been so often redefined and then contravened that no one, it would seem, could be excluded as a potential conspirator.

The creation of new boundaries.   None of the first three persons brought before the Salem magistrates on March 1 deviated significantly from the prevailing stereotypes of the malefic witch. Tituba, Parris's West Indian maidservant, was a plausible suspect if only because of her early involvement in the activities of the afflicted. Even before the young women in Parris's household had been diagnosed as bewitched, Tituba had applied countermagic to help locate their tormentors.[7] On the advice of Mary Sibley, the aunt of one of the afflicted, she had baked a witch cake whose recipe called for a blending of the children's urine with meal. She had then fed the cake to Parris's dog, presumably on the assumption that the animal was a familiar and could thus identify its master. During her interrogation, she required only mild prompting from the magistrates to confess to the charges brought against her.[8] Moreover, she named as her accomplices the other two women who had been arrested the same day.

Sarah Good, one of the women identified by Tituba, was an equally likely candidate for suspicion. By the time of the Salem trials, she and her husband, William, were homeless and destitute, and Sarah had begun to beg for shelter and provisions from neighbors.[9] Her reliance upon scolding and cursing as a means of retaliation against unresponsive neighbors generated a wealth of negative testimony. At least seven witnesses, in addition to the afflicted, testified to her general turbulence and angry mutterings following their refusal to offer charity. Sarah even lacked the support of her husband. At her examination, William informed the court that his wife "either was a witch or would be one very quickly."[10]

The other woman to be examined on March 1, Sarah Osborne, presented a somewhat less tidy portrait of the malefic witch. Although old and sickly, she and her second husband, Alexander, held in trust a large estate that had been bequeathed to her by her former deceased husband. Despite the paucity of popular testimony against her, Sarah was implicated not just by Tituba but by Sarah Good as well. Good, who had been steadfast in affirming her own innocence, was nonetheless persuaded that someone was responsible for the afflictions. When asked by magistrate Hathorne who it was then that tormented the children, she replied quite simply, "it was Osborne."[11]

The examination of Martha Corey on March 19 constituted the first major departure from popular expectations. Though Martha was over sixty at the time of her arrest, her husband, Giles, was a prosperous and respected member of the Salem Village community. Even more important, she was a member in full communion of the village church. It was this feature of her biography that Martha herself had emphasized in a conversation with two of her accusers. According to their testimony, Martha had sought to separate her case from those of Sarah Good and Sarah Osborne by claiming that "they were idle, sloathfull persons and minded nothing that was good." She had argued that her case was different because she "had made a profession of Christ and rejoyced to go and hear the word of God."[12] Nevertheless, Martha's reputation was sufficiently compromised that she did not fully contradict the popular stereotype. That she had given birth to an illegitimate son was in itself a mark of some notoriety.[13] That, in addition, her own husband had offered testimony against her may have further narrowed the social distance between her and the previous suspects.

Not until March 23 with the arrest and interrogation of Rebecca Nurse did the allegations of the afflicted mark a decisive break with the identifications of the past. The prestige enjoyed by the Nurse family was great enough to have shielded any of its members from arrest during the pre-Salem litigations. That Rebecca's husband, Francis, held a sizable estate in Salem Village was not the only unusual feature of the case.[14] Equally significant was the fact that Rebecca had acquired a reputation for exemplary piety that was virtually unchallenged in the community. A petition circulated in her behalf just before her trial in late June included among the signers the near relatives of the very persons who had testified against her in March.[15]

More immediately, Rebecca had powerful allies who were prepared to come to her defense as early as her initial examination. A statement composed by Israel Porter and signed by his wife, Elizabeth, and two prominent villagers arrived in time to be read by Hathorne before his interrogation of the suspect on March 24. Whether because of the contents of this moving chronicle of Rebecca's charity or because Elizabeth was Hathorne's sister, the magistrate displayed an uncharacteristic delicacy in his handling of the interrogation. When the suspect asserted at the outset of her interview, "I can say before my Eternal Father I am innocent and God will clear my innocency," Hathorne replied, "Here is never a one in the assembly but desires it."[16] Despite such judicial misgivings, Rebecca was placed in prison without bail following her examination.

In the next few weeks, the boundaries of conspiracy were further extended. Indeed, on the same day that the afflicted had dared to ignore status considerations, another new constituency for witchcraft was uncovered. Dorcas Good, the daughter of Sarah, was arrested on March 23 and brought in for examination the following day. A confession was produced in which Dorcas also implicated her mother.[17] What was unprecedented about the case, though, was that the suspect was at most five years of age at the time of her hearing.[18] Henceforth in the proceedings, neither youth nor high status would provide immunity against suspicion.

Another boundary was removed several weeks later in the examination of Bridget Bishop. When confronted with the accusations of the afflicted, Bridget entered an objection that would have been appropriate for any of the pre-Salem litigations: "I never saw these persons before, nor I ever was in this place before." In the Salem trials, however, familiarity between victim and accused was no longer a condition for suspicion. Possibly because Bridget's history of problematic relationships with her neighbors so thoroughly typified the career of the malefic witch, this unusual feature of the case went unnoticed in the transcript of her pretrial examination.[19] Nevertheless, this break with precedent vastly extended the range of persons eligible for suspicion.

It was the arrest and examination of George Burroughs that constituted the most dramatic escalation of judicial action during the early phases of the trials, for the Reverend Mr. Burroughs had been the minister of Salem Village from 1680 until 1683. His departure from the community was preceded by a bitter dispute over salary.[20] At the time of his arrest on May 4, he had been serving as pastor of a small town in Maine for nine years. With the discovery of George Burroughs, the magistrates were able to confirm their worst fears about the scope of the conspiracy against New England. The afflicted accorded to Burroughs a position in the invisible world commensurate with his prestigious office in the visible world. As one of his accusers revealed on April 20 after her encounter with his specter, "And he also told me he was above a witch, he was a conjurer."[21] During the examination, the sufferings of the afflicted were so extreme that the magistrates ordered several of the girls to be removed from the court for their own safety. In addition to these demonstrations of Burroughs's power to inflict harm, other witnesses testified to his general mistreatment of his wife and to his remarkable physical strength.[22] The cumulative effect of such testimony was to suggest that the magistrates had finally located one of the central figures in the current diabolical operations.

The correspondence between local opinion and the allegations of the afflicted.   Thus far, even with the arrest and imprisonment of a Puritan minister, the identifications of the afflicted were still more or less in accord with the identifications of the villagers who had accompanied them to the court. Two other groups of accusers in addition to the afflicted had offered testimony against the suspects. The first group consisted of those villagers who accused the suspects of ordinary malefic practice, either by calling attention to the presence of revealing moral and physical signs or by providing accounts of their own victimization. The second group consisted of those villagers who sponsored the allegations of the afflicted. Until May 31, there is evidence to suggest that the suspicions of the afflicted overlapped substantially with the suspicions of one or the other of these two groups.

Of the sixty-nine suspects under arrest at this time, thirty-three approximated the popular expectations for the malefic witch in terms of their conflictual relations with neighbors and/or in terms of their social and demographic characteristics. In addition to Tituba, Sarah Good, and Bridget Bishop, other suspects such as Dorcas Hoar, Wilmot Reed, and Martha Carrier had long held reputations as magical practitioners and were susceptible to charges of malefic witchcraft even without judicial encouragement. According to a lengthy deposition submitted by her minister, John Hale, Dorcas had long practiced the arts of palmistry and fortune-telling. Indeed, some twenty-two years before the trials, she had sought to renounce these occult interests in response to Hale's firm admonitions.[23] More recent testimony indicated that her renunciation had not been wholehearted.

The activities of Wilmot Reed of Marblehead were no less typical of the practices of the pre-Salem witch. In the course of an extended dispute with a neighbor, she had pronounced a curse upon her adversary that she might never urinate or defecate. Apparently the spell was successful until the victim moved to another town.[24] Likewise, Martha Carrier of Andover made use of imprecations in her disagreements with neighbors. In his letter on her behalf, minister Frances Dane, Sr., conceded that Martha had been suspected of malefic witchcraft well before her arrest.[25]

Others resembled the pre-Salem witch less in terms of their demonstrated prowess in magical arts than in terms of their economic dependency. Sarah Buckley's downward mobility prior to her arrest well exemplifies the career of a number of her pre-Salem predecessors. In 1675, her husband, William, was forced to forfeit his house and lands in a judgment over debt.[26] Five years later, Buckley was again sued, on this occasion for debts incurred by his son. As a result, his table, chest, and possibly his cobbler's tools were seized. In the following year, Buckley sold his remaining plot of village land, presumably to avoid complete destitution. By 1692, the Buckleys were approaching the age of sixty without the security of land or property and with no prospects for financial improvement.

Rachel Clinton's descent into destitution was no less precipitous. In a petition to the quarterly court in 1667, Rachel complained that Thomas White, her brother-in-law, had deprived her of an inheritance of thirty pounds bequeathed by her father. She sought compensation from the court in order "that she may not be forced to wander from house to house like an Indian or bruit beast." Such fears were fully realized shortly thereafter. In 1668, her husband, Lawrence, was placed in prison for nonsupport. Six years later, Rachel again complained of her husband's neglect and was awarded an allowance of two shillings a week. In 1678 she sued again for support from her husband. By now, she was willing to settle for a modest allowance since her husband had provided her with only ten pounds over a period of ten years.[27] At the time of the Salem trials, Rachel was reduced to seeking alms from her neighbors in Ipswich. The testimony against her reveals that the villagers of 1692 were no more solicitous of their paupers than were their forebears.

Still other persons, such as Ann Pudeator, Mary Bradbury, and Elizabeth How, who conformed less fully to popular expectations, were nevertheless susceptible to village suspicions, if only because of their intermittently problematic encounters with neighbors. Thus Ann, a widow of approximately seventy years of age, was accused by several of her neighbors in spite of her considerable landholdings in Salem Village.[28] The subsequent discovery by the court that she possessed a large collection of ointments may have added weight to these allegations of malefic practice.[29] Mary Bradbury of Salisbury was an even less likely candidate for suspicion. Her husband had served both as a selectman on the town council and as a deputy representative from Salisbury to the General Court. Despite her husband's reputation, at least four witnesses, in addition to the afflicted, could recall disputes with Mary during which they had suffered preternatural mischiefs.[30] Similarly, Elizabeth How, although also a woman of means, was accused by eight of her neighbors of malefic practices. Indeed, Mather reports that she had earlier been denied membership in the church at Ipswich in part because of suspicion of witchcraft.[31]

Thus, for about half the suspects prior to May 31, some element of continuity was discernible between the identifications of the past and the identifications of 1692. Eleven of the accused had claimed or displayed competence in magical arts, six were either economically vulnerable or completely destitute, and an additional five persons, although neither impoverished nor demonstrably skilled in malefic magic, had histories of problematic encounters with at least some of their neighbors. Eleven others were near relations of these suspects—husbands or daughters in eight cases—who had unsuccessfully risked their reputations in order to defend their kin or were themselves equally susceptible to popular allegations. Not unexpectedly, thirty of the thirty-four persons who approximated popular expectations were women.[32]

A further group of suspects within this cohort appear to have been linked through their involvement in factional conflict with the sponsors of the afflicted. Included within the ranks of the afflicted were several persons who were either the close relations or the wards of members of the pro-Parris faction within Salem Village. In addition to Parris's own niece and daughter, Abigail Williams and Elizabeth Parris, four other bewitched females were connected with the Putnam family—the family from whom Parris derived his principal political support. Ann Putnam, Jr., and Ann Putnam, Sr., were the daughter and wife of Thomas Putnam. Another of the afflicted, Mary Walcott, was Thomas's niece and resided in his household at the time of the trials. The fourth member of this circle, Mercy Lewis, also lived with the Putnam family in the capacity of maidservant. In the course of the proceedings, Mary Walcott, Ann Putnam, Jr., Mercy Lewis, and Abigail Williams emerged as by far the most active accusers among the afflicted. Mary is mentioned in at least fifty-three depositions, Ann in forty-eight, Mercy in thirty-six, and Abigail in thirty-two. Moreover, Thomas Putnam was the most frequent sponsor of the afflicted, followed by Nathaniel Ingersoll, the deacon of the village church, and Jonathan Walcott, Putnam's brother-in-law, with twenty-four, eleven, and ten appearances in court, respectively. Other members of the Putnam family who participated as sponsors were Edward, Nathaniel, and John Putnam, Sr., Thomas's brother and two uncles.[33]

The possibility that a portion of the allegations in Salem Village and Salem Town reflected the lines of conflict between the pro-Parris faction and their political rivals constitutes the central premise in Boyer and Nissenbaum's well-researched investigation. And, indeed, before May 31, at least nineteen of the allegations of the afflicted were directed toward the allies of the Porter family and their relations as well as toward other enemies of the Putnams. Thus, the pious Rebecca Nurse and her sister, Sarah Cloyce, however little they resembled the conventional malefic witch, were nevertheless intimately associated with the anti-Parris faction through their husbands, Francis Nurse and Peter Cloyce. Nurse, along with Daniel Andrew, another of the accused and the brother-in-law of Israel Porter, had been elected to the village committee in October 1691. One of the first actions taken by this committee was to vote against the assessment of a tax for the payment of Parris's salary. Likewise, John Proctor, who had named Porter as trustee of his estate, was accused together with his wife, two sons, and a daughter.[34] Also included among the ranks of the accused were Philip English and his wife, Mary. English was a wealthy Salem Town merchant who had engaged in business dealings with the Porters.[35] An additional nine suspects were either close associates of the Porters through political and commercial alliances or the near relations of these associates.[36]

Accordingly, it may be concluded that, until May 31, the suspicions of the afflicted cannot be clearly disentangled from those of the village groups with whom they were associated. During this first phase of legal action, the pattern of accusation might be roughly described as a conflating of the traditional popular demand with the suspicions of the pro-Parris faction in Salem Village. For about fifty-two of the sixty-nine suspects, the allegations of the afflicted appear to have concurred with at least a segment of local opinion. With regard to another fifteen of the suspects, there is insufficient information even to speculate about their relationship to the community in which they resided. The two remaining cases—those of Mary Warren and Elizabeth Cary—will be discussed below.

Then, on May 31, the afflicted reached farther upward within the prestige hierarchy of Massachusetts to accuse a suspect whose identity would astonish even the court. In selecting Capt. John Alden, Sr., of Boston, son of the already legendary John Alden of the *Mayflower*, the accusers once again moved beyond any of the recognizable parameters of suspicion. Alden had no apparent involvement with the tensions in Salem Village, nor was he known to his accusers. Indeed, when asked by the magistrates who it was that tormented them, one of the afflicted pointed several times to the wrong person.[37] Despite this awkwardness, the testimony was enough to convince the court. According to Alden's own account, "Mr. Gidney [Bartholomew Gedney] said he had known Alden many years and had been at sea with him, and always look'd upon him to be an honest Man, but now he did see cause to alter his judgment."[38] On the day of Alden's examination, Thomas Newton, king's attorney for the Court of Oyer and Terminer, observed in a letter to the governor: "The afflicted spare no person of what quality so ever neither conceale their crimes tho' never so heinous."[39] In the following months, the identification of the afflicted would become increasingly unrelated to popular suspicions.

Further expansions in the boundaries of suspicion. After a period of relative inactivity in June, the afflicted further expanded their allegations across the boundaries of geography. In the middle of July, a resident of Andover requested the help of the afflicted to determine the identity of those responsible for the death of his wife.[40] The result was an intervention that equaled in scale and intensity the previous operations in Salem Village and Salem Town. Between July 15 and September 17, at least fifty persons were cried out upon in a town whose total population was approximately six hundred persons.[41]

The order and pattern of accusations corresponded closely to that established in the earlier activities. The first residents to be accused were persons who satisfied the popular expectations for the malefic witch and the near relations of these persons. The widowed and impoverished septuagenarian, Ann Foster, was arrested on July 15. In the next week, her daughter and granddaughter were charged, together with the sons of Martha Carrier, who herself had been imprisoned two months before the arrival of the afflicted.[42] Ann, by virtue of her economic vulnerability, and Martha, because of her reputation as a practitioner of magical arts, were both unsurprising candidates for suspicion.

Thereafter, the identifications of the afflicted included ever more prominent members of the community. By the middle of August, five more persons had been added to the ranks of the accused, the most conspicuous of whom were the daughter and granddaughter of Andover's minister, Frances Dane.[43] By the end of September, the afflicted had cried out upon the wives of several of the largest landholders in the town as well as the wife of the church deacon. Only the extraordinary intervention of the local justice of the peace prevented a further escalation in the number and prestige of Andover suspects. In what may well constitute the most awkward judicial compromise in the colonial prosecution of witchcraft, Dudley Bradstreet decided against the issuance of any further warrants based on the testimony of the afflicted and at the same time refused to cancel the forty-four warrants he had already signed.[44]

In terms of their demographic characteristics, the Andover suspects were no less heterogeneous than the cohort of suspects accused prior to June. Children under twelve as well as persons over sixty-five years of age, married men and women as well as widows and single women, were all included among the accused. The overall distribution indicates that the afflicted ignored age and status considerations in Andover just as they had in Salem Village and its vicinities. Also, consistent with the pre-June allegations, a disproportionate number of the accused were female—three-quarters of the Andover suspects (thirty-four out of forty-five) as compared to 70 percent of the earlier suspects (fifty out of seventy).[45]

What distinguished the allegations at Andover from the previous allegations was not that they generated new social categories from which candidates might be drawn but rather that they no longer bore any discernible relationship to local discontents. Now it was the youthful accusers who defined the pattern of suspicion and the village laity who were forced to accommodate to this definition. Calef reports that the afflicted even went so far as to accuse John Bradstreet, brother of the justice of the peace, of bewitching a dog, with the result that Bradstreet fled the colony and the animal was eventually put to death. Brattle's narrative mentions the bewilderment of the residents in response to the unpredictable allegations: "Poor Andover does now rue the day that ever the afflicted went among them; they lament their folly, and are an object of great pity and commiseration."[46] In Andover, the afflicted discovered that they could move with impunity not only against venerable individuals but against whole communities as well.

Changes in the composition of the afflicted.   This insensitivity to local concerns was less the consequence of youthful defiance or self-assertion than the by-product of an important development in judicial policy. Early in the proceedings, it became apparent that the magistrates regarded the victim of bewitchment and the perpetrator of bewitchment as easily reversible identities. In practice if not in theory, the judges perceived in each of the afflicted a potential witch and in some of the suspects a potential ally of the court. Indeed, the very first person to be accused of witchcraft, Tituba, was allowed to join the ranks of the afflicted and was thereby spared the ordeal of trial and further prosecution.[47]

From the outset of the investigation, this unspoken premise of official policy had a profound impact upon the evolution of the afflicted as a group. Most significantly, it provided the initial cohort of accusers with an effective sanction against potential apostates. If a member contradicted the attributions of her fellow sufferers, she herself could be accused of witchcraft.

One incident, in particular, well illustrates this risk. In April, Mary Warren, one of the more active accusers, sought to renounce her affiliation with the afflicted and was immediately placed under arrest by the Salem magistrates. At the beginning of her examination on April 19, she pronounced herself innocent of the charge of witchcraft and free of further spectral assaults. During this exchange, the original records indicate that the courtroom was filled with the screams of the other girls. Such palpable demonstrations of suffering abated only when Mary reverted to her prior condition of bewitchment. The transcript of this hearing concludes with a revealing observation: "Note that not one of the sufferers was afflicted during her examination after once she began to confess, tho they were tormented before."[48] Given the narrow options of arrest or bewitchment, it is perhaps not surprising that individuals among the afflicted tended to remain loyal and supportive to each other's attributions throughout the proceedings.[49]

Official policy contributed not only to the solidarity of the afflicted but also to the increase in their numbers. Young women who were susceptible to charges of witchcraft had a clear incentive to present themselves as victims of bewitchment;[50] six of the afflicted were actual targets of accusation prior to their bewitchment.[51] The possibility arises that others may have joined the ranks of the accusers, if not in response to legal action, then in anticipation of legal action.

Another probable source of increase was the tendency of the magistrates to bypass the usual precautions applied to the identification and validation of afflictions. In the early phases of the trials, as in the pre-Salem cases, alleged symptoms of bewitchment were carefully scrutinized by medical and ecclesiastical authorities before they were credited with authenticity. Gradually, however, expressions of suffering among the afflicted became standardized, and the court no longer relied upon the judgments of ministers and physicians to determine their validity. Under these conditions, in which conventional safeguards had been relaxed, claims of bewitchment were unlikely to be questioned whether or not they were offered in good faith.

Thus the cumulative effect of judicial policy was to reinforce solidarity within the original cohort of accusers and to promote a steady increase in their numbers throughout the proceedings. As of March 20, Lawson mentions that the afflicted included about ten females within their ranks.[52] By October, the number of afflicted had grown to thirty-four persons, not including two women in the original cohort who chose not to participate in any legal actions. Twelve persons had been added from Salem Village and vicinity, six from Andover, and eight from other localities in Essex County. Despite six months of intense legal activity against witchcraft, the problem of afflictions had evolved from a local to a provincial concern, and there are strong indications that the number of these disturbances was still increasing even after the investigations had subsided.[53]

Ultimately, it is in terms of these changes in the internal organization of the afflicted as a group that their activities in Andover can best be explained. In March, the afflicted had consisted of a small group of young girls who were linked not only by their residential proximity but also by their allegiance to a village coalition. By July, the ranks of the afflicted had doubled in size, and the members were now geographically dispersed. Moreover, between March and July, the magistrates had come to replace the pro-Parris faction as the primary sponsors of the afflicted. Now it was the members of the court rather than local partisans who determined the composition of the group and who legitimated their suspicions. By the time of their visit to Andover, the afflicted were no longer tied either geographically or politically to the communities that enlisted their aid. Accordingly, the accusers could begin to act without reference to local demands although, increasingly, they were obliged to respond to judicial demands.

Toward the liminal point.   Not until the final phases of the investigation did the afflicted exhibit a willingness to contravene even the generous boundaries allowed by the court. Toward the end of July, the accusers began to cry out against notable figures within the province, some of whom were closely affiliated with the magistrates themselves. Among the first of these personages to be identified was the minister Samuel Willard, who served as pastor of the church to which several of the magistrates belonged.[54] The selection of magistrate Nathaniel Saltonstall showed perhaps even greater audacity since he had served briefly on the very tribunal that directed the Salem prosecutions.[55] Other officials accused in September and October included the secretary of the Colony of Connecticut and Dudley Bradstreet, the Andover justice of the peace.[56] Finally, in October, the afflicted went so far as to cry out against Lady Phips, the wife of the governor of the province.[57]

Such identifications indicate that the afflicted were prepared to accuse not only those who were plausible suspects from the standpoint of the villagers or the magistrates but also those who dared to question the validity of their testimony. The allegations against Bradstreet and Saltonstall in particular suggest that those who expressed even the mildest forms of dissent were in danger of suspicion. Bradstreet was accused shortly after he refused to participate in the arrest of more Andover suspects; Saltonstall was complained of after he had withdrawn in silence from active involvement in the prosecution. Although the charge against Willard occurred before the circulation of his cautiously critical *Dialogue between S. and B.*, his opposition to the proceedings was common knowledge among his contemporaries.[58] And, according to the eighteenth-century historian Thomas Hutchinson, Lady Phips was accused after she had issued a warrant for the discharge of a suspected woman during her husband's absence.[59]

Whatever provoked the afflicted to make these identifications—whether they sought to safeguard their privileged position as seers into the invisible world or merely to defend their mission against Satan from subversive influences—it is clear that they had finally arrived at the liminal point of their credibility. Especially with regard to Willard, the magistrates indicated quite openly that the accusers had overstepped the permissible limits of suspicion. According to Calef, the accuser who cried out against the Boston minister "was sent out of the Court, and it was told she was mistaken in the person."[60] Nor was any legal action taken against Bradstreet, Saltonstall, or Lady Phips. Moreover, other suspects who were also closely linked to the political leadership of the province similarly escaped punishment. No warrants were issued against Mrs. Thacher, mother-in-law of Jonathan Corwin, one of the active magistrates, or against Mrs. John Hale, the wife of one of the few ministers to give encouragement to the proceedings.[61] The exemption of Mrs. Thacher is all the more noteworthy since she had been named as witch by an unusually large proportion of the accusers.[62]

By November, the allegations of the afflicted had ceased to carry legal force. After a brief excursion into Gloucester in late October, which yielded perhaps three or four arrests, the accusers returned to the town at the request of a resident who believed his sister to be bewitched.[63] This time, however, the persons they identified were neither imprisoned nor brought to trial. In the absence of official encouragement, the accusers withdrew from active participation in the proceedings.

Throughout the investigation, the afflicted served as the primary instruments in the production of suspected witches; their testimony was indispensable to the prosecution of all 141 persons whose arrests were recorded. Yet, despite the seriousness with which their allegations were regarded, their opportunities for initiating legal action were clearly limited. The afflicted were free to define the shape of conspiracy only insofar as their formulations did not conflict with those of their official sponsors. If it was the afflicted who established the visible identity of their spectral assailants, it was the magistrates who decided upon the identity of the afflicted as well as upon the validity of their testimony. Not until the accusers began to cry out against civil and ecclesiastical authorities and their near relations did these judicial prerogatives become explicit.

While the magistrates may have exerted only an indirect control over the production of accusations, they were considerably more active in the production of convictions. It is in their efforts to reconcile the terms of accusation with the terms of prosecution that the magistrates came to exercise the full measure of their judicial authority. This open display of authority was occasioned by the debate over the problem of proof.

THE PROBLEM OF PROOF REVISITED

In the debate over the problem of proof, what was decided was nothing less than the question of which group—the village laity, the clergy, or the magistrates—would define the terms of prosecution. But it was not until the setting up of the Court of Oyer and Terminer on May 27, some three months after the initial arrests and examinations, that this critical issue could be addressed. Until the governor constituted this judicial body, the most important questions regarding the guilt or innocence of the suspects remained to be resolved. Now, with over seventy persons already imprisoned, the members of the newly appointed court were obliged to determine which evidences were convictive and which evidences were not.

Few contemporaries would have disputed Governor Phips's own appraisal of his appointments: "The Chief Judge in this Commission was the Deputy Governor and the rest were persons of the best prudence and figure that could then be pitched upon."[64] In addition to Deputy Gov. William Stoughton as chief justice, the original court included six of the most prominent civil leaders in New England: Samuel Sewall, Wait Winthrop, Nathaniel Saltonstall, William Sargent, John Richards, and Bartholomew Gedney.

Judge Sewall, author, scholar, and future overseer of Harvard College, enjoyed a reputation for fairness and even benevolence in his capacity as magistrate. One of his treatises, *The Selling of Joseph*, is regarded as the first antislavery tract to be published in America.[65] Winthrop, the grandson of the first governor of Massachusetts Bay, held the rank of major general in the provincial militia as well as the office of magistrate. Judge Saltonstall also had an illustrious ancestor in his grandfather, Sir Richard, one of the founders of the Bay Colony. The remaining three magistrates were only slightly less distinguished than their associates. John Richards and William Sargent were both wealthy Boston merchants, and Bartholomew Gedney—the only member from Salem Town—was a respected physician and a major in the militia. The selection of so prestigious a commission to officiate in the forthcoming prosecution made clear that the crisis at Salem Village had escalated into a crisis for the entire province.[66]

Nevertheless, it was not the prominence of its members that most distinguished the Court of Oyer and Terminer from previous judicial commissions on witchcraft. On the one hand, the new court encountered external pressures that virtually ruled out the obstructionist strategies of the pre-Salem magistrates. That so many suspects were already imprisoned in the jails of Essex County was in itself a strong incentive for a decisive judicial response. Under these circumstances, a reversion to the dilatory tactics of the earlier courts might have provoked censure from the friends of the accused as well as from the victims of the accused. Moreover, the effects of witchcraft were only too visible, even if the identity of the perpetrators remained to be established. The sufferings of the afflicted had been witnessed and authenticated by both medical and ecclesiastical authorities. That neither group of experts had yet devised a solution to their distress provided a clear warrant for judicial intervention, if only as a last resort.

On the other hand, the demand for legal action may also have been generated from within the court. Several members had already participated in the preliminary hearings that led to the present emergency. Gedney was one of the three Salem magistrates who were in regular attendance at the pretrial examinations. Stoughton had presided at one of these examinations, at least, and Sewall had been an uncritical witness at the hearing of Sarah Cloyce on April 11.[67] It may be assumed that all three members were disposed to accept the findings they had helped to generate. The combined effect of these various internal and external pressures was to create in the Court of Oyer and Terminer a predisposition toward conviction.

Because of this judicial predisposition, the problem of proof posed an even greater dilemma during the Salem prosecutions than it had during the pre-Salem prosecutions. In the earlier legal actions, as discussed above, the magistrates had consistently joined ranks with the clergy, even at the risk of aggravating local tensions. Now that the demand for legal retaliation was sponsored by the magistrates themselves, however, this vital alliance between church and court was threatened.

The problem of proof during the Salem trials was to somehow reconcile the official inclination to validate the findings of the pretrial examinations with the stringent theological constraints on the use of evidence. An open breach between civil and ecclesiastical authorities was virtually unthinkable. For the magistrates to publicly repudiate the advice of the clergy was to question the only acceptable moral and theoretical framework within which action against witchcraft could be justified. At the same time, the clergy could ill afford to challenge the very officials charged with the upholding of ecclesiastical authority.

In spite of these risks, a direct confrontation between the Court of Oyer and Terminer and the church was only narrowly averted. The basis for the conflict lay in the emphasis given to spectral evidence in the gathering of incriminating testimony. While other evidences, including ordinary witchcrafts, witch's marks, puppets, and even secondary signs such as unusual physical strength, had also been admitted into the records of the court, only the spectral evidence had been collected for all the cases.[68] The popular testimony could be disqualified with little or no inconvenience to the court and with few misgivings by the clergy, and because the search for witch's marks and puppets had yielded positive findings for only a small proportion of the suspects, these tests also were of less than critical importance to the prosecution. The deliberations over spectral evidence were more problematic.

On the surface, spectral evidence seemed to offer a happy reconciliation between orthodox doctrine and the new experimental philosophy of Newton and Descartes. The proposition that the devil could use the spectral representations of human forms to wreak harm on his victims rested on sound theological precepts. The sufferings of the afflicted in response to spectral assault provided empirical proof of the validity of this proposition. At last, by means of spectral testimony, the doctrine of spiritual causation could be substantiated through the most careful empirical observation.

Certainly, the afflicted had given the magistrates ample opportunity to probe the workings of the invisible world. During the pretrial examinations, the judges had discovered that a mere glance from the suspect was sufficient to produce fits and other extreme torment in the victim.[69] Gradually, through experimentation, they had also learned that, if the suspect touched the victim, the fits would abate. Moreover, there were other incidents or "curiosities" that provided even more graphic illustrations of spectral agency. On one occasion, a sufferer who had complained of torture by means of some invisible instrument reached out to attack her spectral tormenter and produced an iron spindle before witnesses. On a different occasion, another of the bewitched claimed that she was tormented by a specter wearing a sheet. With a violent motion, she was able to tear a piece from the cloth, which then became visible to spectators as the corner of a sheet.[70]

Yet, for all its apparent promise, spectral evidence was more a legal expedient than a source of theoretical reconciliation. Spectral evidence represented not a synthesis of orthodox doctrine and experimental philosophy but rather a vulgarization of both metaphysical systems. To maintain that the devil revealed his confederates through the testimony of the afflicted was to presume that the intentions of God and Satan were accessible to human understanding. Such a facile interpretation of the preternatural was not consonant with Puritan cosmology; though Satan might indeed make use of spectral representation, it was not within human capacity to decide whether his intention was to inform or to deceive.

Moreover, if there was no theological warrant for identification by means of spectral representation, so, also, there was no philosophical warrant for identification by means of experiments with touch. This method of identification was based upon the assumption that the act of touching would heal the victim of the spectral assault only if performed by the perpetrator, but, as Brattle was later to observe, such a practice could not be reconciled with a mechanistic view of the laws of nature:

The Salem Justices, at least some of them, do assert, that the cure of the afflicted is a natural effect of this touch; and they are so well instructed in the Cartesian philosophy, and in the doctrine of effluvia, that they undertake to give a demonstration of how this touch does cure the afflicted persons. . . . I must confesse to you, that I am no small admirer of the Cartesian philosophy; but yet I have not so learned it. Certainly this is a strain that it will by no means allow of.

Within the framework of Puritan dogma, spectral evidence was a mere presumption; within the framework of Cartesian philosophy, it was mere superstition. Brattle spoke for the clergy as well as for the new men of science when he described it as a method "which we have no rule for, either from reason or religion."[71]

Cotton Mather's letter to magistrate John Richards two days before the first meeting of the Court of Oyer and Terminer well reveals the awkward position of the clergy in the face of judicial determination. As an advocate of legal intervention against witchcraft, Mather could claim to approach the court more as a friend than as a critic. Even someone with these sympathies, however, could not offer theological support for the use of spectral evidence:

And yet I must humbly beg you that in the management of the affair in your most worthy hands, you do not lay more stress upon pure specter testimony than it will bear. When you are satisfied or have good, plain, legal evidence that the demons which molest our poor neighbors do indeed represent such and such people to the sufferers, tho' this be a presumption, yet I suppose you will not reckon it a conviction that the people so repre- sented are witches to be immediately exterminated.

In place of this questionable evidence, Mather proposed that the magis- trates employ aggressive methods—short of the "un-English method of torture"—to obtain confessions. And, if confessions were unobtainable, Mather recommended that the court conduct searches for witch's marks and puppets.[72]

The actions of the court in its first session on June 2 suggest that Mather's tactful advice may have had some impact, for, instead of try- ing suspects in the order in which they had been accused, the magis- trates selected Bridget Bishop as the first of the defendants.[73] If the persons who had been arrested prior to Bridget had been chosen, the court would have been forced to rely almost exclusively on spectral testimony. In the case of the notorious Bridget Bishop, however, a conviction could be justified on the basis of other evidences, including a wealth of popular testimony. At the same time, it is significant that all four of the indictments filed against the suspect were based on the spectral testimony of the afflicted. When Bridget was condemned and sentenced to be executed on June 10, there was still room for uncer- tainty about the methods of the court.

Three days after Bridget Bishop was hanged, there remained enough uncertainty for Governor Phips to request advice from leading minis- ters on the proper procedures for the discovery of witchcraft. Twelve clergymen, including Cotton and Increase Mather, responded on June 15 in a document entitled "The Return of Several Ministers Con- sulted." Cotton Mather was the principal author of the statement. Where the letter to Richards had merely voiced doubts about the va- lidity of spectral evidence, "The Return" was forthright in its repudia- tion of this testimony:

Presumptions whereupon persons may be committed, and, much more, con- victions whereupon persons may be condemned as guilty of witchcrafts, ought certainly to be more considerable than barely the accused person be- ing represented by a specter unto the afflicted, inasmuch as 'tis an undoubted and notorious thing that a Demon may, by God's permission, appear, even to ill purposes, in the shape of an innocent, yea, and a virtuous man. Nor can we esteem alterations made in the sufferers by a look or touch of the accused to be an infallible evidence of guilt, but frequently liable to be abused by the Devil's legerdemains.

The ministers even dared to suggest that the witchcrafts might subside if the evidences were viewed more critically: "We know not whether some remarkable affronts given to the Devils by our disbelieving of those testimonies whose whole force and strength is from them alone, may not put a period unto the progress of the dreadful calamity begun upon us."[74]

The judicial response to this strong statement was not encouraging. Indeed, the period immediately following Bridget Bishop's trial was marked by a further polarization of the church and court. Nathaniel Saltonstall, the one magistrate who concurred with the ecclesiastical opinion, resigned from the court in dissatisfaction with the conduct of the trials.[75] His replacement was Jonathan Corwin, one of the Salem magistrates who had presided in the pretrial examinations. The Court of Oyer and Terminer now included four magistrates who had already committed themselves to the use of spectral evidence.

When this body convened again on June 30, there was little indication of internal dissension. Judicial policy had become fully consolidated in favor of accepting the findings of the pretrial court. Five more of the accused, including the well-respected Rebecca Nurse, were sentenced and condemned on the basis of spectral evidence. In the remaining sessions of the Court of Oyer and Terminer, this policy was not altered.

No further ecclesiastical advice was solicited or granted during the following three sessions of the court. Most of the clergy accommodated to judicial intransigence by keeping their silence. Perhaps the most tortured response of all was that of Cotton Mather. In subsequent writings, in *Wonders of the Invisible World,* and in his various exchanges with Calef, Mather endeavored to somehow reconcile the decisions of the court with the ecclesiastical prohibitions against spectral evidence.[76] Earlier a critic of the court, although sympathetic to its goals, Mather became a reluctant apologist for the court.

The debate over the problem of proof was not so much resolved as it was declined. For one brief moment during the Salem trials, the magistrates and the clergy faced each other as potential adversaries. In that moment of confrontation, it was the policy of the court that prevailed over ecclesiastical dissent. An institutional crisis was averted, but only at a considerable cost to the clergy. The price of alliance was the default of the church.

Later, in the aftermath of the Salem trials, the alliance between church and court would once again be placed in jeopardy. And, once again, measures would be taken to conceal this disunity from public view. Nevertheless, the suspicion would linger that the Court of Oyer and Terminer had sacrificed theological principles for the sake of legal expedience and that the clergy had been their accomplices in this betrayal.

In spite of their defiance of the church, it would be misleading to suggest that the magistrates were entirely unaffected by ecclesiastical opinion. Even in the early stages of the proceedings, the magistrates endeavored to reconcile the terms of prosecution with the theological requirements for the crime. From the outset, it is clear that the court preferred to use spectral testimony not as a final proof of witchcraft but rather as a means for securing a final proof. From the standpoint of the magistrates as well as the clergy, the most satisfactory basis for conviction was the confession.

Certainly there was ample precedent in England and New England for granting spectral evidence the status of presumption. In his cautionary note to Magistrate Richards, Mather himself had explicitly conceded presumptive validity to the testimony of the afflicted,[77] although "The Return of Several Ministers" later recommended against this policy. If spectral evidence were allowed as a strong presumption, then the strategy devised by Perkins and Bernard was applicable to the Salem trials. As discussed in chapter 7, both ministers had recommended the use of alert and vigorous cross-examination to elicit the convictive testimony of the confession from the more easily generated presumptive evidences. Whether or not it was this specific strategy that guided the actions of the magistrates, it is apparent that the persons who were accused by the afflicted entered the court under at least a strong presumption of guilt.

Perhaps no trial more fully reveals the judicial predisposition toward conviction than that of Rebecca Nurse on June 30. After her interrogation, the jury was sent out and returned a verdict of not guilty. In a dramatic reversal of previous official policy toward witchcraft, the magistrates urged reconsideration of the verdict. According to the foreman of the jury, Rebecca had remarked after hearing the accusation of a confessed witch, "What, do these persons give in Evidence against me now, they used to come among us." The magistrate chose to interpret this statement as a tacit admission of complicity, although Rebecca herself later declared to the court, "I intended no otherways, then as they were Prisoners with us, and there did then, and yet do judge them not legal Evidence against their fellow Prisoners."[78] Nevertheless, on second deliberation, the jury returned a verdict of guilty, and the prisoner was condemned to be executed.

The presumption of guilt was evident as well in the actual cross-examinations. The account of Nathaniel Cary, a prominent shipbuilder from Charlestown, provides a graphic description of the aggressive conduct of the magistrates. The examination he attended began with a prayer by a minister, followed by the calling in of the prisoners. During the interrogation, each prisoner was required to stand about seven or eight feet from the magistrates, and the accusers were placed between them and the bench. Extreme precautions were taken to protect the afflicted from further assault. Officers were appointed to hold each of the prisoners' hands, "least they should therewith afflict them." In addition, the court ruled that the "Prisoners Eyes must be constantly on the Justices," in order to shield the victims from ocular assault.[79] After intensive cross-examination, the suspects were required to recite the Lord's Prayer, on the assumption that a true confederate of Satan would be unable to speak the holy words without committing blasphemy.[80] Finally, the magistrates would ask of the afflicted, "Which of you will go and Touch the Prisoner at the Bar?" Here the afflicted persons would be seized with fits that would abate only when they established physical contact with the suspect.

In other instances, official harassment verged upon torture. Cary's own wife was accused shortly after his arrival in Salem and was brought in for examination on May 28. Throughout her interrogation, she was obliged to stand with her arms stretched outward. When she complained that she was about to faint, Magistrate Hathorne replied, according to Cary's narrative, that "she had strength enough to torment those persons, and she should have strength enough to stand."[81] John Proctor, one of the accused who was later executed, described the following event in a letter from Salem Prison on July 23:

My son, William Proctor, when he was examin'd, because he would not confess that he was Guilty, when he was innocent, they tyed him Neck and Heels till the Blood gushed out at his Nose, and would have kept him so 24 hours, if one more merciful than the rest, had not taken pity on him, and caused him to be unbound.[82]

According to Proctor, two other boys did confess after being subjected to similar physical trials.

In spite of these aggressive measures, the proportion of confessors among the accused remained disappointingly low until the later part of

July. Even such likely candidates as Bridget Bishop and Sarah Good
not only refused to yield to judicial pressure but also failed to display
any sign of remorse at their execution. Indeed, on July 19, in response
to minister Nicholas Noyes's attempts to elicit a confession, Good had
cried out from the scaffold, "you are a lyer; I am no more a witch than
you are a Wizard, and if you take away my life, God will give you
blood to drink."[83] Before July 21, only five confessions had been obtained from more than eighty imprisoned suspects.[84]

Then, only two days after the execution of July 19, four suspects
from Andover confessed on the same day. Before August 1, at least
seven more prisoners had offered confessions. As Cotton Mather noted
in his letter of August 5 to John Cotton, these sudden acknowledgments of guilt occurred at a most opportune moment:

Our good God is working of miracles. Five witches were lately executed,
impudently demanding of God a miraculous vindication of their innocency.
Immediately upon this, our God miraculously sent in five Andover witches,
who made a most ample, surprising, amazing confession of all their villain-
ies, and declared the five newly executed to have been of their company.[85]

Mather need not have thanked God for the timely vindication, however. In a decision virtually without legal precedent for capital offenders in Massachusetts Bay, the magistrates chose to exempt confessors
from execution.[86] While the precise date of introduction of the policy
is unknown, it is hardly surprising that the first large wave of confessions should follow so closely upon the first wave of mass hangings.
For those suspects who survived the executions of July 19, the benefits of confession were not easily declined.

Yet, for some of the prisoners, even the promise of life was not
enough. Of the fifteen persons who were condemned in the trials of
September 9 and September 15, eight refused to surrender to judicial
pressure.[87] Like the persons who had preceded them to the gallows on
August 19, they were reported by contemporary witnesses to have
protested their innocence up to the very moment of their hanging. Indeed, one of the condemned prisoners, Samuel Wardwell, retracted a
previous confession only barely in time to join the others on the scaffold. Wardwell, a self-acknowledged dabbler in the magical arts, had
been one of the few convicted witches to be genuinely convinced, albeit only temporarily, of the validity of the charges against him.[88]

Perhaps the most dramatic retraction of all was that of Margaret Jacobs on the day before the execution of August 19. Margaret, a young
woman from Salem Village, had implicated John Willard, George
Burroughs, and her grandfather, George Jacobs, Sr., in an earlier con-

fession. On August 18, she withdrew her confession and, according to Calef, begged forgiveness from Burroughs. Her declaration of innocence, later presented to the magistrates at Salem, is worth quoting at some length if only because it well described a dilemma faced by most of the confessors:

That whereas your poor and humble declarant being closely confined here in Salem jail for the crime of witchcraft, which crime, thanks be to the Lord, I am altogether ignorant of, as will appear at the great day of judgment. May it please the honoured court, I was cried out upon by some of the possessed persons, as afflicting of them; whereupon I was brought to my examination, which the persons at the sight of me fell down, which did very much startle and affright me. The Lord above knows I knew nothing, in the least measure, how or who afflicted them; they told me, without doubt I did, or else they would not fall down at me; they told me if I would not confess, I should be put down into the dungeon and would be hanged, but if I would confess I should have my life; the which did so affright me, with my own vile wicked heart, to save my life made me make the confession I did, which confession, may it please the honoured court, is altogether false and untrue.[89]

Nevertheless, Margaret's retraction effected no change in judicial policy. Burroughs, Willard, and her grandfather were executed on schedule, and Margaret was returned to Salem dungeon the following day and again placed in fetters.

For most of the imprisoned suspects, however, the advantages of confession proved irresistible. Dorcas Hoar, condemned to be executed during her trial of September 9, finally yielded on the day before her scheduled hanging after months of defiance. Several ministers petitioned on her behalf, and she was granted a one-month stay of execution—long enough to survive the dismantling of the court.[90] Likewise, the execution of Samuel Wardwell may have helped to overcome any lingering moral qualms in his wife, Mercy, or his daughter Sarah, both of whom held to their confessions of September 1.

Other confessors later claimed that they had been victims of intimidation. In a petition submitted to Stoughton in early October, six Andover women explained that they had vacillated between professions of guilt and innocence until persuaded to confess by some local gentlemen: "they telling us, that we were witches, and they knew it, and they knew that we knew it, which made us think that it was so."[91] One of the six women reported that she had even begun to suspect herself after witnessing the sufferings of the afflicted: "the afflicted persons crying out of her as afflicting them made her fearful of herself." Two other Andover women also eventually acknowledged that they had confessed under duress.[92]

Just prior to her execution, Mary Easty, one of the few condemned witches to refuse the judicial pardon, included in her petition to the court: "I would humbly beg of you, that your Honours would be pleased to examine some of those confessing witches, I being confident there are several of them have belyed themselves and others, as will appear, if not in this World, I am sure in the World to come, whither I am going."[93] These suspicions were later confirmed when only three out of more than fifty confessors continued to declare their guilt after the Court of Oyer and Terminer had been dissolved. Perhaps the most disturbing irony of the Salem trials was that those who were most able to sustain faith in divine justice were least likely to survive the justice of the court.

The judicial improvisation on confessions may well constitute the most enigmatic feature of the entire proceedings, particularly since the magistrates appear not to have disclosed the grounds for the policy even to contemporaries. Indeed, Cotton Mather's almost offhand suggestion in his letter of May 31 survives as the only formulation available to historical observers:

What if some of the lesser criminals be only scourged with lesser punishments, and also put upon some solemn open, public, and explicit renunciation of the devil? . . . Or what if the death of some of the offenders were either diverted or inflicted, according to the success of their renunciation?[94]

From this standpoint, the allowance of confession as a mitigating factor could be viewed as a gesture of Christian charity. Those who were guilty but fearful of judicial retaliation would be rewarded for openly renouncing their allegiance to Satan.

Yet the accounts of contemporary publicists reveal no such understanding of the policy. For Calef, the most striking feature of the innovation was its failure to comply with legal precedent: "And though the confessing witches were many: yet not one of them that confessed their own guilt, and abode by their confession were put to death." Brattle's concern was with the harshness of the policy, the "violent, distracting, and draggoning" methods used to elicit confessions. And Hale, in his commentary some five years after the trials, referred to the policy only to draw attention to one of its potential shortcomings: "And as for the condemned confessors at the Bar (they being reprieved) we had no experience whether they would stand to their self-condemning confessions, when they came to dye."[95]

In the absence of any clarification by the magistrates themselves, it is tempting to view the innovation as merely a desperate legal expedient to restore confidence in judicial authority. At the time of the first wave of confessions, the court had placed itself in potential conflict with the village laity and the clergy. Five persons had just been executed on the basis of controversial evidence, two of whom, Rebecca Nurse and Elizabeth How, were believed by many of their neighbors to be women of high moral character. The timely confessions of July 21 provided the first unassailable proof that drastic measures had been necessary. Under these conditions, the possibility arises that the magistrates may have disregarded legal precedent in the case of capital offenders in order to produce the evidence required to maintain the credibility of their investigation.

However, such an interpretation overlooks the fact that the members of the province attached a symbolic meaning to the act of confession that far transcended its significance as mere evidence. What led the magistrates to improvise so recklessly in their pursuit of the confession had less to do with the mechanics of institutional control than with the imperatives of covenant theology. The confession offered not just a proof of witchcraft but a means of communal expiation.

If self-vindication had been the only objective of the court, then the production of a few confessions might have been sufficient, but because the more important goal was that of communal regeneration, the magistrates could afford no relaxation in their diligence. Brattle has reported that even after the mass confessions of July, the judicial pressure did not abate. New methods of torture and harassment were devised for the more stubborn suspects:

You may possibly think that my terms are too severe; but should I tell you what a kind of Blade was employed in bringing these women to their confession; what methods of damnation; with what violence urged . . . I am sure that you would call them, (as I do) rude and barbarous methods.[96]

The penitent witch who renounced her alliance with the devil acted not only on her own behalf but on behalf of the entire community. Indeed, several among the accused had been asked to confess specifically in order to uphold the good reputation of their towns and villages.[97] Within the framework of covenant theology, the only durable solution to the conspiracy of Satan was communal regeneration. The fifty or more suspects who acknowledged their treason before the court and before God furnished the means by which this regeneration would be achieved.

10

The Salem Witchcraft Prosecutions:

The Invisible World at the Vanishing Point

IT WAS NOT LONG after the last confession had been elicited that the members of Massachusetts Bay began to reinterpret the events of the preceding eight months. By September, the magistrates had accumulated information from the reports of confessors that confirmed their worst suspicions about the activities of the invisible world. In the following months, however, this official version of the prosecution began to break down. The findings of the Court of Oyer and Terminer were called into question, and decisions that had previously seemed necessary and sensible were now perceived as problematic.

Thus, in the aftermath of the Salem trials, the inhabitants of Massachusetts Bay came to experience the shock of demystification as the hidden dynamics of witchcraft prosecution came into public view. In the light of these disturbing revelations, contemporaries faced an agonizing dilemma: how to repudiate the policies of the magistrates without hastening the collapse of the state and without jeopardizing New England's covenantal relationship with God.

It is one of the objectives of this chapter to describe how and in what terms members accomplished the reformulation of official policy. It is the other objective to show how public reconsideration of the problem of the Salem trials entailed a reconsideration of the problem of witchcraft in general.

THE POPULAR RESPONSE TO OFFICIAL INITIATIVE

Villagers did not perceive any serious incompatibility between the popular and the official approaches to the problem of witchcraft until well after the trials had begun. That the magistrates routinely included allegations of malefic harm among the evidences against the suspects may have delayed this recognition. That, moreover, most of the early suspects, such as Sarah Good, Susanna Martin, and Bridget Bishop, were as likely to be accused by their neighbors as by the afflicted may have convinced some of the villagers, in varying degrees, that their concerns were well represented by official policy.

What eventually estranged the villagers from the court was not that the magistrates took seriously the evidence of the afflicted or even that they were willing to sign warrants against persons of unblemished reputations. Apart from such luminaries as Thomas Brattle and possibly a few iconoclasts, the majority of residents in Essex County were as persuaded by the sufferings of the accusers as were the members of the court. And, although the arrest of such notables as Rebecca Nurse, Philip English, and John Alden was hardly reassuring for their neighbors, there were other occasions prior to the Salem trials in which reputable men and women had come under suspicion of witchcraft.

The truly provocative feature of judicial policy was that it rendered the allegations of the afflicted utterly irreversible. Whereas in earlier legal actions the villagers had been able to defend themselves and others against accusations either by questioning the reputation of the complainant or by making public their own good reputation, the Court of Oyer and Terminer made any such appeals to status considerations futile. Whereas the identity of the pre-Salem witch had been crystallized only after a lengthy process of negotiation between her supporters and her adversaries, the Salem witch passed through the several phases of legal action entirely unaffected by local opinion. Judicial policy during the Salem trials not only allowed persons of good reputation to be placed under suspicion, it also deprived these persons of the traditional safeguards that would have protected them against further legal jeopardy.

In spite of these new limitations on public action in behalf of the defendant, villagers were slow to depart from established channels of legal redress. Perhaps no expression of popular support was more painfully respectful of judicial authority than that offered by Ephraim Wilds in defense of his mother, Sarah Wilds. Unhappily, Ephraim had just been elected constable of Topsfield at the time that a warrant was filed against his mother on April 22. It was thus his duty to perform the arrest. To resolve this conflict of loyalty, the sheriff first delivered his mother to prison and then offered as counterevidence her conscientious discharge of parental responsibilities:

I never saw any harm by her upon any such account neither in word nor action as she is now accused for she hath always instructed me well in the Christian religion and the way of God ever since I was able to take instructions and so I leave it to this Honored Court to consider it.[1]

Such filial praise notwithstanding, Sarah was among the first of the convicted witches to be hung on July 19.

In other cases, popular support was more substantial, although still well within the bounds of traditional modes of appeal. Local opinion appears to have been sharply divided in the case of Elizabeth How of Rowley, arrested on May 28. About a dozen of her neighbors gave evidence of her malefic powers, while an equal number testified to her good character and to the sincerity of her religious convictions. More significantly, included among her advocates were the two ministers of the Rowley congregation, and both were prepared to openly challenge the testimony of one of the afflicted girls who had accused her. According to ministers Samuel Philips and Edward Paison, the girl had cried out against Elizabeth only after strong prompting by members of her family.[2] Nevertheless, even ecclesiastical support was not enough to protect the defendant from being condemned and then executed on July 19.

Public opinion was less equivocal in the cases of Rebecca Nurse, John and Elizabeth Proctor, and Mary Bradbury. More than thirty-five neighbors in Topsfield and Salem Village, including several of the wealthiest landholders in both communities, testified that Rebecca had never given them grounds to suspect her of witchcraft.[3] Two petitions were filed in behalf of the Proctors, one of which was similar in content to the Nurse petition.[4] The other petition—submitted by thirty-one residents of Ipswich—was possibly the first public document in the Salem trials to question the validity of spectral evidence. Using an argument that would shortly gain wider acceptance, the signers urged the magistrates to consider whether God might permit Satan "to personate, Dissemble and thereby abuse innocents."[5] Finally, the efforts expended in behalf of Mary Bradbury of Salisbury may well have represented the exhaustion of conventional means for legal redress. In addition to favorable testimonials from the local minister, James Allen, and from magistrate Robert Pike, 118 persons signed a petition in which Mary was described as a "lover of the ministry in all appearance and a diligent attender upon God's holy ordinances."[6] In spite of these strong expressions of public support, the Court of Oyer and Terminer condemned all four of the accused to be executed.

Under these circumstances in which the usual protections against witchcraft accusations were no longer viable, some of the suspects and their families began to defend themselves in a less orthodox manner. Daniel Andrew and George Jacobs, both of Salem Village, were among the first of the accused to resist judicial authority by fleeing the colony. The two men collaborated in their escape shortly after May 14 when warrants were issued for their arrest.[7]

By the middle of July, there are clear indications that an effective underground had been organized to help suspects with sufficient political and economic resources. Philip English and his wife, Mary, were enabled to leave the colony soon after his capture in Boston on May 31.[8] Among his confederates was John Alden, who also was helped to escape prison after fifteen weeks of detention.[9] Likewise, Captain Bradbury managed to rescue his wife, Mary, only days before her scheduled execution on September 22.[10] By early October, at least twelve suspects were in flight from the law, and, like Mary Bradbury, most had tried to defend themselves by conventional means before engaging in more extreme forms of resistance.[11]

Several incidents, however, suggest that segments of the public were willing to take far more drastic action against judicial authority. Although the mounting number of escapes from prison may have created practical difficulties in law enforcement and though the gathering of support for individual cases may have helped to focus public discontent, neither response directly challenged the legitimacy of judicial policy. When such a challenge did arise in May, the judges did not hesitate to reply. A petition circulated by the Reverend Mr. Milborne of Boston included objections not only to the imprisonment of persons of high status but also to the entire framework of judicial procedure. Milborne was arrested for these activities on June 25.[12]

On August 19, a more spontaneous form of collective protest was only barely contained. While on the scaffold, condemned witch George Burroughs had delivered, in addition to an inspired oration, a perfect rendering of the Lord's Prayer, a feat believed impossible for confederates of Satan. Magistrate Sewall recorded in his diary that the spectators were strongly sympathetic to Burroughs, and Calef mentions that the executions had to be delayed for fear of mob violence.[13] A speech by Cotton Mather, which justified the decisions of the court, helped to calm the crowd, and the hangings proceeded without further interruption.

When Governor Phips ordered a moratorium on legal action on October 12, public opposition had begun to escalate from dissatisfaction with individual cases to rejection of the entire proceedings. On the same day, the governor received the first of several petitions from the residents of Andover for the release of their relatives from the harsh conditions of prison.[14] On October 18, the two ministers of Andover together with twenty-four residents sent a more strongly worded petition to the governor, the Governor's Council, and the General Court in which judicial policy was directly criticized:

Our troubles, which hitherto have been great, we foresee are like to continue and increase if other methods be not taken than as yet have been, for there are more of our neighbors of good reputation and approved integrity who are still accused, and complaints have been made against them. And we know not who can think himself safe if the accusations of children and others who are under a diabolical influence shall be received against persons of good fame.[15]

Moreover, the signers of the petition alleged that a number of the Andover confessions had been obtained under duress. This charge was promptly investigated by Increase Mather on the following day. From his interviews in the Salem jail, Mather discovered that the persons in question did in fact complain of extortion and were now eager to retract their confessions.[16]

A week later, on October 26, popular discontent was translated into more effective political action. The elected representatives of the villagers passed a bill proposing a convocation of ministers to decide upon an alternative course of action. The bill was tactful and merely stated that "Notwithstanding Indefatigable Endeavors" of the magistrates, the number of cases of witchcraft had grown rather than diminished.[17] Nevertheless, the implications of passing such a bill were obvious, and Sewall noted in his diary, "The reason and manner of doing it, is such, that the Court of Oyer and Terminer count themselves thereby dismissed."[18] Yet, since the bill was not sanctioned by the Governor's Council, the status of the court remained uncertain for a few days. Sewall's own request for clarification was met with silence. Not until October 29, in response to another inquiry about the next sitting of the court, did the governor formally terminate the commission.

That the public came to oppose the Salem prosecution is less surprising than that this opposition should have emerged so slowly, for the villagers had been presented with anomalous decisions as early as April when persons were identified who thoroughly contradicted their expectations for the malefic witch. Moreover, the court had further confounded the popular understanding by honoring the allegations of victims who had never met the persons they accused. Perhaps even more significantly, the magistrates had chosen to disregard the counterevidence upon which defendants had traditionally relied to protect their reputations. In spite of these striking departures from the popular approach to witchcraft, the bill of October 26 passed only by a narrow margin of thirty-three yeas to twenty-nine noes, and as Sewall indicates, the difference can be attributed to the votes of relatives of the accused and other interested parties.[19] Even after the Court of Oyer and Terminer had been discontinued, several residents of Gloucester had invited the afflicted to help investigate new acts of malefic witchcraft.

The persistence of popular support becomes more comprehensible once it is recognized that there were areas of agreement as well as areas of disagreement between the popular and official approaches to witchcraft. If the selection of reputable persons as suspects was problematic, the selection of disreputable men and women was not. The Court of Oyer and Terminer was the first judicial commission in over thirty years to have acted decisively to protect villagers against malefic harm. And, while some residents may have been troubled by the imprisonment of their more respectable neighbors, others were undoubtedly relieved to be spared further contact with persons whom they had suspected for years.

For persons such as John Alden, Philip English, and possibly Rebecca Nurse and her relations, the Salem trials may have constituted a thoroughly unnecessary judicial adventure. Villagers of their stature did not ordinarily participate in witchcraft proceedings either as defendants or as accusers. It was these persons and their friends and relatives who were the earliest to oppose judicial policy by means of petitions and other countermeasures, and it was largely through their efforts that the court was dismantled. But those of their neighbors who were less prosperous and who were forced to deal directly with reputed practitioners of malefic magic such as Wilmot Reed or Susanna Martin had a different outlook. The Court of Oyer and Terminer was one of the very few official tribunals to have taken their suffering seriously. It is not so surprising, after all, that requests for legal protection continued well into November of 1692 and that, for some members of the village laity, the court was terminated before it had finished its work.

THE REFORMULATION OF OFFICIAL POLICY

Steps were taken to mitigate judicial policy even before the Court of Oyer and Terminer had been dismissed.[20] In October, the governor began to accept petitions for the release of imprisoned relatives on bond. Bond was also accepted for persons accused only on the basis of spectral evidence. Moreover, Brattle mentions in his letter of October 8 that several of the suspects who had eluded capture were no longer actively pursued.[21]

Nevertheless, such halfway measures served only to dramatize the need for more drastic changes in judicial policy. By late October, dozens of suspects roamed the villages neither cleared of the charges against them nor under threat of immediate prosecution. Others languished in prison uncertain of when and in what terms their legal status would be resolved. Meanwhile, as more accusations filtered into the courts, the magistrates awaited direction from the governor. Any further equivocation in the official response toward witchcraft was politically untenable.

It was under these precarious circumstances that the governor undertook to reverse the findings of the Court of Oyer and Terminer.

The state versus the covenant.   From a purely theological standpoint, the invalidation of the findings of the Court of Oyer and Terminer posed no problem at all. That the rejection of spectral evidence was fully compatible with orthodox doctrine had been communicated to Governor Phips in "The Return of Several Ministers" of June 15. In case the governor harbored any further misgivings about the doctrinal propriety of these opinions, by October 3 Increase Mather had already completed a manuscript entitled *Cases of Conscience Concerning Evil Spirits Personating Men,* in which spectral evidence and the tests that accompanied it were discredited on impeccable theological grounds. The work had been in preparation since at least August 1, and there can be little doubt that it represented the official ecclesiastical statement on the subject. The foreword to the discourse consisted of an enthusiastic endorsement signed by fourteen ministers, including Samuel Willard and the venerable Michael Wigglesworth. In addition to Mather's work, the governor received yet another authoritative ecclesiastical statement in the second week of October. In reply to questions submitted by the Chief Justice of the Province of New York, a panel of Dutch ministers had declared unequivocally that spectral evidence was unreliable and that it would be "the greatest imprudence" to convict persons on the basis of such testimony.[22]

If there were no serious theological objections to the voiding of spectral evidence, there were nevertheless other reasons for extreme caution. Brattle's letter was the earliest public document to make explicit the real difficulty that confronted civil and ecclesiastical authorities. What distinguished his contribution from other writings of the period was his forthright assertion that an injustice of major proportions had already been perpetrated. After presenting various criticisms of the use of spectral evidence, Brattle concluded his letter with the dire prophecy, "I am afraid that ages will not wear off that re-

proach which these things will leave behind them upon our land."[23]
While others had challenged the testimony of the afflicted with equal
force, no one else had dared to openly acknowledge the obvious implications. If it were allowed that spectral evidence was insufficient
for conviction, then the magistrates were responsible for the deaths
of innocent persons as well as for the hardships imposed upon scores
of others who had been unfairly imprisoned.

In the aftermath of the Salem trials, the governor and his supporters
faced a test no less severe than that which had been imposed upon the
confessors. To acknowledge error was to invite political disaster. If it
were conceded that the court was guilty of injustice, then were not
those who legitimated its policies as well as those who participated in
the implementation of these policies also responsible for the punishment and execution of innocent persons? In his letter of October 12,
Phips had complained that his enemies were already using the Salem
trials to challenge his authority.[24] And if the charge of complicity were
extended to the governor who had appointed the magistrates, then it
also could include the sheriffs, examiners, jailkeepers, and other legal
functionaries who had obeyed their orders as well as the jurymen who
had accepted their rules of evidence. Indeed, the lines of complicity
could be extended to include even those suspects who had offered
testimony against others among the accused. For the sake of political
stability, the error would have to be denied.

For the sake of the national covenant, however, the error would
have to be acknowledged. Within the covenantal framework, the believing Christian was obliged to avow his sins before God, not only in
his own behalf but in behalf of the community to which he belonged.
The sins committed during the Salem trials reflected not only on the
perpetrators but on the whole of New England. To fail to confess
these sins was to incur divine wrath against an unrepentant community.

It is impossible to understand the terms in which official policy was
reformulated without an appreciation of this tension between the political imperatives of the state and the moral imperatives of the covenant. Civil and ecclesiastical authorities were faced with stark alternatives. To acknowledge the errors of the Court of Oyer and Terminer
was to risk the collapse of Phips's regime. To deny error was to erode
the moral pledge that had sanctified New England's special relationship with God. The one choice would result in the withdrawal of
divine favor; the other choice would undermine the stability of the
state.

Thus, in the period following the Salem trials, the crisis of witchcraft was transformed into a crisis of legitimacy. The state could be preserved, but the moral pledge that justified the state would have to be sacrificed. Or the pledge could be reaffirmed while a beleaguered community lived through yet another moment of political uncertainty.

In the short run, the official solution was to uphold the state in default of the covenant. Spectral testimony was disqualified, but the implications of this disqualification were deliberately ignored. Eventually, however, the leaders of Massachusetts Bay would be reminded of the imperatives of covenant theology both in the personal misfortunes visited upon those most responsible for the trials and in the political and economic adversities suffered by the community as a whole.

The affirmation of the state.   No single administrative act more fully reveals the terms in which official policy was reformulated than does the governor's decision on October 12 to impose a ban on the printing of all publications relating to witchcraft. So volatile had the subject become that any discussion whether in defense of or in opposition to the proceedings was perceived as a direct threat to political stability. As Phips explained in his letter to the home government, "I have [also] put a stop to the printing of any discourses one way or other, that may increase the needless disputes of people upon this occasion, because I saw a likelyhood of kindling an inextinguishable flame if I should admit any publique and Open Contests."[25] It was not by mere coincidence that the official ban followed so closely the publication of Willard's "Dialogue between S. and B." and the circulation of Brattle's letter.

In the next few months, the official solution to the Salem predicament would be implemented rapidly and without public debate. On November 25, a new court, the Superior Court of Judicature, was constituted to replace the Court of Oyer and Terminer. To expedite the disposition of the remaining cases, a special order was issued on December 16 to reschedule the first sessions of the court from November 1693 to January of the same year.[26] Apparently, it was not until the court actually convened on January 3 that the jurors were informed of a change in the rules of evidence. According to Calef, when some members of the jury asked what weight was to be given to spectral evidence, the magistrates' answer was "as much as of Chips of Wort."[27] On this basis, only twenty-one of over fifty persons were indicted, and only three of these twenty-one defendants were found guilty.[28]

The most striking characteristic of the court, however, was that four of its five members were the same magistrates who had served on the Court of Oyer and Terminer. Although the policies of the earlier court had been rejected, the men who had enforced these policies were quietly reinstated.

The only threat to this semblance of continuity between the two courts was the intransigence of magistrate William Stoughton. After Phips had issued a reprieve for the three persons who had just been condemned as well as for five others who had previously been convicted, Stoughton resigned from the court in angry protest.[29] In his letter to the home government on February 21, 1693, Phips observed that Stoughton "hath from the beginning hurried on these matters with great precipitancy."[30] In the immediate aftermath of the Salem trials, this exchange constitutes the only open acknowledgment of dissension within the ranks of civil and ecclesiastical authorities.

In the final two sessions of the new court, a verdict of not guilty was returned in five cases, and in one other case, that of John Alden, the defendant was discharged by proclamation. Finally, as Hale's account indicates, a rapid if somewhat precipitous settlement was obtained for persons under arrest or in prison after May of 1693: "Some brake prison and ran away, and were not strictly searched after, some acquitted, some dismissed and one way or other, all that had been accused were set at liberty."[31] Within eight months after the dissolution of the Court of Oyer and Terminer, the governor had virtually cleared the courts and prisons of all cases linked to the Salem trials.

Thus it was by means of silence and by force of administrative fiat that an interim solution was achieved for the Salem predicament. The rules of evidence were reformulated, but the act of reformulation was divested of its controversial overtones. In theory, the magistrates were merely concluding the investigations they had begun in Salem Village; in practice, they were repudiating the very findings they had helped to generate.

The governor did not act alone, however, in his attempt to discourage criticism of the members of the Court of Oyer and Terminer. Once again, the clergy found themselves hard-pressed to avoid the implications of their own pronouncements. If spectral evidence were disqualified according to the recommendation of the church, did this not imply that the representatives of ecclesiastical authority were in open disagreement with the representatives of civil authority? Yet, for all the embarrassment the magistrates might have occasioned, such lack of unity was no more desirable now than it had been earlier. In a period of political transition in which the franchise had been extended to include Quakers, Anglicans, and other dissident groups, the alliance between church and state was all the more necessary to preserve Puritan hegemony.

It was Cotton Mather who clearly foresaw the risk of political in-
stability and who, together with his father, helped to formulate an
ecclesiastical defense of judicial conduct, albeit with the tacit consent
of other members of the clergy. Mather recognized that *Cases of Conscience*, in spite of its broad acceptance among the clergy, raised as
many problems as it solved. Even if read only as a theological tract,
Increase's work was a bold statement. In the present political climate,
Cotton believed that *Cases* was a potentially incendiary document. In
a letter of October 20, he explained why he had not signed the introduction to the work.

I did, in my conscience, think that as the humors of this people now run,
such a discourse going alone would not only enable our witch-advocates
very learnedly to cavil and nibble at the late proceedings against witches,
considered in parcels, while things as they lay in bulk, with their whole
dependences, were not exposed; but also evermore than so, produce a public
and open contest with the judges, who would (tho' beyond the intention of
the worthy author and subscribers) find themselves brought unto the bar
before the rashest mobile.[32]

The obvious danger was that if the authority of the church were used
to justify the invalidation of spectral evidence, then this same authority
might be invoked to discredit the magistrates.

It was in part to forestall this calamity, "to prevent such a bloodly
quarrel between Moses and Aaron as would be bitterness in the later
end,"[33] that Cotton Mather wrote his *Wonders of the Invisible World*.
Wonders was the only work to somehow escape Phips's censorship of
materials pertaining to witchcraft, and, although no formal exemption
was granted, there is reason to believe that the treatise was accorded a
privileged status. Mather indicates that the governor encouraged him
in its preparation, and the reverse of the title page in the first edition
contains the inscription, "Published by the Special Command of his
Excellency, the Governor of the Province of Massachusetts-Bay in
New England."[34]

As mentioned above, Mather's work presented a version of the Salem
trials that articulated the standpoint of the magistrates. What is equally
significant is that this version represented judicial policy as if it had
never deviated from the ecclesiastical recommendations. In Mather's
account, five cases were presented as illustrative of the Salem prosecutions: the trials of George Burroughs, Bridget Bishop, Susanna Martin,
Elizabeth How, and Martha Carrier. Because the evidence for each of
these cases included an unusual number of allegations of malefic practice in addition to other testimonies, it was possible for the author to

imply that spectral evidence had been granted only presumptive weight in the actual proceedings.[35] Each case was thoroughly summarized except that of How; here Mather chose to ignore the evidence submitted in behalf of the defendant. Thus, in *Wonders*, Mather produced a history that effectively obscured the major points of disagreement between civil and ecclesiastical authorities.

When *Cases of Conscience* was finally published in June 1963, it was included in a single volume with *Wonders*, but in retrospect this precaution seems hardly to have been necessary. Increase subscribed fully to the approach formulated by his son. After denouncing the use of spectral evidence—"To take away the Life of any one, merely because a Spectre or Devil, in a bewitched or possessed person does accuse them will bring the Guilt of Innocent Blood upon the land"—Increase continued: "Mercy forbid that it should (and I trust that as it has not it never will be) in New England."[36] And, in case this exculpatory note failed to reassure the magistrates, Increase added a postscript in which he not only approved the conduct of the court but also claimed to be in complete agreement with the account given by his son.[37]

In seeking to conceal judicial error, the Mathers committed themselves to so transparent a deception that their reputations would suffer for the remainder of their lives. Cotton, in particular, continued to be haunted by the publication of a painfully compromised work long after others had found the room to place the Salem trials firmly behind them. In his prolonged and bitter quarrel with Calef, he would defend a position that had become even more questionable with the passage of time than it had been in 1692. Meanwhile, the entries in his diary reveal a man plagued by an uneasy conscience. Publicly, Mather was never quite able to acknowledge his culpability; privately, he was never quite able to convince himself of his innocence.

Perhaps, though, it is less important that Phips and the Mathers promoted such easily deflatable fictions than that these fictions went unchallenged by their contemporaries, for the official ban on publications cannot by itself account for the virtual absence of public reference to the trials between 1692 and 1696. No mention of the subject is to be found in sermons or in legislative records or in town records, except those of Salem Village. Even here the references are veiled and ambiguous. It is almost as if members sought to expunge the trials not only from their history but from their memory as well. If the leaders of Massachusetts Bay had disposed of the Salem predicament by devious means, they did so with the tacit cooperation of their compatriots.

Ultimately, the denial of judicial error was more than just a simple act of political deception; it was a refusal to acknowledge a totally unacceptable outcome. That the magistrates were possibly guilty of judicial murder was disturbing enough, but that they had committed injustices in defense of the Puritan mission was a contradiction that could not be readily assimilated. That the confessions had failed to deliver the country from the judgment of afflictions was also distressing, but that these expressions of collective guilt were later revealed to be the product of judicial extortion was an enormity beyond comprehension.

There was more at stake in the failure of the Salem trials than the political future of Phips's regime. The magistrates had applied the same remedial measures to the judgment of witchcraft that earlier generations had applied to other providences such as famine, war, and sickness. Yet the results of this intervention had been not the expiation of the community from its collective sins but a further aggravation of the collective guilt. The failure of the Salem trials left members with questions not only about the methods of the court but also about the entire framework of meanings by which they had interpreted the misfortunes that befell them. In the years immediately following 1692, there were few who dared to probe these questions too closely.

The affirmation of the covenant.   Until 1696, federal affairs were conducted as if the Salem trials had never occurred. Only the continuation of factional conflict in Salem Village threatened to disturb the official silence, for among the more damning indictments against the Salem trials is that they failed utterly to resolve the local tensions of which they were in part an expression. Once again, it proved impossible to contain the conflicts in Salem Village within the safe limits of local politics.

Early in 1693, several members of the village congregation moved to call a convocation of ministers to inquire into their grievances against Parris.[38] The implications of the request were obvious: Merely to allow such a meeting was to acknowledge that the grievances might be legitimate. Parris refused the request on April 20, 1693, but his opponents persisted in their efforts and submitted a petition to Governor Phips to have the dispute arbitrated by disinterested observers. By October 1693, it is clear that Parris had become an embarrassment to the ecclesiastical leadership and could no longer count on the support of his colleagues. Three neighboring ministers from Salem Town and Beverly wrote Parris to advise him to comply with the request for arbitration.[39]

Parris accepted the advice but was able to use his considerable political skills to delay the convocation for two years. At length, on April 3 and 4, 1695, a prestigious assembly of seven ministers and ten church elders convened in the Salem Village meetinghouse. Increase Mather served as moderator for the group. The panel's recommendations were a model of administrative restraint. No direct reference was made to the recent prosecutions, nor did the members of the panel commit themselves to either side of the dispute. The problem was defined as one of mere incompatibility between the minister and several members of his congregation. The dissenting brethren were given permission to join with another church, and Parris was gently advised to terminate his present employment: "If the distempers in Salem Village should be (which God forbid!) so incurable, that Mr. Parris, after all, find that he cannot, with any comfort and service, continue in his present station, his removal from thence will not expose him unto any hard character with us."[40]

Nevertheless, the resolution satisfied neither party to the dispute. The anti-Parris leaders quickly submitted another petition in which they urged that Parris be removed from the village immediately.[41] This was followed by yet another petition in which Parris's supporters urged with equal conviction that the minister be retained.[42] Ultimately, it was Parris's own wearying of the struggle that ended the controversy. Late in 1695, the minister evidently concluded that his position was no longer tenable, and he notified the elders in April 1696 that he would not continue in his current appointment beyond its date of expiration on July 1. Yet it was not until the summer of 1697, after still further debate over financial matters, that Parris finally severed his ties with Salem Village.[43]

Parris was the only major figure among the strong advocates of prosecution to receive the full brunt of public recrimination. He was also the first of the advocates to offer a public apology. In a dramatic encounter on November 26, 1694, Parris read his congregation the grievances of his opponents and then responded with his own sermon of reconciliation, "Meditations for Peace." He conceded that if the same situation should arise again, "I should not agree with my former apprehension in all points."[44] For one thing, he had changed his opinion about the validity of spectral evidence: "I question not but God sometimes suffers the Devil (as of late) to afflict in the shape of not only innocent but pious persons, or so to delude the sense of the afflicted that they strongly conceive their hurt is from such persons, when indeed it is not."[45] For another, he had come to see his own writings and sermons as part of the problem: "through weakness and sore exercise, I might sometimes, yea and possibly sundry times, unadvisedly expressed myself."[46] Unhappily, Parris's apology was delivered too late to improve his relations with his local adversaries and too early to be received and acknowledged by his ecclesiastical colleagues. After reading an advance copy of the sermon, one of the dissenting brethren declared that he was "much affected" but then commented bitterly, "if half so much were said formerly, it had never come to this."[47]

By 1696, however, there were others who were willing to make public confessions, and by this time civil and ecclesiastical authorities were prepared to accept them. The recent misfortunes visited on the province had made any further denials of collective guilt intolerable. A disappointing harvest coupled with inflationary prices in grain had yielded an extreme scarcity of food.[48] That the winter of 1696 was among the most severe to have been experienced by the colonists may well have seemed a further judgment against an unregenerate people.[49] Meanwhile, as the community underwent these disasters, there were several among the central participants in the trials who had come to believe that they were the special objects of divine disfavor. Calef undoubtedly spoke to these anxieties when, in his *More Wonders of the Invisible World*, he cataloged the crippling illnesses, the unusual accidents, and the other reversals of fortune suffered by those persons who had most encouraged the prosecutions.[50]

It was under these circumstances that the House of Representatives appointed a Committee of Religion to draw up a proposal for a Day of Humiliation. The document was composed by Cotton Mather, and it followed the standard jeremiad format of enumerating the sins of the community. Included among these evils for the first time was a clear acknowledgment of the guilt incurred during the Salem trials:

Wicked sorceries have been practiced in the land; and, in the late inexplicable storms from the Invisible world thereby brought upon us, we were led, by the Just Hand of Heaven unto those Errors whereby Great Hardships were brought upon Innocent persons, and (wee feare) Guilt incurr'd which wee have all cause to Bewayl, with much confusion of our Face before the Lord.[51]

The bill was passed in the House on December 10 but promptly vetoed in the Governor's Council on December 11. Apparently, the members of the council objected to the bill as an invasion of their prerogative to initiate public policy. After several days of debate, a compromise bill originating in the council and calling for a Day of Humiliation on January 14 was passed by the House. The final document was far more guarded than the earlier proposal; it conceded only that mistakes may have been made, and it contained no reference to the sufferings of innocent persons.[52]

In spite of the official caution, contemporaries well understood that the Day of Humiliation was an occasion for collective and personal atonement for the events of 1692. On the day of the fast, Judge Sewall presented his minister, Samuel Willard, with a bill to be read before the entire congregation. The statement was at once a personal apology and a reaffirmation of faith in an accessible God. The opening clause— "Samuel Sewall, sensible of the reiterated stroke of God upon himself and family"[53]—established that the magistrate's private sufferings were directly linked to his participation in the Court of Oyer and Terminer. The remainder of the statement was an assertion that his sufferings had been well deserved.

On the same day, twelve members of the jury that had served with the court submitted an apology in which they acknowledged the "Guilt of Innocent Blood."[54] No further confessions were offered, although there is evidence that others were deeply affected. On the day after the fast, Cotton Mather recorded in his diary that he had been "afflicted last night with discouraging thoughts as if unavoidable marks of Divine Displeasure must overtake my family for not appearing with vigor enough to stop the proceedings of the judges."[55]

Even after the expiatory rituals of 1697, the Salem trials remained a live political issue. Although it was now widely accepted that innocent persons had suffered during the prosecutions, the victims themselves as well as their families had not yet benefited from this reappraisal. Elizabeth Proctor's petition of June 10, 1696, well illustrates the survivors' dilemma. She had wished to file an appeal to contest her husband's will. Because she had been convicted of witchcraft, however, she was, in her own words, "dead in the law."[56] Although Phips had cleared the jails in 1693, he had not resolved the legal status of those persons found guilty by the court. Accordingly, Elizabeth petitioned the General Court for a reversal of attainder to restore her legal rights.

No action was taken on this request for the next seven years until several more petitions had been submitted. Then, in July 1703, the House of Representatives passed a bill formally disallowing spectral evidence but reversing attainder only for those cases for which petitions had been filed.[57] In principle, the bill cleared all persons who had been convicted on the basis of spectral testimony; in fact, it applied only to the three persons who had been represented by formal appeals.

Nevertheless, by this time, there was growing support for a more complete and equitable settlement. In 1704, Michael Wigglesworth invoked the national covenant in behalf of a plea for further compensation for the victims. In a letter to Increase Mather, he contended that God's controversy with New England over the witchcraft prosecutions had not yet been ended: "I believe the whole country lies under a curse to this day, and will do till some effectual course be taken by our honored governor and General Court to make them [the families of the accused] some amends and reparations."[58] Five years later, the General Court received a direct request to act on Wigglesworth's recommendation. In May 1709, Philip English and twenty-one others who had themselves been convicted of witchcraft or whose parents had been convicted presented the government with a bold petition in which they demanded both a reversal of attainder and compensation for their financial losses.[59]

The first request was fulfilled on October 17, 1711, when the General Court passed a bill to reverse the judgments against twenty-two persons who had been convicted of witchcraft.[60] However, the Court did what it had been asked to do and no more. Seven of the convicted witches, for whom petitions had not been filed, were not included in the reversal of attainder. The second request was granted on December 17 when the governor authorized the payment of 578 pounds, 12 shillings, to be distributed among the survivors and their relatives.[61] Most accounts were settled within the year. In a few cases, notably that of Philip English and the Burroughs family, legal questions pertaining to the amount of the payment or to the rightful recipient of the payment were not resolved for decades.

Thus, in the twenty years since the Salem prosecutions, official policy had come full circle. By 1696, members had come to believe that those actions originally designed to salvage the covenant had instead placed the covenant in serious jeopardy. And, by 1711, the Province of Massachusetts Bay became one of the few governments ever to voluntarily compensate persons who had been victimized by its own policies.

The failure of the Salem trials precipitated another historical development at least as significant as the retroactive exoneration of convicted witches. The reformulation of public policy with regard to the Salem trials was accompanied by a change in public policy toward witchcraft in general. After 1692, members began to doubt not just whether the Court of Oyer and Terminer had used proper rules of discovery but whether witchcraft was discoverable at all.

THE PROBLEM OF PROOF: THE FINAL SOLUTION

Even before the Salem trials, there are ample indications that the clergy regarded the discovery of witchcraft as problematic. In the pre-Salem litigations, adherence to theological strictures had rendered the translation of popular suspicions into convictive proofs inoperational. During the Salem trials, the ecclasiastical recommendations of June 15 had advised against the use of spectral evidence without offering any alternative criteria for the validation of imputations of witchcraft. Now, in the aftermath of the Salem trials, some members of the clergy were prepared, however reluctantly, to reexamine the epistemological assumptions in terms of which acts of witchcraft and the identity of witches were believed to be humanly ascertainable.

It is in this context that Increase Mather's *Cases of Conscience* may be appreciated as a final resolution to the long-standing theological uncertainties about witchcraft, for in spite of its conciliatory stance toward the magistrates, Mather's treatise was far more than an exercise in political diplomacy. The questions Mather raised about spectral evidence were questions that applied to other forms of evidence as well. *Cases* was a demonstration within the framework of orthodox doctrine that the workings of the invisible world were not available to human understanding and that, accordingly, errors in the discovery of witchcraft could be neither controlled nor eliminated.

As Mather formulated it, the testimony of the afflicted was unreliable not because it overestimated the powers of witchcraft but because it underestimated the powers of Satan. The use of spectral evidence was based upon an assumption that was crucial to the discovery of witchcraft in general, namely, that God imposed humanly recognizable limits upon Satan's capacity for evil. It followed from this assumption that God would make the activities of Satan and his confederates available to humanity, either by preventing a witch from reciting the Lord's Prayer or by refusing Satan the power to impersonate innocent men and women in spectral representations or by some other sign. It was this belief about the laws of supernatural causation that allowed courts of law to proceed with confidence in their determination of responsibility for acts of witchcraft.

Mather's work undermined this confidence by positing an inscrutable God who would permit Satan to act in ways that were too subtle for human comprehension. Thus, with regard to spectral evidence, Mather argued that it was entirely possible for Satan to represent the images of innocent and pious persons to the victims of bewitchment.[62] Indeed, Satan was so cunning that, in order to deceive the unwary, he could arrange for concomitances between empirically observable events. Accordingly, the recovery of afflicted persons when touched by their alleged assailants was as likely to be a diabolical trick as a providential sign.[63] Even the question of how to distinguish between possession and bewitchment could not be decided with certainty. It was quite conceivable that afflicted persons might only appear to be in conflict with the devil when, in fact, they were instruments of Satan's will. The outcome of Mather's critique was to suggest that human perceptions could not be trusted at all in matters relating to afflictions.

For Mather, however, the exclusion of spectral evidence as a method for the detection of witchcraft entailed the exclusion of all other forms of evidence in which it was assumed that the activities of Satan could be comprehended by humanity. The testimony of confessed witches was dismissed as the devil's testimony, and popular allegations of maleficia were not even granted the status of presumptions. What remained as criteria for the validation of imputations of witchcraft were most unlikely to furnish a basis for successful convictions.

Mather allowed as sufficient proofs, first, the free and voluntary confessions of the defendant and, second, the sworn testimony of two credible witnesses that the accused party and not any spectral representation had performed supernatural feats. With respect to the second criterion, Mather urged extreme caution: "It were better that ten suspected Witches should escape, than that one innocent person should be condemned."[64] Henceforth, the criteria for the validation of imputations of witchcraft—confession and the two-person rule—would in no way differ from the criteria applied to the validation of other capital crimes.

In the course of formulating the theological grounds for the rejection of spectral evidence, Mather arrived at conclusions he himself was at pains to disclaim. Indeed, it is clear that he was no less ambivalent about the theological implications of his work than he had been about its political implications. The postscript to Cases included reassurances not only to the magistrates but to all believers in witchcraft. For those among his readers who might be troubled by possible deviations from orthodox doctrine, Mather promised to publish another discourse in which he would demonstrate the existence of witches and the need for decisive action against them.[65] Nevertheless, the promised sequel to Cases was not published, and Mather's drastic reformulation of the rules of evidence was left to stand as one of the final statements by a New England divine on the subject of witchcraft.

Ultimately, it was a later work by another minister that most directly confronted the epistemological problems relating to witchcraft. John Hale's Modest Inquiry into the Nature of Witchcraft made explicit the full theological implications of Mather's dissertation. Hale's work was published posthumously in 1702, some five years after it had been written. That the work evoked strong reactions from readers familiar with the manuscript may account for the delay. Despite his own public misgivings about the Salem trials, Sewall noted in his diary on November 19, 1697: "Mr. Hale and I lodg'd together; He discours'd me about writing a History of the Witchcraft; I fear lest he go into the other extream."[66]

Hale's critique of the evidences used in the Salem trials added little to what had already been articulated in *Cases of Conscience.* The criteria he recommended for the discovery of witchcraft were identical to those proposed by Mather.[67] What was distinctive about Hale's work was not its recommendations for future prosecutions but rather its analysis of past prosecutions, including the Salem trials. Hale's accomplishment was to formulate the problem of error in the Salem trials in such a way as to call into question the entire history of witchcraft prosecution in New England. Of all the contemporary commentators on witchcraft, it was Hale alone who dared to suggest that what made the Salem trials problematic made the discovery of witchcraft problematic altogether.

Certainly, by 1697, there were few inhabitants of Massachusetts Bay who would have challenged the claim that errors had been committed during the Salem trials. Far more controversial was the question of what errors had been committed. For some members, it was enough merely to note the consequences of judicial action. As the bill of October 26, 1692, had stated, the trials had resulted in the indictment and arrest of an extraordinarily large number of persons, many of whom were individuals of exemplary piety. Accordingly, the number and quality of the defendants were proof in themselves that mistakes had been made. More often, members pointed to the judicial reliance on spectral evidence. For some critics, the magistrates had violated the theological recommendations on the use of such testimony; for others, the court had confounded afflictions with possessions. In general, however, the tendency of contemporary postmortems was to rescue witchcraft from the Salem trials by conceiving of the errors of the Court of Oyer and Terminer as specific to the events of 1692 rather than as applicable to all witchfinding activities.

For Hale, the problem of error was more complex. He himself had been one of the most active supporters of witchcraft prosecutions among the clergy, and he had not offered this support on the basis of spectral evidence alone. The problem posed by the Salem trials was not that the rules of evidence were treated lightly but rather that they had been taken so seriously. The Court of Oyer and Terminer had organized the most cautiously empirical and systematic investigation into witchcraft ever to occur in New England. In addition to collecting spectral evidences as well as allegations of malefic harm, the magistrates had conducted searches for witch's marks, puppets, and special healing potions. Moreover, they had gathered testimony from confessed witches who implicated other suspects. They had even conducted experiments in the courtroom in order that the devil might reveal his confederates before witnesses.

The cumulative effect of this testimony was to corroborate in detail the magistrates' version of conspiracy. Indeed, during the trials, one of the best educated of the defendants, George Burroughs, conceded that the testimony against him was convictive in view of the fact that eight confessed witches had identified him as their leader.[68] Since he nevertheless claimed he was innocent because his accusers were false witnesses, Hale proceeded to question one of the confessors who had named him. She stood by her account even after Hale had urged her to reconsider her statement while Burroughs was still alive.

As Hale understood it, the Salem trials constituted a faithful and valid application of approved theological recommendations for the discovery of witchcraft. The failure of the Salem trials was the failure of a paradigm:

If there were an Error in the proceedings in other places and in New England, it must be in the principles proceeded upon in the prosecuting of the suspected, or in the misapplication of the principles made use of. Now, as to the case at Salem, I conceive it proceeded from some mistaken principles made use of.[69]

That the identifications of the Court of Oyer and Terminer were in error was an anomaly that could not be explained in terms of the principles embodied either in earlier legal actions against witchcraft or in authoritative texts for the discovery of witchcraft. If the Salem trials had been based upon mistaken assumptions, then so also were the prosecutions against Margaret Jones, Ann Hibbins, and others in which an earlier generation of New England divines had participated.[70] If the policies followed by the Court of Oyer and Terminer were ill advised, then so also were the recommendations of Richard Bernard, Richard Baxter, and other revered authorities on witchcraft. For Hale, an acknowledgment of the errors of the Salem trials entailed an acknowledgment of past errors as well: "May we not say in this matter . . . We have sinned with our fathers?"[71]

While Hale's specific criticisms of the rules of evidence were primarily extensions of Mather's thesis on the inadequacy of human perceptions in understanding Satan's intentions, he went beyond *Cases* in another respect. Where Mather's work had expressed doubt about the possibility of objective criteria for the determination of witchcraft, there are intimations that Hale had arrived at an even more extreme attitude of disbelief. Various passages in *Modest Inquiry* verge on the radical interpretation that witchcraft might have no ontological basis apart from the perceptions of believers.

Thus Hale explained that the efficacy of charms, curses, and puppets as instruments of malefic harm had little to do with invisible forces:

And probably the cause may be, that Satan, the Lord permitting him, may inflict his mischief on the person, the Spectators or Actors herein supposed to be concerned, suiting thereby his design to man's faith about it. And, if so, the reason why any suspected person is hereby concerned is not because they are guilty but because they are suspected.[72]

Elsewhere he offered a similar interpretation of imputations of malefic witchcraft:

Some persons will put an evil construction upon an innocent person, and so raise an evil fame against a person; and then others believing it, are apt to look upon other actions with a squint eye, and through the multiplying glass of their own jealosies, make a Molehill seem a mountain.[73]

Modest Inquiry was very nearly the work that Sewall had feared it might be. It was an indication that at least one member of the New England clergy had begun to reflect on witchcraft from outside the context of belief.

Cases of Conscience and *Modest Inquiry* articulate the theological closure around the problem of witchcraft. Together, the two works constitute an admission that witchcraft was no longer available as a demonstration of the existence of the invisible world. To be sure, Mather and Hale had met doctrinal requirements by acknowledging the reality of witchcraft, but such acknowledgments notwithstanding, both authors had served notice that, in the future, theological confirmation of imputations of witchcraft as real empirical events was most unlikely. The new rules of evidence virtually precluded the further production of witches. On the one hand, no provision had been made for the translation of popular suspicions into theologically acceptable proofs. On the other hand, the allowance for free and voluntary confessions as a sufficient proof was a condition that had been fulfilled by only a single earlier prosecution in Connecticut. In the aftermath of the Salem trials, witchcraft had become an impossible crime.

Symptomatic of the altered epistemological status of witchcraft was a proposal for the recording of special providences, signed by eight leading ministers on March 5, 1695.[74] The reasons for this undertaking

were the same as those given in Increase Mather's earlier proposal of
1681: to help demonstrate the existence and agency of the invisible
world. This time, however, there was a significant deletion in the list
of unusual occurrences about which information was to be gathered.
No mention was made of witchcraft. In this act of omission, the clergy
tacitly acknowledged that witchcraft no longer had a place within
orthodox doctrine. In the future, New England divines would look to
other signs for the presence of God.

THE DECLINE OF WITCHCRAFT PROSECUTIONS

For all its apparent suddenness, the decline of witchcraft prosecutions
after the Salem trials involved no marked discontinuities with the past.
Apart from the events of 1692, popular allegations had formed the
primary basis for legal action against witchcraft, and these testimonies
had ceased to carry convictive weight after the last execution in 1656.
Furthermore, though allegations of maleficia were included among the
evidences gathered by the Court of Oyer and Terminer, there is no
reason to believe that they were regarded with greater seriousness in
1692 than in the earlier prosecutions. Now, in the light of a further
separation between popular and theological understandings of the
problem of witchcraft and in view of the new rules of evidence,
witchcraft soon disappeared entirely from the legal records of Massachusetts Bay.[75] Within two years after the Salem trials, witchcraft was
no longer an actionable legal offense.

The final case to be recorded, that of Mary Watkins, well demonstrates that, by 1693, the legal possibilities for witchcraft as a valid
form of deviant imputation had been exhausted. Mary, a Boston servant, confessed to witchcraft shortly after failing in an attempt at suicide.[76] She was brought before a magistrate, and a bill of indictment
was presented to the grand jury of the Superior Court of Judicature
on April 25, 1693. The jury refused the bill in spite of the confession.
This time, when asked by the magistrates to reconsider their verdict,
the jurors maintained their original finding of ignoramus. Although the
grounds for the decision are not mentioned, it is likely that the defendant was judged to be distracted and therefore not competent to
offer credible testimony. This possibility notwithstanding, the case of
Mary Watkins was an indication that, after the Salem trials, not even
voluntary confessions would be accepted as proof of witchcraft.

The decline of witchcraft prosecutions by no means coincided with
the decline of witchcraft accusations. Despite official and ecclesiastical
discouragement, villagers continued to believe in the efficacy of ma-

lefic witchcraft until well into the eighteenth century.[77] Indeed, fragmentary records indicate that, even without the benefit of legal authority, witchcraft allegations remained an effective weapon against suspected adversaries. An account in 1728 by a Massachusetts minister, the Reverend Mr. Turell of Medford, furnishes a detailed description of the local response in a small community in 1720 to three children believed to be afflicted. The report makes clear that the children and their supporters were able to mobilize local opinion against the woman whom they identified as responsible for their condition.[78] And, in the town of Colchester in neighboring Connecticut in 1724, one woman regarded the suspicions against her with sufficient seriousness to sue her accusers for 500 pounds in damages.[79]

At the same time, the outcome of these events suggests that if, in certain communities, popular beliefs in mystical harm had not changed greatly in the thirty years since the Salem trials, the response of civil and ecclesiastical authorities had nevertheless changed appreciably. In his narrative, Turell questioned not only the validity of the accusations but also the motives of the accusers. According to Turell, the afflictions were not only not genuine, they were deceitful strategies employed by the children to attract attention to themselves.[80] Similarly, the decision rendered in the Connecticut case also reveals an inclination to view as problematic not the behavior of the accused but the perceptions of the accuser. On appeal, the complainant was awarded a nominal compensation of one shilling in damages. More significantly, the same ruling included a judgment that the defendants were not insane. In the decades following the Salem trials, public attention began to focus less on the guilt of the accused and more on the credibility of the accuser.

Ultimately, the withdrawal of legal recognition from imputations of witchcraft entailed far more than the decriminalization of a category of deviant behavior. The loss of witchcraft as an actionable offense divested contemporary theories of supernatural causation of their last remaining claim to legal authority. With the decline of witchcraft prosecutions, questions about the availability of the invisible world ceased to be a matter of practical concern for the state.

Witchcraft in Historical and

Sociological Perspective

THIS STUDY DIFFERS from previous investigations of New England witchcraft in that it attempts to deal systematically not just with the Salem prosecutions but with the entire history of witchcraft prosecutions in Massachusetts Bay. From this perspective, the events of 1692 become comprehensible neither as a sudden, aberrational manifestation of witchcraft belief nor as a simple amplification of earlier patterns of prosecution. The difference between the pre-Salem and the Salem prosecutions in terms of both the scale of operation and the social distribution of witches was indeed the outcome of different expressions of the idiom of witchcraft. But to acknowledge this difference does not require that one pattern be defined as normal and the other as abnormal or pathological. The two periods of legal action generated different patterns because they were produced by different audiences who proceeded according to different interpretations of witchcraft.

In the pre-Salem prosecutions, the witch emerged as the living embodiment of those attributes that were most despised by her neighbors. She was not only the agent of misfortune and disaster in the lives of those around her; she was also someone who contravened local norms of propriety and neighborliness. By her violent and intemperate outbursts, she disturbed the tranquillity of the community. In her open defiance of authority, she challenged the very assumptions that made orderly social transactions possible. Typically, she was described as quarrelsome, scornful of her neighbors, contemptuous of her near relations, and vengeful if her unreasonable demands were not met. In short, the pre-Salem witch was a destructive presence in both her worldly and her otherworldly activities.

In contrast, the Salem witches were notable for other qualities. Not infrequently, they were persons who commanded respect both from their family and from members of their community; indeed, several

I B

*enemy
of
Church*

were renowned in the colony as models of Christian virtue. Such
worldly displays of good character, however, rendered their activities
all the more sinister, for what defined the Salem witches was their involvement in an organized conspiracy against God and the state—and
what better way was there of pursuing their real objectives in the invisible world than by inspiring trust and confidence in their dealings
in the visible world? As one confessor revealed late in the proceedings,
"And the design was to Destroy Salem Village, and to begin at the
Ministers House, and to destroy the Church of God, and to set up
Satans Kingdom, and then all will be well."[1] Where the pre-Salem
witch emerged as the enemy within the community, the Salem witch
was above all the enemy within the church.

*I
B*

   That the pre-Salem and the Salem prosecutions embodied approaches
to the problem of witchcraft that were divergent and even conflicting
is of historical and sociological significance. Once it is recognized that
unified collective action against witchcraft was increasingly difficult
to achieve throughout the seventeenth century in New England, the
decline of witchcraft prosecutions after 1692 appears not so much a
sudden reversal in public policy as an understandable resolution to a
long-standing predicament. The coexistence of competing conceptions
of witchcraft furnished the ideal conditions for the emergence of
doubt and disbelief. The believers who embraced the popular version
of witchcraft as represented in the pre-Salem prosecutions eventually
came to perceive the actions of the Court of Oyer and Terminer as
illegitimate and unwarranted. At the same time, the attitude of clergy
and magistrates toward the pre-Salem witch was one of growing skepticism over the sources of village suspicion.

   From a historical standpoint, New England witchcraft emerges not
as a prime illustration of the idiom of witchcraft belief but as a manifestation of this belief just prior to its disappearance. Sociologically, it
presents the unusual spectacle of a form of deviance in which collective mobilization against a perceived problem proved to be more divisive than unifying. Some brief remarks on how the two perspectives
complement each other are in order.

THE SOCIAL SOURCES OF DISBELIEF

To suggest that the different approaches to witchcraft were ultimately
socially divisive is not to overlook their potential utility for the groups
that advanced them. In directing accusations toward particular members of the community, the villagers of pre-Salem Massachusetts were
able to define norms of neighborly conduct and, at the same time, to

tacitly condone the breaching of these norms when the responsibilities of neighborliness appeared too onerous. Similarly, the activities of the Court of Oyer and Terminer were also responsive to the social conditions that produced them. The Salem prosecutions are more accurately described as a witch-finding movement than as a witch hunt—the goal of the magistrates was not so much to execute witches as to bring about their conversion.[2] By gathering together suspects from the different villages of the colony under strong pressure both to confess their guilt and to rededicate themselves to the church, the actions of the court can be seen as a device to reintegrate the community during a period of pronounced political uncertainty.

Political uncertainty

Whether as doer of malefic deeds or as arch-conspirator, the witch served the interests of the groups that mobilized against her. In the socially and culturally differentiated society of seventeenth-century New England, however, this harsh utilitarianism was not enough to insulate proponents of either conception of evil from public challenge. The witch may have helped to define the priorities of one group, but attempts to impose these priorities on other groups by intimidation, by force, by threat of extralegal action, or even by judicial fiat were likely to encounter some form of public resistance. It is under these circumstances that the laws against witchcraft became politically dangerous to enforce.

Against this background of conflict, members began to divest witchcraft of its status as an objectively knowable crime with enforceable sanctions. The stages of this process are most readily discerned in the recurring debates over the problem of proof. Efforts by expert diagnosticians such as clergy and jurists to transform the volatile issue of whose interests the courts would serve into the safer technical issue of which tests to apply to the discovery of witchcraft were never entirely successful. In New England, the political problem of deciding whose definition would prevail kept intruding upon the legal problem of how to apply either definition.

In the pre-Salem prosecutions, the cross-pressures generated by popular and theological audiences were a constant source of embarrassment for the court. On the one hand, popular definitions had to be taken seriously if only because of the aggressive manner in which they were advanced. By the time the suspect came to the attention of legal authorities, villagers were likely to have already convinced themselves of her guilt. It required years of tense relationships to produce the malefic witch, and the villagers who appeared in court were prepared to exert strong pressure for a quick and decisive resolution to this tension.

On the other hand, the theological requirements for adequate proof virtually ruled out conviction on the basis of popular testimony. Because the one sure proof from the theological standpoint—the confession—was only rarely obtained, efforts were made to meet the exacting standards of the clergy in other ways. An abundance of texts was produced in seventeenth-century England to assist in the translation of popular allegations into terms compatible with theological criteria, but the manuals with which the New England clergy were most familiar tended rather to widen the gap between popular and theological definitions than to reduce it.

Richard Bernard's influential guide, for example, ostensibly a work of mediation in order to ease the judicial predicament, did not conceal the author's skepticism toward the popular version of the crime. What villagers perceived as the evil deeds of the witch, Bernard interpreted as the product of their own suspicions. Just as the devil could corrupt the witch, so also could he deceive the accuser.

1. [The devil works] a slavish feare.
2. Upon this fear, he suggesteth a suspition of this or that party to be a witch.
3. The suspition a little settled, hee then stirreth the man or woman to utter the suspition of this or that neighbor.
4. The Divell worketh credulity in those neighbors, and withal sets them on worke to second the relation, with openings of these suspicious thoughts to the same partie: and withall, to tell what they have either heard from others, or observed from themselves.
5. Through this credulity, this relation, and rumouring this suspition, from one talking group to another, it is taken for granted that such an one is a witch.[3]

Such an analysis did more than challenge the validity of village accusations. It justified a categorical devaluation of the legal weight to be given to the popular version of the crime. For Bernard, Perkins, and others, evidences that conformed to popular understandings were granted the status of mere presumptions and evidences that conformed to theological understandings were treated as convictions. The problem of how to elicit convictive proofs from presumptive evidences remained disturbingly unresolved, however. Other attempts to simplify the problem of translation by means of quasi-objective tests such as witch's marks, swimming the witch, and so forth, were rejected either on theological grounds as judicial magic or on medical grounds as unreliable.

The official disposition of the pre-Salem cases well reflected the stalemate between popular demands and theological strictures. After years of equivocal and indecisive verdicts in which defendants were neither convicted nor cleared of suspicion, the magistrates finally arrived at a policy in which they would repudiate popular definitions of witchcraft but respect popular demands for legal protection. Such a compromise yielded verdicts in which the suspect was released from confinement on condition that she leave the community that despised her. In effect, the pre-Salem witch was cleared of charges of witchcraft but convicted on grounds of gross unpopularity.

That accusations of witchcraft generated convictions in the Salem prosecutions should not be taken as an indication that the magistrates who presided in these legal actions were any less scrupulous in the weighing of evidence than were their predecessors who rendered judgments in the pre-Salem prosecutions. To the contrary, the methods employed during the Salem trials represented perhaps the most conscientious attempt in the history of Anglo-American prosecutions to reconcile the conflicting directives of popular and theological audiences. A thorough search was made for evidences that were compatible with both orientations to witchcraft. The allegations of maleficia and other village testimonies were supplemented with examinations for witch's marks as well as evidence of competence in magical arts. Confessions were obtained and the testimony of confessors was used to provide information on other suspects. The spectral evidence that figured so crucially in the prosecution was validated by means of tests and experiments derived from contemporary doctrines of spiritual causation. Throughout the investigation, the magistrates sought to follow legal precedent and authoritative opinion in the formulation of the rules of evidence, to make these rules explicit, to apply the rules consistently, and to collect corroborative evidence wherever possible. As the minister John Hale observed, the Court of Oyer and Terminer approached the prosecution of witchcraft far more systematically than did any previous judicial commission on witchcraft in New England.

It is one of the ironies of New England witchcraft that this most systematic of prosecutions was also the most socially disruptive. For all its rigor, the official solution to the problem of proof was compatible with neither popular nor theological approaches to witchcraft. The replacement of allegations of maleficia with impartially administered tests applied to spectral evidence rendered the actions of villagers, whether for or against the suspect, utterly irrelevant to the outcome of the case. As a result, the magistrates managed to imprison and convict precisely those persons who would have been least vulnerable to suspicion in village-initiated legal actions. The validation of spectral evidence by means of experiments in court did violence to theological understandings about the availability of the invisible world to human perceptions. The consequence of this innovation was to usurp the prerogative of the clergy to define the terms in which God communicated his intentions to humanity. The eventual alliance of popular and theological audiences in opposition to the findings of the court constituted one of the very few occasions in the history of witchcraft prosecutions in Massachusetts in which these two groups were able to find a point of agreement.

Ultimately, Increase Mather's conclusion that the activities of the devil were too elusive for human understanding may be read not only as theology but also as sociology. Human perceptions could not be trusted to reveal the truth about witchcraft, and the rules of evidence that invested these perceptions with validity would have to be revoked. Mather had interviewed a number of the confessors just after publishing *Cases of Conscience* and, as he listened to their recantations, he learned that the magistrates had been deceived. Just as the villagers had not foreseen that it was their "rumouring" that generated the context of suspicion out of which accusations would later arise, so the magistrates had not perceived that it was their aggressive policies that had induced the large number of confessors.

It was a mark of Satan's subtlety that he did not need miracles to accomplish his evil; the materials of the visible world would suffice. The devil could achieve his goal in the invisible world because the villagers and magistrates could not see how their actions in the visible world affected the actions of others. The invisible world of witchcraft derived from that part of the social world that somehow escaped awareness. Given the human susceptibility to being deceived by this world, the best response to the mystery of witchcraft was silence.

Appendix A

List of Legal Actions against Witchcraft

Prior to the Salem Prosecutions

Note: The gathering of information on pre-Salem legal actions against witchcraft in Massachusetts Bay entailed use of a variety of sources. The most important sources were the published legal records of the quarterly courts, the Court of Assistants, and the General Court. Nevertheless, because the bulk of quarterly court records are still available only in manuscript form and because the records of the Court of Assistants were not kept continuously between 1643 and 1673, other, less trustworthy sources were indispensable. The gap in the records of the Court of Assistants is particularly significant because this judicial body was charged with the responsibility for deciding capital crimes, including witchcraft.

Among the other sources consulted were contemporary narratives and local histories or surveys in which the author had access to records since destroyed or not publicly available. Because of the uneven quality of scholarship on witchcraft, certain precautions were taken to insure greater reliability in the use of these sources. Cases derived from contemporary narratives were included only if they were reported by two or more publicists. In addition, in those instances where local histories and surveys constituted the only source for a particular case, the scholarship of the author in question was checked by matching references to known witchcraft cases against surviving legal records.

The following list represents a compilation of pre-Salem legal actions against witchcraft from published legal records and from reliable secondary sources. I have not included cases in which the names of the accused are not recorded. Nor have I included the few recorded instances of informal accusations that did not lead to legal action.

At the same time, there is no doubt that far more legal actions occurred than are here reported. In a letter dated in 1686, John Dunton mentioned that twenty cases had recently been tried in the colony, although only nine cases can be retrieved from the legal records between 1680 and 1686; see Thomas Hutchinson, "The Witchcraft Delusion of 1692," p. 385, n.6. The Reverend John Eliot observed in a letter dated July 4, 1651, that four persons had recently been detected as witches in Springfield, but records survive for only two of the cases; see Poole, "Witchcraft in Boston," p. 37. A note in the legal records of the county court in Springfield on January 5, 1675, indicates the occurrence of other unrecorded cases: "There havinge beene many Suspitiones of Witchcraft at Northampton and severall testemonyes concerning the same, of Persones suspected . . . Exhibited to last County Corte in Sept. Last at Springfield by Persones then and there comeing Voluntarilie some to give in Evidence and others appearing also without Sumondes to Cleare themselves of soe execrable a Crime"; see Trumbull, *History of North-ampton*, I: 230–31. Information is available for only one of these cases. Finally, a deposition against Rachel Fuller in 1680 mentioned ten witches who had been recently tried in Hampton, of which only two can be identified by the historical observer; see Drake, *Annals*, pp. 150–56. It is no exaggeration to suggest that the true number of legal actions against witchcraft may well be twice that of the known number of legal actions against witchcraft.

The omission of so many witchcraft cases from contemporary records can be only partially explained in terms of deficiencies in seventeenth-century bookkeeping practices. More likely, the missing cases were less the product of error than the result of a deliberate policy of silence on the part of civil and ecclesiastical authorities. Undoubtedly, publicists were reluctant to give specific information, particularly about minor cases, in part to protect the reputation of the parties involved and perhaps in part to avoid a defamation suit. But, as discussed earlier, it may be that such underreporting figured as part of a general strategy to contain popular anxieties about the extent of the threat of witchcraft.

In any case, it is interesting that seventeenth-century histories of New England witchcraft such as Cotton Mather's *Wonders of the Invisible World* or John Hale's *Modest Inquiry into the Nature of Witchcraft*, which claim to be comprehensive, vastly underestimate the number of pre-Salem legal actions against witchcraft. Possibly, witchcraft prosecutions form a distinctive class of events, along with political purges, security actions, and other aggressive official measures directed against internal populations, which are necessarily shrouded in secrecy. Certainly, seventeenth-century records of witchcraft in Massachusetts Bay reflect the contemporary ambivalence about the subject.

Case number	Name	Location	Date of initial complaint
1	Goodwife Batchellor	Ipswich	Mar. 30, 1654
2	John Bradstreet	Rowley	Oct. 28, 1652
3	Christopher Brown	Unknown	Dec. 24, 1674
4	Goodwife Burt	Lynn	Nov. 1, 1669
5a	Eunice Cole	Hampton	Sept. 1656
5b	Eunice Cole	Hampton	Oct. 12, 1672

Outcome	Comments	Source
Unknown	Only initial complaint before county court recorded	EQCR, 3:403, 404.
Fine of 20 shillings or whipping	Occupation was laborer; previously convicted for lying	Drake, *Annals*, pp. 74–75; RSW, 2:250; Joseph B. Felt, *History of Ipswich, Essex, and Hamilton* (Cambridge, Mass, 1834), p. 267; EQCR, 1:265.
Case dismissed with warning to defendant		RSW, 2:250.
Unknown	Was practitioner of magical arts	RSW, 2:262–67.
Verdict of guilty; sentenced to life imprisonment		Massachusetts Archives, vol. 135, docs. 2, 3; Dow, *History of Hampton, N.H.*, 1:54, 57.
Not guilty but suspected of witchcraft	Petition of husband for release granted by General Court on condition that she leave colony	Massachusetts Archives, vol. 135, docs. 4–13, 15–17; Dow, *History of Hampton, N.H.*, 1:68, 79; 2:644.

Case number	Name	Location	Date of initial complaint
5*c*	Eunice Cole	Hampton	Sept. 1680
6	Anna Edmunds	Lynn	1673
7	James Fuller	Springfield	May 1683
8	Rachel Fuller	Hampton	July 14, 1680
9	Margaret Gifford	Lynn	June or July 29, 1680
10	Mary Clover	Boston	1688
11*a*	John Godfrey	Lack of stable residence noted by court	Mar. 1659
11*b*	John Godfrey	Uncertain	Feb. 1666
12	Mary Hale	Boston	Mar. 1 or 15, 1681
13	Ann Hibbins	Boston	Verdict given May 14, 1656

Outcome	Comments	Source
Imprisoned on suspicion of witchcraft; fetters attached to legs; released; died Oct. 1680		Drake, *Annals*, pp. 99–103.
Acquitted of charge of witchcraft; accusers ordered to pay cost of witnesses	Accusers themselves later charged with murder of mother and son for which they had blamed Edmunds	RCA, 1:11.
Acquitted of charge of witchcraft but fined 5 pounds and given 30 stripes for lying		RCA, 1:228–29.
Discharged	Was a magical healer or healing witch; jury of inquest noted sign on corpse of infant whom Rachel was alleged to have murdered by witchcraft	Drake, *Annals*, pp. 150–56; *Documents and Records Relating to the Province of New Hampshire*, ed. Nathanial Bouton, 1:415–19.
Did not appear in court; no record of further legal action		RSW, 2:262.
Executed Nov. 16, 1688		Cotton Mather, *Memorable Providences*, in Burr, *Narratives*, pp. 103–6; Calef, *More Wonders*, pp. 151–52.
Verdict not known, although he was imprisoned		Upham, *Salem Witchcraft*, 2:428–33; EQCR, 2:157–60; Demos, "John Godfrey and His Neighbors," pp. 242–65.
Equivocal verdict; suspicious, but not legally guilty of witchcraft	Between 1660 and 1666, was involved in at least 16 civil suits as plaintiff or defendant	RCA, 3:151–52, 158–61. For background of litigation between Godfrey and his accusers, see EQCR, 3:345, 405; 2:366–67; Demos, "John Godfrey and His Neighbors," pp. 242–65.
Acquitted		RCA, 1:189–90.
Executed June 19, 1656		For transcript of Ann's excommunication prior to

Case number	Name	Location	Date of initial complaint
14	Mary Holman	Cambridge	June 1659
15	Winifred Holman	Cambridge	June 1659
16	Margaret Jones	Charlestown	Unknown
17	Thomas Jones	Charlestown	Arrested in 1648
18	Mrs. Kendal	Cambridge	Case tried in 1651
19	Mrs. H. Lake	Dorchester	Case tried in 1650

Outcome	Comments	Source
		the charge of witchcraft, see Demos, *Remarkable Providences*, pp. 221–39. For background of defendant and discussion of the case, see Drake, *Annals*, pp. 98–99; Poole, "Witchcraft in Boston," pp. 139–41; Burr, *Narratives*, p. 410, n. 1. For verdict, see Massachusetts Archives, vol. 135, doc. 1; MCR, 4, 1:269.
Acquitted		Lucius Paige, *History of Cambridge*, p. 356.
Acquitted	Winifred and Mary Holman were mother and daughter	Paige, *History of Cambridge*, p. 356.
Executed June 15, 1648	Was a skilled healing witch deeply feared by her neighbors	For background of defendant, see Poole, "Witchcraft at Boston," pp. 135–36; Hutchinson, "Witchcraft Delusion," p. 384, n. 4; Drake, *Annals*, pp. 58–61. For verdict, see MCR, 3:126, 2:242; EQCR, 4:207–8. For additional information, see Samuel G. Drake, *History of Boston from 1630–1700* (Boston, 1856), pp. 308–9.
Probably released	Husband of Margaret	Drake, *Annals*, pp. 58–61.
Executed	Hale mentions this case as miscarriage of justice; accuser suspected in crime of infanticide by witchcraft, for which Kendal was hanged	Hutchinson, "Witchcraft Delusion," p. 385, n. 6; Hale, *Modest Inquiry*, pp. 18–19.
Probably executed in Boston		Hutchinson, "Witchcraft Delusion," p. 384, n. 4; Hale, *Modest Inquiry*, p. 17; Burr, *Narratives*, pp. 408–9, n. 4.

Case number	Name	Location	Date of initial complaint
20	Susanna Martin	Amesbury	Apr. 1669
21	Elizabeth Morse	Newbury	Jan. 7, 1680
22	Bridget Oliver	Salem Village	Dec. 1679
23	Mary Oliver	Boston	1649
24	Hugh Parsons	Springfield	Mar. 1, 1651

Outcome	Comments	Source
Sent to prison on bond of 100 pounds	Actually a defamation suit in which Susanna as plaintiff was charged with witchcraft	EQCR, 4:129–33.
Trial, May 20, 1680; verdict of guilty, May 27, 1680; reprieve by governor and magistrates, June 1, 1680; petitions by husband for more humane treatment, May 14 and 18, 1681; new trial granted, May 24, 1681; final verdict, June 1, 1681	See chap. 7 for extended discussion of case	See Drake, *Annals,* pp. 258–96, for transcript of evidence and depositions presented both before Commissioner John Woodbridge at Newbury on Jan. 7, 1680, and before Court of Assistants on May 20, 1680. See Massachusetts Archives, vol. 135, docs. 11–19, for depositions against Elizabeth, for her reprieve, for complaint about her reprieve, and for two petitions of William Morse on behalf of his wife. See Hale, *Modest Inquiry,* pp. 21–22, for résumé of magistrates' decision in granting reprieve. For ofcial record of retrial and final verdict, see *RCA,* 1:159, 189–90. Further reliable historical accounts are available in Upham, *Salem Witchcraft,* 2:449–54; Joshua Coffin, *History of Newbury* (1845), pp. 127–34; Drake, *Annals,* pp. 140–50.
Referred to Court of Assistants; outcome of this court unknown	Later executed for witchcraft in Salem prosecutions under her new married name, Bishop	EQCR, 7:329–30.
Unknown; may have confessed to witchcraft		Drake, *Annals,* p. 64.
Imprisoned; verdict of guilty May 12, 1652, not consented to by magistrates; acquitted	Hugh was the husband of Mary Parsons	For evidence against Parsons, see Drake, *Annals,* pp. 219–58; for official actions, see MCR, 3:273;

Case number	Name	Location	Date of initial complaint
25	Mrs. Joseph Parsons	Northampton	Sept. 29, 1674
26	Mary Parsons	Springfield	Feb. or Mar. 1651
27	Caleb Powell	Resident at Newbury at time of trial	Dec. 3, 1679
28	Mary Randall	Springfield	Sept. 29, 1691
29	Isabel Towle	Hampton	Sept. 7, 1680
30	Jane Walford	Portsmouth	Trial Apr. 18, 1656
31	Mary Webster	Hadley	Mar. 27, 1683
32	Thomas Wells	Ipswich	1669

Outcome	Comments	Source
May 31, 1652		4, pt. 1:96. For additional information, see Drake, *Annals*, pp. 64–73.
Acquitted May 13, 1675		RCA, 1:31, 33; Trumbull, *History of Northampton*, 1:42–52, 230–35.
Acquitted of witch-craft but convicted of murder of child and executed May 29, 1651		For reliable summary of case, see Smith, *Colonial Justice in Western Massachusetts*, pp. 20–24; also MCR, 4, pt. 1:47, 73; Drake, *Annals*, pp. 218–56.
Acquitted but ordered to pay charges on grounds of suspicious practice		RSW, 2:251–62; Upham, *Salem Witchcraft*, 1:449–54; Burr, *Narratives*, pp. 23–32.
Released on good behavior		Drake, *Annals*, pp. 185–86.
Arrested but later released		*Documents and Records of New Hampshire*, p. 368; see also p. 430 for previous conviction on charges of theft.
Freed on condition of good behavior		*Documents and Records of New Hampshire*, 1:217–20; Drake, *Annals*, pp. 103–7; Burr, *Narratives*, pp. 60–61.
Acquitted Sept. 4, 1683		RCA, 1:233; Sylvester Judd, *History of Hadley* (Springfield, Mass.: H. R. Hasting & Co., 1905), p. 228. The case of Mary Webster was linked to the death of selectman Philip Smith; see Drake, *Annals*, pp. 167–69, and Burr, *Narratives*, pp. 131–34.
Wells was not indicted		EQCR, 4:75, 79.

Case number	Name	Location	Date of initial complaint
33	Robert Williams	Hadley	Mar. 29, 1670
34	Mary Wright	Oyster Bay, under juris-diction of Massachusetts Bay	1660

Outcome	Comments	Source
Fined 5 pounds and given 15 stripes for lying		Smith, *Colonial Justice in Western Massachusets,* p. 108.
Acquitted of witch-craft but banished for being a Quaker		Drake, *Annals,* pp. 117–18.

Appendix B

List of Defamation Suits Involving Witchcraft

in Seventeenth-Century Massachusetts Bay

Note: This appendix lists alphabetically and numbers all those persons who are named in the published legal records of seventeenth-century Massachusetts Bay as plaintiffs in defamation suits involving allegations of witchcraft. Some historical observers have expressed surprise that suspects did not file defamation suits during the Salem trials in view of the fact that such legal actions were generally successful prior to the Salem trials. This is to ignore the vastly different circumstances in which suspects found themselves in the two periods of witchcraft prosecutions. In defamation suits prior to Salem, plaintiffs were frequently able to mobilize formidable support against their potential accusers in anticipation of a witchcraft accusation. Moreover, the accuser was often someone of low social standing in the community. In the Salem trials, however, accusations occurred so suddenly and unpredictably that suspects had little opportunity to avail themselves of these preventive measures. Furthermore, the accusers were supported by the highest civil authorities in the province. Even if potential suspects had somehow managed to file defamation suits, the probability of a favorable decision would have been extremely low.

Name of plaintiff and date of defamation suit	Defendant and charge
1. Christopher Collins in behalf of his wife, Mar. 29, 1653	Enoch Coldam for calling Jane Collins a witch
2. Mordecai Crawford in behalf of his wife, June 1667	Anthony Ashby for calling Edith Crawford a witch
3. Goodman Dutch in behalf of his wife, Sept. 4, 1653	Edward Marshall for claiming Goodwife Dutch was under suspicion of being a witch
4. Goodman Evens in behalf of his wife, Sept. 4, 1653	Edward Marshall for claiming that Goodwife Evens was under suspicion of being a witch
5a. John Godfrey, June 28, 1659	William and Samuel Symonds for calling Godfrey a witch
5b. John Godfrey, Mar. 29, 1664	John Singletarry for saying of Godfrey: "Is this witch on this side of Boston Galloes yet?"
5c. John Godfrey, June 29, 1669	Daniel Ela for stating that Godfrey was in two places at once, thus suggesting super-

Verdict	Sources
For defendant; Jane imprisoned for 10 weeks	EQCR, 1:274, 276, 348
Suit withdrawn; Edith had previously been prosecuted for setting fire to Ashby's house	EQCR, 3:420–21
For plaintiff; defendant ordered to make public acknowledgment at meetinghouses of Salem, Ipswich, and Gloucester within 14 days	EQCR, 1:301
See case 3, above	EQCR, 1:301
For plaintiff, with qualification: "notwithstanding doe conceive that by the testimonyes he is rendered suspicious"	EQCR, 2:157
For plaintiff; defendant ordered to make public acknowledgment or pay fine of 10 shillings	EQCR, 3:120–22
For defendant, terms not recorded	EQCR, 4: 152–55

Name of plaintiff and date of defamation suit	Defendant and charge
	natural powers
6. Mary Holman, Apr. 3, 1660	John Gibson, Sr., for alleging that his daughter was afflicted by Mary and her mother, Winifred
7. Winifred Holman, Apr. 3, 1660	See case 6, above
8. Elizabeth Hooper, Jan. 11, 1679	Richod Holman for referring to Elizabeth as "bare old baud and spirited old witch"
9a. Jane James, Sept. 1646	Peter Pitford for calling Jane a witch
9b. Erasmus James in behalf of his wife, Sept. 1650.	Peter and Edward Pitford for calling Jane James a witch
9c. Jane James, June 25, 1667	Richard Rowland for claiming he had been throttled by Jane's specter
10. Widow Marshfield, 1649	Hugh and Mary Parsons for calling Marshfield a witch
11. George Martin in behalf of his wife, Apr. 1669	William Sargent for calling Susanna Martin a witch
12. Joseph Parsons in behalf of his wife, Oct. 7, 1656	Sarah Bridgman for calling Mrs. Parsons a witch
13. Goodman Perkins in behalf of his wife, Sept. 4, 1653	Edward Marshall for claiming that Goodwife Perkins was under suspicion of being a witch
14. Thomas Crawley in behalf of Goodwife Sawyer, Oct. 1650	Rolfe Hall for alleging that Crawley had called Sawyer a witch
15. William Thomson, Sept. 25, 1676	Hanna Downing for calling Thomson "a devil, a black dog, and an ugly witch"
16. Goodwife Tope, June 30, 1674	Lawrence Carpenter for calling Tope a witch
17. Goodman Vincen in behalf of his wife, Sept. 4, 1653	Edward Marshall for claiming that Goodwife Vincen was under suspicion of being a witch
18a. Thomas and Jane Walford in behalf of Jane, Oct. 3 or Nov. 3, 1648	Nicholas and Elizabeth Roe for calling Jane a witch
18b. Jane Walford, June 28, 1670	Robert Couch for calling Jane a witch

Verdict	Sources
For plaintiff; defendant ordered to make public acknowledgment or pay fine of 5 pounds	Lucius Paige, *History of Cambridge*, pp. 354–64
Uncertain; probably for defendant; plaintiff ordered to pay cost of court	Paige, *History of Cambridge*, pp. 354–64
Not recorded	EQCR, 6:387
Not recorded	EQCR, 1:108
For plaintiff; defendant ordered to pay cost of court, 50 shillings	EQCR, 1:204
For plaintiff; defendant ordered to pay cost of court, £1 7s. 6d.	EQCR, 3:403–4
For plaintiff; defendants ordered to pay 24 bushels of Indian corn and 20 shillings	Drake, *Annals*, pp. 71–72; Smith, *Colonial Justice*, pp. 219–20
For defendant; Susanna committed to prison on bond of 100 pounds; note that magistrate did not concur in verdict of jury	EQCR, 4:129, 133
For plaintiff; defendant to make public acknowledgment in places where parties dwell; in case of default, husband of defendant to pay 10 pounds and cost of court	Trumbull, *History of Northampton*, pp. 43–50
See case 3, above	EQCR, 1:301
Not recorded	EQCR, 1:200
Not recorded	EQCR, 6:237–38
For plaintiff; defendant fined 10 shillings and cost of court	*Documents and Records of New Hampshire*, p. 304
See case 3, above	EQCR, 1:301
For plaintiff; Elizabeth Roe ordered to acknowledge slander in public meeting within a month or pay fine of 5 pounds	*Documents and Records of New Hampshire*, 1:38
For plaintiff; defendant ordered to pay fine of 5 pounds and cost of court	*Documents and Records of New Hampshire*, 1:258

Appendix C

List of Persons against Whom Legal Actions
Were Initiated during Salem Prosecutions

Note: This appendix lists alphabetically all persons against whom legal action was taken on charges of witchcraft during the Salem prosecutions of 1692. The list was compiled directly from the Salem Witchcraft Papers, vols. 1, 2, and 3, designated as SWP, 1, 2, and 3 in the notes to each chapter. It should be emphasized that the list does not include persons who were accused of witchcraft but against whom no formal action was taken.

With regard to other entries in the list, I have taken as the date of the initial legal action the date on which warrants or complaints were first filed. In some cases, as indicated, the date is either unknown or can only be approximated as to the month.

Because of irregularities in legal procedure after the dismissal of the Court of Oyer and Terminer, the final outcome is not clear for every case. In some instances, particularly in regard to those suspects who were accused late in the proceedings, it is not possible to determine whether arrests were made in each case for which a warrant was issued. In other instances, among those who were convicted but who were not mentioned in the reversal of attainder of 1711, the cases remain unresolved even after the passage of legislation as recent as 1957; see Powers, *Crime and Punishment,* pp. 508, 509, 632. I have included the legal history of each of the cases for only 1692 and 1693.

The modal career of the Salem suspects entailed arrest, imprisonment, and eventual release and acquittal by the Superior Court of Judicature. Accordingly, I have included length of imprisonment as part of the outcome even if the suspect was later acquitted. For the most part, this information was taken directly from petitions filed by suspects and their relatives for reversal of attainder.

Finally, I have used asterisks (*) to indicate those suspects who were accused not only of tormenting the afflicted but also of ordinary witchcrafts. I have also abbreviated references to the Superior Court of Judicature (SCJ).

Name	Location	Date of initial legal action	Outcome
Nehemiah Abbot, Jr.	Topsfield or Ipswich	Apr. 21	Released; the only case in which the afflicted withdrew their complaint
Capt. John Alden	Boston	May 31	Imprisoned 15 weeks; escaped; cleared by SCJ on Apr. 25, 1693
Daniel Andrew	Salem Village	May 14	Escaped; pardoned in 1693
Abigail Barker	Andover	Sept. 8	Imprisoned 18 weeks; acquitted by SCJ on Jan. 6, 1693
Mary Barker	Andover	Aug. 29	Imprisoned 6 weeks; acquitted by SCJ in May 1693
William Barker, Sr.	Andover	Aug. 29	Imprisoned; acquitted by SCJ in May 1693
William Barker, Jr.	Andover	Aug. 29	Imprisoned 6 weeks; acquitted by SCJ in May 1693
Sarah Bassett	Lynn	May 21	Imprisoned; case dismissed by SCJ on Jan. 3, 1693
Bridget Bishop*	Salem Village	Apr. 18	Convicted June 2; executed June 10, 1692
Edward Bishop	Salem Village	Apr. 21	Imprisoned 18½ weeks; escaped; case dismissed by SCJ
Sarah Bishop	Salem Village	Apr. 21	Imprisoned 18½ weeks; escaped; case dismissed by SCJ
Mary Black	Salem Village	Apr. 22	Imprisoned 8 months; pardoned in 1693
Mary Bradbury*	Salisbury	Apr. 26	Imprisoned 6 months; convicted and condemned Sept. 9; escaped; pardoned in 1693
Mary Bridges, Sr.	Andover	July 28	Imprisoned; acquitted by SCJ in Jan. 1693
Mary Bridges, Jr.	Andover	Aug. 25	Imprisoned; acquitted by SCJ in May 1693
Sarah Bridges	Andover	Aug. 25	Imprisoned; acquitted by SCJ in Jan. 1693
Hannah Bromage	Haverhill	July 30	Imprisoned; case dismissed by SCJ
Sarah Buckley	Salem Village	May 18	Imprisoned over 8 months; acquitted by SCJ on Jan. 3, 1693
George Burroughs*	Wells, Me.	Apr. 30	Convicted Aug. 5; executed Aug. 19

Name	Location	Date of initial legal action	Outcome
Candy	Salem Town	June 1	Imprisoned; acquitted by SCJ in Jan. 1693
Andrew Carrier	Andover	July 21	Imprisoned; case dismissed by SCJ
Martha Carrier	Andover	May 28	Convicted Aug. 5; executed Aug. 19
Richard Carrier	Andover	July 21	Imprisoned; case dismissed by SCJ
Sarah Carrier	Andover	. . . . .	Imprisoned; case dismissed by SCJ
Thomas Carrier	Andover	July 21	Imprisoned; case dismissed by SCJ
Hannah Carroll	Salem Town	Sept. 10	No record of further legal action
Bethia Carter, Sr.	Woburn	May 8	Imprisoned; either pardoned or case dismissed
Bethia Carter, Jr.	Woburn	May 8	No information
Elizabeth Cary	Charlestown	May 28	Imprisoned; escaped; either pardoned or case dismissed by SCJ
Mary Clarke	Haverhill	Aug. 3	Either pardoned or case dismissed by SCJ
Rachel Clinton*	Ipswich	Mar. 29	Imprisoned; either pardoned or case dismissed by SCJ
Sarah Cloyce	Salem Village	Apr. 4	Imprisoned; case dismissed by SCJ in Jan.
Sarah Cole*	Lynn	Oct. 3	Imprisoned 17 weeks; acquitted by SCJ on Jan. 31, 1693
Elizabeth Colson	Reading	May 10	Possibly escaped; no records of further legal action
Mary Colson	Reading	Sept. 5	Case dismissed by SCJ on Jan. 5, 1693
Giles Corey*	Salem Village	Apr. 18	Pressed to death for refusal to testify, Sept. 19, 1692
Martha Corey*	Salem Village	Mar. 19	Convicted Sept. 9; executed Sept. 22
Deliverance Dane	Andover	. . . . .	Imprisoned 13 weeks; case dismissed by SCJ
Mary De Rich	Salem Village	May 23	Imprisoned about 6 months; case dismissed by SCJ in Jan. 1693

Name	Location	Date of initial legal action	Outcome
Elizabeth Dicer	Gloucester	Sept. 3	No record of further legal action
Rebecca Dike	Gloucester	Nov. 5	No record of further legal action
Ann Doliver	Gloucester	June 6	Imprisoned; pardoned in 1693
Joseph Draper	Andover	Sept.	Imprisoned; either pardoned or case dismissed by SCJ
Lydia Dustin*	Reading	Apr. 30	Imprisoned; acquitted by SCJ on Jan. 31, 1693
Sarah Dustin*	Reading	May 8	Imprisoned; acquitted by SCJ on Jan. 31, 1693
Rebecca Eames	Boxford	Aug. 19	Convicted and condemned Sept. 17; reprieved for confession; imprisoned 7 months; pardoned
Mary Easty*	Salem Village	Apr. 22	Convicted Sept. 9; executed Sept. 22
Esther Elwell	Gloucester	Nov. 5	No record of further legal action
Martha Emerson	Haverhill	July 22	Case dismissed by SCJ in Jan. 1693
Joseph Emons	Manchester	Sept. 5	Imprisoned; case dismissed by SCJ
Mary English	Salem Town	Apr. 21	Imprisoned at least 6 weeks; escaped; pardoned
Philip English*	Salem Town	Apr. 30	Escaped; pardoned
Thomas Farrer	Lynn	May 14	Imprisoned 5 months; case dismissed by SCJ
Edward Farrington	Andover	Sept. 17	Probably imprisoned and then pardoned
Abigale Faulkner, Sr.	Andover	Aug. 11	Convicted and condemned Sept. 17; reprieved; pardoned
Abigail Faulkner, Jr.	Andover	Sept. 17	Imprisoned 1 month; cleared by SCJ in May 1693
Dorothy Faulkner	Andover	Sept. 16	Imprisoned 1 month; cleared by SCJ in May 1693
Capt. John Flood	Rumney Marsh	May 28	No record of further legal action
Elizabeth Fosdick	Malden	May 28	No record of further legal action

Name	Location	Date of initial legal action	Outcome
Ann Foster	Andover	July 15	Convicted and condemned Sept. 17; reprieved; died in prison
Nicholas Frost	Manchester	Sept. 5	No record of further legal action
Eunice Fry	Andover	Sept.	Imprisoned 15 weeks; acquitted by SCJ in May 1693
Dorcas Good	Salem Village	Mar. 23	Imprisoned 7 months; case dismissed by SCJ
Sarah Good*	Salem Village	Feb. 29	Convicted June 30; executed July 19
Mary Green	Haverhill	.....	No record of further legal action
Elizabeth Hart	Lynn	May 14	Imprisoned 7 months; case dismissed by SCJ
Margaret Hawkes	Salemn Town	July 1	Imprisoned; either pardoned or case dismissed by SCJ
Sarah Hawkes	Andover	Sept. 1	Imprisoned 5 months; acquitted by SCJ in Jan. 1693
Dorcas Hoar*	Beverly	Apr. 30	Convicted and condemned Sept. 9; reprieved; pardoned
Abigail Hobbs*	Topsfield	Apr. 18	Convicted and condemned Sept. 9; reprieved; pardoned in 1693
Deliverance Hobbs	Topsfield	Apr. 21	Imprisoned; released after confession
William Hobbs	Topsfield	Apr. 21	Imprisoned 8 months; case dismissed, possibly in Dec. 1692
Elizabeth How*	Topsfield	May 28	Convicted June 30; executed July 19
John Howard	Rowley	Aug. 5	Imprisoned; no record of further legal action
Francis Hutchins	Haverhill	Aug. 18	Imprisoned; no record of further legal action
Mary Ireson	Lynn	June 4	Imprisoned; no record of further legal action
John Jackson, Sr.	Rowley	Aug. 5	Imprisoned; case dismissed by SCJ on Jan. 7, 1693
John Jackson, Jr.	Rowley	Aug. 5	Imprisoned; case dismissed by SCJ on Jan. 7, 1693

Name	Location	Date of initial legal action	Outcome
George Jacobs, Sr.*	Salem Town	May 10	Convicted Aug. 5; executed Aug. 19
George Jacobs, Jr.	Salem Village	May 14	Escaped; pardoned
Margaret Jacobs	Salem Village	May 10	Imprisoned at least 2 months; acquitted by SCJ on Jan. 3, 1693
Rebecca Jacobs	Salem Village	May 14	Imprisoned 6 months; acquitted by SCJ on Jan. 3, 1693
Abigail Johnson	Andover	Aug. 29	Imprisoned 5 weeks; case dismissed by SCJ on Jan. 7, 1693
Elizabeth Johnson, Sr.	Andover	Aug. 29	Imprisoned 25 months; acquitted by SCJ in Jan. 1693
Elizabeth Johnson, Jr.	Andover	Aug. 10	Imprisoned 6 months; convicted by SCJ in Jan.; reprieved by governor
Rebecca Johnson	Andover	. . . . .	Imprisoned 8 months; case dismissed by SCJ in Jan.
Stephen Johnson	Andover	Sept. 1	Imprisoned 5 weeks; case dismissed by SCJ in Jan.
Mary Lacey, Sr.	Andover	July 21	Convicted and condemned Sept. 17; reprieved; pardoned
Mary Lacey, Jr.	Andover	July 20	Imprisoned 10 weeks; acquitted by SCJ in Jan.
John Lee	. . . . .	Apr. 1	No record of further legal action
Jane Lilly	Malden	Sept. 5	Case dismissed by SCJ on Jan. 31, 1693
Mary Marston	Andover	Aug. 29	Imprisoned 5 months; acquitted by SCJ in Jan. 1693
Susanna Martin*	Amesbury	Apr. 30	Convicted June 30; executed July 19
Mary Morey	Beverly	May	Imprisoned 35 weeks; no record of further legal action
Sarah Murrill	Beverly	May 2	Imprisoned 35 weeks; no record of further legal action
Rebecca Nurse*	Salem Village	Mar. 23	Convicted June 30; executed July 19
Sarah Osborne	Salem Village	Feb. 29	Imprisoned 9 weeks; died in prison

Name	Location	Date of initial legal action	Outcome
Mary Osgood	Andover	Sept. 8	Imprisoned 15 weeks; acquitted by SCJ in Jan.
Elizabeth Paine	Charlestown	May 30	No record of further legal action
Alice Parker*	Salem Town	May 12	Convicted Sept. 9; executed Sept. 22
Mary Parker	Andover	Sept. 2	Convicted Sept. 9; executed Sept. 22
Sarah Pease	Salem Town	May 23	Imprisoned; no record of further legal action
Joan Peney	Gloucester	Sept. 20	No record of further legal action
Hannah Post	Boxford	Aug. 25	Imprisoned; acquitted by SCJ in Jan.
Mary Post	Andover	Aug. 2	Imprisoned 8 months; convicted by SCJ in Jan. 1693; reprieved by governor; released May 1693
Susanna Post	Andover	Aug. 25	Imprisoned; acquitted by SCJ in May 1693
Margaret Prince	Gloucester	Sept. 5	No record of further legal action
Benjamin Proctor	Salem Village	May 23	Imprisoned; case dismissed by SCJ
Elizabeth Proctor*	Salem Village	Apr. 4	Convicted and condemned Aug. 5; reprieved; released from prison in 1693
John Proctor*	Salem Village	Apr. 11	Convicted Aug. 5; executed Aug. 19
Sarah Proctor	Salem Village	May 21	Imprisoned; cleared by SCJ in Jan.
William Proctor	Salem Village	May 28	Imprisoned; cleared by SCJ in Jan.
Ann Pudeator*	Salem Town	May 12	Convicted Sept. 9; executed Sept. 22
Wilmot Reed*	Marblehead	May 28	Convicted Sept. 17; executed Sept. 22
Sarah Rice	Reading	May 28	Imprisoned; no record of further legal action

Name	Location	Date of initial legal action	Outcome
Abigail Roe	Gloucester	Nov. 5	No record of further legal action
Susanna Roots	Beverly	May 21	Imprisoned; no record of further legal action
Henry Salter	Andover	Sept. 7	No record of further legal action
John Sawdy	Andover	Sept.	Imprisoned; released; no record of further legal action
Margaret Scott*	Rowley	Sept.	Convicted Sept. 17; executed Sept. 22
Ann Sears	Woburn	May 8	Imprisoned; released; no record of further legal action
Abigail Somes	Salem Town	May 13	Imprisoned; case dismissed by SCJ in Jan.
Martha Sparks	Chelmsford	.....	Imprisoned 12 months (see Massachusetts Archives, vol. 135, doc. 4)
Mary Taylor	Reading	Sept. 5	Acquitted by SCJ on Jan. 31, 1693
Tituba	Salem Village	Feb. 29	Imprisoned 13 months; released in 1693
Jerson Toothaker	Billerica	May 24	No record of further legal action
Mary Toothaker	Billerica	May 28	Acquitted by SCJ on Jan. 31, 1693
Roger Toothaker*	Billerica	May 18	No record of further legal action
Job Tukey*	Beverly	June 4	Acquitted by SCJ in Jan. 1693
Hanna Tyler	Andover	Sept. 16	Imprisoned; released; acquitted by SCJ on Jan. 5, 1693
Martha Tyler	Andover	Sept. 16	Imprisoned; released; acquitted by SCJ on Jan. 7, 1693
Mercy Wardwell	Andover	Sept. 1	Imprisoned; acquitted by SCJ on Jan. 10, 1693
Samuel Wardwell*	Andover	Sept. 1	Convicted Sept. 9; executed Sept. 22.
Sarah Wardwell	Andover	Sept. 1	Imprisoned; convicted by SCJ on Jan. 10, 1693; reprieved by governor

Name	Location	Date of initial legal action	Outcome
Mary Warren	Salem Village	Apr. 18	Briefly imprisoned; then released as accuser
Sarah Wilds*	Topsfield	Apr. 21	Convicted June 30; executed July 19
Ruth Wilford	Haverhill	Aug. 18	No record of further legal action
John Willard*	Salem Village	May 10	Convicted Aug. 5; executed Aug. 19
Sarah Wilson, Sr.	Andover	Sept. 17	Imprisoned 15 weeks; released from prison Jan. 13, 1693
Sarah Wilson, Jr.	Andover	Sept.	Imprisoned 6 weeks; released from prison Jan. 13, 1693
Mary Witheridge	Salem Village	May 18	Imprisoned; acquitted by SCJ on Jan. 3, 1693

Appendix D

List of Confessors during Salem Prosecutions

Note: Under "Date of Confession," two or more dates are given in those instances in which the confessor provided more than one account. Dates and text of confessions are available in SWP, vols. 1, 2, and 3 unless otherwise indicated.

Name	Date of confession	Sources
Abigail Barker	. . . . .	
Mary Barker	Aug. 29	
William Barker, Sr.	Aug. 29; Sept. 5	
Mary Bridges, Sr.	. . . . .	
Mary Bridges, Jr.	Aug. 25	
Sarah Bridges	Aug. 25	
Hannah Bromage	July 30	
Candy	July 2	
Andrew Carrier	July 23	
Richard Carrier	July 22	
Sarah Carrier	Aug. 11	
Thomas Carrier	July 21	
Sarah Cole	Oct. 3	
Deliverance Dane	. . . . .	
Joseph Draper	Sept. 16	
Rebecca Eames	Aug. 19	
Martha Emerson	July 23	
Edward Farrington	Sept. 17	
Abigail Faulkner, Jr.	Sept. 17	
Dorothy Faulkner	Sept. 17	
Ann Foster	July 15, 16, 18, 21	
Margaret Hawkes	July	
Sarah Hawkes	Sept. 1	
Dorcas Hoar	Shortly before Sept. 22	Burr, *Narratives,* p. 366, n. 3
Deliverance Hobbs	Apr. 22; May 3	
John Jackson, Jr.	. . . . .	

Name	Date of confession	Sources
Margaret Jacobs	Before Aug. 19	Only fact of confession is preserved; see Burr, *Narratives,* pp. 364–66
Elizabeth Johnson, Sr.	Aug. 30	
Elizabeth Johnson, Jr.	Aug. 11	
Rebecca Johnson	.....	
Stephen Johnson	Sept. 1	
Mary Lacey, Sr.	July 21	
Mary Lacy, Jr.	July 21	
Mary Marston	Aug. 29	
Mary Osgood	.....	
Hannah Post	Aug. 25	
Susanna Post	Aug. 25	
Tituba	Feb. 29	RSW, 1:43–48
Mary Toothaker	July 30	
Hanna Tyler	Sept. 16	
Martha Tyler	Sept. 16	
Mercy Wardwell	Sept. 1	
Samuel Wardwell	Sept. 1	
Sarah Wardwell	Sept. 1	
Mary Warren	Apr. 21; May 12	
Sarah Wilson, Sr.	Sept. 17	
Sarah Wilson, Jr.	.....	

Appendix E

List of Allegations of

Ordinary Witchcrafts by Case

Note on use of records: Information on accusers was derived primarily from depositions. The sources for these depositions are given in Apps. A and C. I have included only those allegations that meet the criteria for ordinary witchcrafts described in chapter 4.

In some instances, where the age of the plaintiff is not given in the records, I have inferred the information from the age of the plaintiff's spouse or sibling. I have indicated these inferences by placing a *c.* before the given age. Marital status is indicated by M (married), S (single), or W (widowed).

Name of suspected witch	Name of accuser(s)	Accuser's age	Accuser's marital status
Bridget Bishop	John Bly	?	M
	Rebecca Bly	?	M
	John Louder	c.30	M
	Samuel Shattuck	41	M
	Sarah Shattuck	?	M
	William Stacey	36	M
Mary Bradbury	James Carr	c.45	M
	Richard Carr	?	?
	Samuel Endicott	?	M
	Zerubabel Endicott	?	M
George Burroughs	Elizer Keyzar	45	M
G'wife Burt	Bethiah Carter	c.25	M
	Thomas Farrer (Ffarer)	50	M
	Jacob Knight	25	?
	John Knight	47	M
	John Pearson	19	S
	Madeleine Pearson	50	M
	Philip Read	45	M
Rachel Clinton	William Baker	?	M
	Thomas Boorman	?	M
	Mary Edwards	?	M
	Mary Fuller, Sr.	41	M

Name of suspected witch	Name of accuser(s)	Accuser's age	Accuser's marital status
Sarah Cole	John Browne	25	M
	Mary Eaton	?	M
Giles Corey	Benjamin Gould	23	?
Martha Corey	Giles Corey	c.80	M
Mary Easty	Margaret Redington	c.70	W
	Samuel Smith	25	?
Philip English	William Beale	c.60	M
Rachel Fuller	Elizabeth Denham	?	?
	John Godfrey	48	M
	Mary Godfrey	36	M
	Sarah Godfrey	16	S
	Hazen Levit	36	M
	Nathaniel Smith	20	?
Mary Glover	G'wife Hughes	?	M
John Godfrey	Ephraim Davis	?	?
	James Davis, Sr.	?	M
	Isabel Holdred	?	M
	Jane Huseldin	?	M
	John Huseldin	?	M
	Jonathan Singletarry	22	M
	Benjamin Swett	?	M
	Job Tyler	40	M
	Abraham Whitaker	?	M
Sarah Good	Mary Abbey	38	M
	Samuel Abbey	45	M
	Sarah Gadge	40	M
	Henry Herrick	21	S
Dorcas Hoar	Edward Hooper	15	S
	Deborah Morgan	43	M
	Joseph Morgan	46	M
	John Tuck	18	S
Elizabeth How	Thomas Andrews	50	M
	Isaac Cummins, Jr.	27	M
	Isaac Cummins, Sr.	60	M
	Mary Cummins	c.60	M
	Jacob Foster	29	M
	John How	50	M
	Francis Lane	27	M
	Samuel Perley	52	M
	Timothy Perley	39	M
	Joseph Safford	60	M
Susanna Martin	John Allen	45	M
	John Atkinson	56	M
	John Kimball	45	M

Name of suspected witch	Name of accuser (s)	Accuser's age	Accuser's marital status
	B. Peach	43	M
	John Pressy	53	M
	Mary Pressy	46	M
Elizabeth Morse	John Chase	?	M
	Zachariah Davis	?	M
	G'wife Goodwin	?	M
	John Mighell	44	M
	Caleb Moody	41	M
	Josh Richardson	30	M
	Susan Toppan	74	W
	David Wheeler	54	M
Rebecca Nurse	Sarah Holton	?	W
Alice Parker	Samuel Shattuck	41	M
	John Westgate	40	M
Hugh Parsons	Symon Beman	c.25	S
	Blanche Bodortha	?	M
	William Branch	c.35	M
	Sarah Edwards	c.25	M
	Anthony Dorchester	c.35	M
	Samuel Marshfield	c.25	S
	Thomas Miller	29	M
	Reverend Mr. Moxon	48	M
	Jonathan Taylor	?	?
Ann Pudeator	John Best, Sr.	48	?
Wilmott Reed	Sarah Dod	?	M
	Charity Pitman	29	M
Margaret Scott	Philip Nelson	?	M
	Sarah Nelson	?	M
	Frances Wycom	?	M
Jane Walford	Nicholas Roe	?	?
	Susannah Trimmings	?	M
Sarah Wilds	John Andrew	37	M
	Joseph Andrew	33	M
	Thomas Dorman	53	M
	John Gould	56	M
	Elizabeth Symonds	50	M
John Willard	Bray Wilkins	c.80	W
	Samuel Wilkins	19	S

Appendix F

List of Persons Diagnosed as Afflicted in Seventeenth-Century Massachusetts Bay

Note: In this appendix, I have included only those persons whose sufferings were verified as afflictions by civil and ecclesiastical authorities. Even a casual glance at the legal records will reveal that far more persons experienced the torments of afflictions than were identified as such and that, according to the perceptions of villagers, such preternatural assaults were not unusual occurrences. Moreover, there are indications in contemporary narratives that afflictions were underreported in spite of ecclesiastical encouragement, perhaps to protect the reputations of the parties involved. Also, it is clear that others besides children and social subordinates were predisposed to similar kinds of sufferings although contemporaries were reluctant to include males or self-sufficient adults within the category of afflicted persons.

Name	Location	Year	Age	Marital status
Alice Booth	.....	1692	...	M
Elizabeth Booth	Salem Village	1692	18	S
Sarah Bridges	Andover	1692	c.18	S
William Brage	Salem Town	1692	Under 20	S
Mary Brown	Reading	1692	...	S
Sarah Churchill	Salem Village	1692	20	S
Johanna Dod	Marblehead	1692	c.20	S
John Doritch	.....	1692	16	S
Mary Fitch	Gloucester	1692	...	S
Rose Foster	Andover	1692	18	S
Goodall	Probably Salem Village	1692	Over 40	M
Benjamin Goodwin	Boston	1688	5	S
John Goodwin, Jr.	Boston	1688	11	S
Martha Goodwin	Boston	1688	13	S
Mercy Goodwin	Boston	1688	7	S
Mary Herrick	Wenham	1692	17	S
Mary Hill	Salem Town	1692	Under 20	S
Elizabeth Hubbard	Salem Village	1692	17	S

Name	Location	Year	Age	Marital status
John Indian	Salem Village	1692	...	M
Elizabeth Knapp	Groton	1671–72	16	S
Mary Lacey, Jr.	Andover	1692	15	S
Mercy Lewis	Salem Village	1692	19	S
Mary Marshall	Reading	1692	Over 40	W
Abigail Martin	Andover	1692	16	S
Elizabeth Parris	Salem Village	1692	9	S
Hanna Perley	Topsfield	1692	10	S
Sarah Phelps	Andover	1692	Under 20	S
Bethshaa Pope	Probably Salem Village	1692	Over 40	M
Ann Putnam, Jr.	Salem Village	1692	13	S
Ann Putnam, Sr.	Salem Village	1692	*c.*30	M
Margaret Rule	Boston	1693	*c.*18	S
Susannah Sheldon	Salem Village	1692	18	S
Mercy Short	Boston	1692	*c.*18	S
Martha Sprague	Boxford	1692	16	S
Tituba	Salem Village	1692	...	M
Rebecca Towne	Topsfield	1692	*c.*19	S
Peter Tufts's maidservant	Charlestown	1692	...	...
Sarah Vibber	Wenham	1692	36	M
Mary Walcott	Salem Village	1692	17	S
Mary Warren	Salem Village	1692	20	S
Elizabeth Weston	Reading	1692	...	S
Rebecca Wilkins	Salem Village	1692	19	S
Abigail Williams	Salem Village	1692	12	S

Sources: All information on age, marital status, and location was obtained directly from SWP, vols. 1, 2, and 3, except for the following: Goodall–reported by Lawson, "A Brief and True Narrative," in Burr, *Narratives*, p. 155. Goodwins–Burr, *Narratives*, pp. 99–131. Herrick–Burr, *Narratives*, p. 369, n. 1. John Indian–Thomas Hutchinson, *The History of the Colony and Province of Massachusetts Bay*, 2:21–22. Knapp–Green, *Groton in the Witchcraft Times*, pp. 7–22. Perley–*RSW*, 2:74–75. Pope–Burr, *Narratives*, p. 155. Rule–Burr, *Narratives*, pp. 324–41. Short–Cotton Mather, "A Brand Pluck'd out of the Burning," in Burr, *Narratives*, pp. 255–87.

Notes

I INTRODUCTION

1 Marvin Harris, *Cows, Pigs, Wars, and Witches*, pp. 225–58.
2 For samples in the literature on New England witchcraft, see Winfield S. Nevins, *Witchcraft in Salem Village in 1692*; George Bancroft, *History of the United States of America*, 2:53–54; James Truslow Adams, *The Founding of New England*, pp. 454–55; and Thomas J. Wertenbaker, *The Puritan Oligarchy*, pp. 252–91.
3 The best-known thesis equating witchcraft with psychopathology is Gregory Zilboorg, *The Medical Man and the Witch during the Renaissance*. For other statements of this position, see Albert Deutsch, *The Mentally Ill in America*, pp. 24, 31, 32; Ilza Vieth, *Hysteria*, pp. 70–73. For a critique of Zilboorg, see Thomas Szasz, *The Manufacture of Madness*, pp. 75–78. A strong case is made that analogies between psychiatric categories and witchcraft-related phenomena have been overextended in Stanley Jackson and Joan K. Jackson, "Primitive Medicine and the Historiography of Psychiatry," in *Psychiatry and Its History*, ed. George Mora and Jeanne L. Brand, pp. 195–222, and Thomas J. Schoeneman, "The Role of Mental Illness in the European Witch Hunts of the Sixteenth and Seventeenth Centuries: An Assessment," pp. 337–51. For a statement regarding the use of psychotropic drugs, see Michael J. Harner, "The Role of Hallucinogenic Plants in European Witchcraft," in *Hallucinogens and Shamanism*, ed. Michael J. Harner, pp. 127–50. For a critique of this thesis, see Norman Cohn, *Europe's Inner Demons*, pp. 219–24.
4 See, for example, formulations of Howard S. Becker, "Labeling Theory Reconsidered," in Paul Rock and Mary McIntosh, eds., *Deviance and Social Control*, pp. 126–62; David Matza, *Becoming Deviant*; Edwin M. Schur, *Interpreting Deviance*, pp. 120–88.
5 Howard S. Becker, *Outsiders*, p. 9.
6 For examples of this interpretation of the interactionist perspective, see contributions in Walter R. Gove, ed., *The Labelling of Deviance*; for criticisms of this interpretation, see comments by Edwin Schur and John I. Kitsuse included therein, pp. 273–94. Recent efforts by critics to point out limitations in the perspective by offering evidence that groups are sometimes reluctant to impose sanctions on rule-breaking members or that the invoking of rules may correct rather than stabilize deviant behavior are ultimately irrelevant to the acceptance or rejection of the perspective. What finally distinguishes proponents of the inter-

actionist framework from their critics is their assumption that acts cannot be analyzed independently of their meanings. For a useful attempt at disentangling the various interpretations of this perspective, see Prudence Rains, "Imputations of Deviance: A Retrospective Essay on the Labeling Perspective," pp. 1–11.

7 An excellent discussion of this paradox and its implications for research is Melvin Pollner, "Constitutive and Mundane Versions of Labeling Theory," pp. 269–88.

8 For a general discussion of the relationship between deviance and the sociology of knowledge that is compatible with the approach taken in this investigation, see Peter Conrad and Joseph W. Schneider, *Deviance and Medicalization*, especially chap. 2.

9 This is not to suggest that the issue of rationality with reference to occult beliefs is not debated in anthropology. For discussion of this issue, see contributions of Stephen Lukes and Ernest Gellner, in *Rationality*, ed. Bryan Wilson.

10 Mary Douglas addressed exactly the same issue in her introduction to *Witch-craft Confessions and Accusations*, p. xiii, although she arrives at different conclusions. Also see Keith Thomas, "The Relevance of Social Anthropology to the Historical Study of English Witchcraft," ibid., pp. 47–79.

11 See, for example, Clyde Kluckhohn, *Navaho Witchcraft*.

12 H. C. Erik Midelfort, "Were There Really Witches?" p. 190.

13 Notable examples are John Middleton's *Lugbara Religion* and Victor Turner's *Schism and Continuity in an African Society*.

14 For the clearest articulations of this thesis, see Cohn, *Europe's Inner Demons*, pp. 251–55; Richard Kieckhefer, *European Witch Trials;* and Richard A. Horsley, "Who Were the Witches? The Social Roles of the Accused in the European Witch Trials," pp. 689–715.

15 Keith Thomas, *Religion and the Decline of Magic*.

2 THE CRIME OF WITCHCRAFT IN MASSACHUSETTS BAY

1 H. C. Lea, *Materials towards a History of Witchcraft*, 1:137–43; see also idem, *History of the Inquisition in the Middle Ages*, 1:429–33.

2 Julio Baroja, *The World of the Witches*, p. 18.

3 There are far more recent examples of this tendency. Indeed, it has been the routine practice of missionaries to attempt the suppression of both sorcery and countersorcery in non-European cultures. See Lucy Mair, *Witchcraft*, pp. 120–45. Some of the destructive consequences of this suppression are described in Deward E. Walker, Jr., "Nez Perce Sorcery," pp. 66–96.

4 For example, in the King James version, Lev. 19:26: "You shall not practice augury or witchcraft"; Lev. 20:27: "A man or a woman who is a medium or a wizard shall be put to death"; 1 Kings 9:22; 2 Kings 21:6, 23:24; and so forth. In the most famous edict, Exod. 22:18 ("Thou shalt not suffer a witch to live"), the Hebrew term for magical practitioner has been variously translated into English as "sorcerer" or "poisoner." See Rossell Robbins, *Encyclopedia of Witchcraft and Demonology*, p. 46.

5 Jeffrey Burton Russell, *Witchcraft in the Middle Ages*, pp. 15–16.

6 Peter Brown, "Sorcery, Demons, and the Rise of Christianity," in Douglas, *Witchcraft Confessions and Accusations*, p. 35.

7 Lea, *Materials*, 1:306–36, for general discussion of the background of the *Malleus Maleficarum*.

Notes

8 Russell, *Witchcraft*, p. 230.

9 Ibid.

10 Jacob Sprenger and Heinrich Institoris, *Malleus Maleficarum*, pt. 1, q. 2; hereafter cited as *Malleus*. Russell, *Witchcraft*, pp. 230–31 et passim.

11 Robbins, *Encyclopedia*, p. 415; Russell, *Witchcraft*, pp. 230–31.

12 Lea, *Materials*, 1:306.

13 For acceptance of classical formulation by German Lutherans, see Hans C. Erik Midelfort, "The Social and Intellectual Foundations of Witch-Hunting in Southwestern Germany, 1562–1684," pp. 70 ff.

14 For the earliest statement of this position by Margaret Murray, see *The Witch-Cult in Western Europe*, pp. 21–24. A more moderate statement of this thesis is developed in Arne Runeberg's *Witches, Demons, and Fertility Magic*. For a thoughtful and balanced critique of the conclusions of the Murray school, see Elliot Rose, *A Razor for a Goat*.

15 Russell, *Witchcraft*, pp. 141–42, 177–81.

16 For a balanced discussion of this issue, see Midelfort, "Were There Really Witches?"

17 Indeed, the authors of the *Malleus* encouraged the active participation of secular officials, although their own authority derived from the church. See *Malleus*, pt. 3.

18 Elliot Currie, "Crimes without Criminals," p. 12.

19 *Malleus*, p. 217.

20 Ibid., p. 231.

21 Midelfort, "The Social and Intellectual Foundations of Witch-Hunting," pp. 153–54.

22 *Malleus*, p. 210. The *Malleus* equivocates even on admitting the testimony of "mortal enemies": "But it is mortal enemies that are spoken of, and it is to be noted that a witness is not necessarily to be disqualified because of every sort of enmity."

23 Robbins, *Encyclopedia*, p. 221. Midelfort, pp. 351–52 et passim.

24 Lea, *Materials*, 1:244.

25 H. C. Erik Midelfort, *Witchhunting in Southwestern Germany, 1562–1684*, p. 147.

26 Robert Mandrou, *Magistrats et sorciers en France au XVIIe siecle*, pp. 94, 111; E. William Monter, *Witchcraft in France and Switzerland*, pp. 49, 105.

27 Russell, *Witchcraft*, p. 336, n. 12.

28 For background on the literary controversy in England, I am indebted to the discussion of Wallace Notestein, *A History of Witchcraft in England from 1558 to 1718*.

29 For the dispute between Scot and King James, see ibid., chaps. 3 and 4. In his discussion of the nature of spirits, Scot was quite aware that he was dealing with the most theologically controversial issue in his entire polemic. Thus, in the introduction to his discussion of Satan's powers, he observed that there "is no question nor theme . . . so difficult to deale in nor so noble an argument to dispute on, as this of devils and spirits. For that being confessed or doubted of, the eternitie of the soule is either affirmed or denied." Reginald Scot, *The Discoverie of Witchcraft*, p. 489.

30 E. L'Estrange Ewen, *Witch Hunting and Witch Trials*, p. 13. Transcriptions of the English enactments appear on pp. 13–21.

31 Ibid., pp. 15–16.

32   Ibid., p. 20.
33   Contained in the "Body of Liberties" of 1641; see William H. Whitmore, ed., *The Colonial Laws of Massachusetts*, p. 55. For Connecticut laws, the same phrasing was used; see *Public Records of the Colony of Connecticut*, J. Hammond Trumbull, 1:77.
34   Thorp Wolford, "The Laws and Liberties of 1648," in David Flaherty, ed., *Essays in the History of Early American Law*, p. 182.
35   George Haskins, *Law and Authority in Early Massachusetts*, pp. 36–38. The assumption of consensus in early Massachusetts with regard to both social and legal propriety allowed magistrates to exercise considerable discretionary powers.
36   G. Lincoln Burr, ed., *Narratives of the Witchcraft Cases, 1648–1706*, p. 380, n. 3.
37   Alan Macfarlane, *Witchcraft in Tudor and Stuart England*, p. 24. This confirms Ewen's findings in *Witch Hunting*, pp. 102–10.
38   See Currie, "Crimes without Criminals," pp. 7–32, for a discussion of the adversary system in sixteenth- and seventeenth-century England.
39   The practice of law was viewed with suspicion in seventeenth-century New England. Prior to 1648, a lawyer could not charge fees for services rendered in court; see Edwin Powers, *Crime and Punishment in Early Massachusetts, 1620–1692*, pp. 434–35. Thomas Lechford, an outspoken member of the English bar who arrived in Boston in 1638 and returned to England three years later, recounts how his colonial practice was discouraged in *Plaine Dealing; or, Newes from New-England*.
40   For a discussion of the disallowance of torture, see E. L'Estrange Ewen, *Witchcraft and Demonianism*, pp. 120–26.
41   Cotton Mather, *Selected Letters of Cotton Mather*, p. 38.
42   Ewen, *Witch Hunting*, p. 31.
43   Macfarlane, *Witchcraft*, p. 57.
44   Powers, *Crime and Punishment*, p. 61.
45   *Records of the Governor and Company of the Massachusetts Bay in New England*, ed. Nathaniel B. Shurtleff, 1:169; hereafter cited as *MCR*.
46   Records of trial collected and reprinted in James Russell Trumbull, *History of Northampton*, 1:230–35.
47   In the actual legal records, this date is written as January 5, 1674/5. Until 1752, England and its colonies in New England used the Julian calendar. For the sake of convenience and ease of reading, I have given the year according to the Gregorian calendar.
48   Witch's marks consisted of special bodily markings or growths on the person of the witch. These marks were believed to result from the forming of a pact with the devil. A more detailed discussion is included in chapter 7.
49   For example, Kittredge writes, "The witch beliefs of New England were brought over from the Mother Country by the first settlers"; George I Kittredge, *Witchcraft in Old and New England*, p. 373. Although most of the work is devoted to English witchcraft, this is consistent with Kittredge's point that the colonial approach to witchcraft was almost entirely derivative.
50   Burr's painstaking and meticulous scholarship is compromised by his tendency to condemn belief in witchcraft before having described it. For example, on Puritan beliefs, he writes, "I am forced to admit that it [Puritan beliefs in witchcraft] was superstitious and bigoted and cruel, even by the standards of their own

time"; G. Lincoln Burr, "New England's Place in the History of Witchcraft,"
p. 215.
51 Information and location of suspected witches available for thirty-four of
thirty-seven presentments.
52 Estimates derived from Evarts B. Greene and V. D. Harrington, *American
Population before the Federal Census of 1790*, pp. 14–20; U.S. Bureau of the
Census, *Historical Statistics of the U.S.: Colonial Times to 1957*, p. 756. I am
assuming that since the population of Essex and Norfolk counties together never
exceeded 30 percent of the total population of Massachusetts Bay, the addition of
the thinly populated Hampshire County could not have increased the proportion
beyond one third of the total population.
53 It is suggestive that Essex and Norfolk counties appear to have had less per
capita wealth than the counties of Suffolk and Middlesex. According to Robert
Wall, *Massachusetts Bay*, pp. 35–37, estate inventories for the two northeastern
counties averaged about 100 pounds lower per capita than for Suffolk and Middlesex counties.

3 WITCHCRAFT AND PURITAN BELIEF

1 Among the better-known polemics against New England Puritanism that either
center on witchcraft or give it prominence are Charles W. Upham, *Salem Witchcraft;* Burr, "New England's Place," pp. 195–221; Wertenbaker, *Puritan Oligarchy*,
pp. 252–91.
2 For example, Clifford Shipton, "The New England Clergy in the Glacial Age,"
pp. 24–54; Chadwick Hansen, *Witchcraft at Salem.*
3 A review of the extensive literature on Cotton Mather's contribution to
witchcraft belief is given by Richard H. Werking, " 'Reformation Is Our Only
Preservation' " pp. 281–90. The debate over Mather's participation in the Salem
trials has been waged for over a century; for a review of nineteenth-century literature on the subject, see W. F. Poole, "Cotton Mather and Salem Witchcraft,"
pp. 337–97.
4 Thomas J. Holmes, *Cotton Mather.* Holmes lists over 400 published works,
not including unpublished manuscripts and extensive correspondence.
5 Perry Miller, *The New England Mind: From Colony to Province*, p. 191.
6 The exception is Cotton Mather, *Magnalia Christi Americana;* see especially
books 6 and 7, art. 6.
7 Deodat Lawson, *Christ's Fidelity the Only Shield against Satan's Malignity*,
p. 11. The most thorough discussion of the New England sermon literature on
Satan is Edward K. Trefz, "A Study of Satan with Particular Emphasis upon His
Role in the Preaching of Certain New England Puritans."
8 Cotton Mather, "A Discourse on the Power and Malice of Devils," in *Memorable Providences Relating to Witchcrafts and Possessions*, pp. 19, 21; idem,
Wonders of the Invisible World, pp. 188–89; Lawson, *Christ's Fidelity*, p. 21.
9 Increase Mather, *Remarkable Providences*, pp. 88–92.
10 Increase Mather, *Angelographia*, p. 24.
11 Samuel Willard, *Christian's Exercise against Satan's Temptation*, p. 9.
12 Ibid., p. 62.
13 Lawson, *Christ's Fidelity*, p. 34.
14 Ibid., p. 37.

15 Willard, *Christian's Exercise*, pp. 129, 203.

16 Robert Calef, *More Wonders of the Invisible World*, pp. 313–14. For an informative discussion of Mather's Manichaean tendencies, see Robert Middlekauff, *The Mathers*, pp. 327–28.

17 William Perkins, *Discourse on the Damned Art of Witchcraft*, p. 33.

18 Cotton Mather, "Discourse on Witchcraft," in David Levin, ed., *What Happened in Salem?*, p. 96.

19 "Mather–Calef Paper on Witchcraft," p. 244.

20 In Levin, *What Happened in Salem?*, p. 100.

21 Burr, *Narratives*, pp. 131–34.

22 Lawson, *Christ's Fidelity*, p. 85.

23 In Levin, *What Happened in Salem?*, p. 100.

24 For general background, I have relied upon Perry Miller's discussion in *The New England Mind: The Seventeenth Century*, book 2.

25 Edward Johnson, *Wonder-Working Providence of Sions*, pp. 185–86.

26 Michael Wigglesworth, Diary, p. 416.

27 Miller, *The New England Mind: The Seventeenth Century*, p. 288.

28 Thomas, *Religion and the Decline of Magic*, pp. 224–25; D. P. Walker, *Spiritual and Demonic Magic from Picino to Campanella*, pp. 199–202.

29 William D. Stahlman, "Astrology in Colonial America," pp. 552–53; Thomas, *Religion and the Decline of Magic*, pp. 282–323; Jon Butler, "Magic, Astrology, and the Early American Religious Heritage, 1600–1760," pp. 320–23.

30 Thomas, *Religion and the Decline of Magic*, p. 72.

31 Quoted in Perry Miller, *Errand into the Wilderness*, p. 66.

32 The entry of Boston merchant John Hull in his diary in 1668 illustrates the kind of event that believers regarded as especially noteworthy: "A man at Ipswich repeating a sermon, and, because it was darkish, stood at a door or window, as a flash of lightning stunned him; but no hurt, His Bible being under his arm, the whole book of Revelation was carried away, and other parts of the Bible left untouched"; John Hull, Diary, p. 231. It may be noted that Hull did not offer a specific interpretation of the "curiosity" as an omen or prophecy. To interpret divine intentions would have been construed as a presumption.

33 Increase Mather, *Remarkable Providences*, preface.

34 Ibid.

35 For example, it would be a miracle for a tree to cry, but for a tree to fall down could be achieved either by natural causes or by a special providence, with God replacing the natural cause.

36 Joseph Glanvill, *Saducismus Triumphatus*. For a review of Glanvill's work on witchcraft, see Moody E. Prior, "Joseph Glanvill, Witchcraft, and Seventeenth-Century Science," pp. 167–92.

37 For example, Glanvill is cited in Cotton Mather, *Memorable Providences*, introduction; John Hale, *A Modest Inquiry into the Nature of Witchcraft*, p. 28.

38 This source is pointed out in James R. Jacob, " 'The Phantastick Air,' " p. 74.

39 Cotton Mather, *Wonders*, pp. 161–62. When Mather says "unlawful," he is referring to divine law rather than the laws of nature.

40 Samuel Eliot Morison, *Harvard College in the Seventeenth Century*, 1:283.

41 "Mather–Calef Paper," p. 250.

42 Increase Mather, *Remarkable Providences*, p. 88.

43 Increase Mather, *Cases of Conscience Concerning Evil Spirits*, p. 237.

44 In Levin, *What Happened in Salem?*, p. 99.

45 Richard Bernard, *Guide to Grand-Jury Men*, p. 256.
46 Ibid., p. 98.
47 Lawson, *Christ's Fidelity*, p. 77.
48 In Levin, *What Happened in Salem?*, p. 102.
49 Parris's sermon of March 27, 1962, is reprinted in Paul Boyer and Stephen Nissenbaum, *Salem Village Witchcraft*, p. 131; hereafter cited as Boyer and Nissenbaum (1).
50 Perkins, *Discourse*, pp. 41–42.
51 "Mather–Calef Paper," p. 258.
52 Bernard, *Guide to Grand-Jury Men*, p. 106.
53 Lawson, *Christ's Fidelity*, p. 25.
54 In Levin, *What Happened in Salem?*, p. 102.
55 Perkins, *Discourse*, p. 168.

4 WITCHCRAFT AND MAGIC

1 Abstracted from transcript of trial of Hugh Parsons, reprinted as appendix in Samuel G. Drake, *Annals of Witchcraft in New England*, pp. 219–58. See App. A, case 24, herein.
2 Thomas, *Religion and the Decline of Magic*, pp. 229, 437, mentions that the rise of Renaissance neo-Platonism helped to give intellectual support to these beliefs. That many of the popular beliefs can be traced back to antiquity is documented in Kittredge's *Witchcraft in Old and New England*, pp. 22–36 et passim. Also see Butler, "Magic and Religious Heritage," pp. 323–34.
3 For a discussion of specific folk practices, see Ralph Merrifield, "Witch Bottles and Magical Jugs," pp. 195–207; Katherine Briggs, "Some Seventeenth Century Books on Magic," pp. 445–62.
4 Lawson, *Christ's Fidelity*, p. 75.
5 For a discussion of method of "sieve and shears," see Kittredge, *Witchcraft in Old and New England*, pp. 198–99; for "Bible and Key" method of divination, see pp. 196–98. The "sieve and shears" was one of the simpler methods of divination: "Stick a pair of shears in the rind of a sieve and let two persons set the top of each of their forefingers upon the upper part of the shears holding it with the sieve up from the ground steadily; and ask Peter and Paul whether A, B, or C hath stolen the thing lost; and at the nomination of the guilty person the sieve will turn round" (reprinted in Thomas, *Religion and the Decline of Magic*, p. 213). The reader familiar with African divination techniques will recognize the close similarity between this formula and the African use of oracles; for example, see E. Evans-Pritchard, *Witchcraft, Oracles, and Magic among the Azande*, pp. 175–76; Middleton, *Lugbara Religion*, pp. 80–81.
6 Kittredge, *Witchcraft in Old and New England*, pp. 167, 200.
7 The depositions that mention use of this procedure are located as follows: W. Elliot Woodward, ed., *Records of the Salem Witchcraft*, 2:26–27, 160 (hereafter cited as *RSW*); Drake, *Annals*, pp. 151–52, 275–77.
8 Reported in Calef, *More Wonders*, pp. 184–85.
9 Boyer and Nissenbaum (1), p. 278.
10 For extended discussion of cunning folk in England, see Macfarlane, *Witchcraft*, pp. 115–34, and Thomas, *Religion and the Decline of Magic*, pp. 212–52 et passim. The demand for these practitioners was often so great that local clergy found it necessary to accommodate rather than oppose their village presence.

11   Cotton Mather, "Discourse on Witchcraft," in Levin, *What Happened in Salem?*, p. 99; Increase Mather, *Remarkable Providences*, p. 190.

12   For example, see *Sarah Hale* vs. *Caleb Powell, RSW*, 2:258–59; *Madgett Mirack* vs. *Elizabeth Morse*, in Drake, *Annals*, p. 287.

13   For further information on these suspected witches, see App. A, cases 4, 8, 16, 20, 24, and 31; App. B, case 7.

14   See Drake, *Annals*, pp. 281–82.

15   See App. A, case 27.

16   *RSW*, 2: 262–63.

17   This point is developed further in chapter 6.

18   Thomas, *Religion and the Decline of Magic*, pp. 250–51.

19   John Gaule, *Select Cases of Conscience*, pp. 85–86.

20   The attitude of ridicule is apparent in the remarks of Calef, *More Wonders*, p. 287, regarding the admission of such allegations as testimony: "As it is not to be supposed that such as these could Influence any Judge or Jury, so not unkindness to relations, or God's having given to one Man more strength than to some others, the over-setting of carts, or the death of Cattle . . . Much less any persons illness, or Cloaths rent when a Spectre has been well banged, much less the burning of the Mares fart, mentioned in the Tryal of [Elizabeth] How." Indeed, until recently, there has been a general tendency in the historiography of American witchcraft to approach popular beliefs disparagingly. Thus, for example, in reproducing a transcript from an early defamation suit, one local historian found it necessary to apologize to his readers: "A recital of this testimony is tedious, but it may be excused inasmuch as it shows on what frivolous grounds the charge of witchcraft was made two hundred years ago"; Lucius Paige, *History of Cambridge*, p. 357.

21   For a related approach to the differentiation of witchcraft accusations according to their meaning for the accuser, see I. M. Lewis, "A Structural Approach to Witchcraft and Spirit-Possession," in *Witchcraft Confessions and Accusations*, ed. Mary Douglas, pp. 293–311.

22   I have modernized the spelling and punctuation of both depositions in order to improve their readability.

23   *Records and Files of the Quarterly Courts of Essex County, Massachusetts, 1636–1683*, 3:6–7; hereafter cited as *EQCR*.

24   The structure of witchcraft accusations is elaborated further in chapter 6.

25   I use "her" rather than "him" because the vast majority of these victims were female.

26   Thus making it possible and plausible that multiple accusations might issue from the same victim.

27   Lawson, "Appendix to Christ's Fidelity," p. 103, included in second edition of *Christ's Fidelity*.

28   Typically, the sponsors of the bewitched were not themselves victims of malefic witchcraft.

29   As developed further in chapter 9, such interventions might also be of strategic value to the victim.

30   *RSW*, 2:266–67.

31   Ibid., pp. 169–71.

32   As suggested by John Demos, "Underlying Themes in the Witchcraft of Seventeenth-Century New England," p. 1316.

33   John Demos, *A Little Commonwealth*, p. 82.

34 For a general discussion of the legitimation of the husband's superiority, see Edmund S. Morgan, *The Puritan Family*, pp. 19–21.

35 For examples of court actions, see ibid., p. 40; for statutes on protection of wife against physical abuse, see Powers, *Crime and Punishment*, p. 542.

36 Powers, *Crime and Punishment*, p. 542.

37 For examples, see Morgan, *Puritan Family*, p. 58; Demos, *Little Commonwealth*, pp. 85–86.

38 For a general discussion of the greater matrimonial benefits for the wife in New England than in England, see Richard B. Morris, *Studies in the History of American Law*, chap. 3.

39 Morgan, *Puritan Family*, pp. 74–78.

40 For further information, see App. F, cases of Sarah Churchill, Elizabeth Hubbard, Mercy Lewis, Mary Walcott, Mary Warren, and Abigail Williams.

41 See App. F, cases of John Indian, Tituba, and Sarah Vibber.

42 See App. F, cases of Bethshaa Pope and Ann Putnam, Sr.

5 THE INTERRELATIONSHIP BETWEEN POPULAR AND
THEOLOGICAL MEANINGS OF WITCHCRAFT

1 Possibly the most comprehensive statement of the differences between magic and religion is still to be found in William Goode's *Religion among the Primitives*, pp. 52–55. The question of whether magic and religion are analytically and empirically distinct has been debated in recent years by anthropologists with inconclusive results. For a review of this literature, see Dorothy Hammond, "Magic," pp. 1349–56. But there can be no doubt of the validity of this distinction in the context of early modern European history. The opposition between magic and religion was explicit in post-Reformation England and New England.

2 *Malleus*, p. 4 et passim.

3 The *Canon Episcopi*, which can be traced to approximately 906 A.D., constitutes one of the earliest attempts to formulate a coherent ecclesiastical policy against witchcraft. The text refers not to witchcraft specifically but rather to the pagan practice of a Dianic cult. For discussion of the *Canon episcopi* and text, see Russell, *Witchcraft*, pp. 75–80, 291–93.

4 Thomas, *Religion and the Decline of Magic*, p. 54.

5 Ibid., p. 365.

6 Ian Breward, ed., *The Works of William Perkins*, pp. 574–75.

7 For a discussion of the political implications of this opposition, see Perry Miller, *Orthodoxy in Massachusetts*, chap. 1.

8 Thomas, *Religion and the Decline of Magic*, p. 367.

9 Ibid.

10 Stahlman, "Astrology in Colonial America," pp. 559–60.

11 Morison, *Harvard College*, 1:214, n. 4.

12 Ibid.

13 Breward, *Works of Perkins*, pp. 6–7.

14 Calvin himself had defended the need for this uncertainty: "Let it . . . be our first principle that to desire any other knowledge of predestination than that which is expounded by the work of God, is no less infatuated than to walk where there is no path, or to seek light in darkness. Let us not be ashamed to be ignorant in a matter in which ignorance is learning"; quoted in Thomas, *Religion and the Decline of Magic*, p. 370.

15 Increase Mather, *Kometographia*, p. 17.
16 Ibid., p. 141.
17 Merton's discussion of the overlap between the value systems of Puritanism and the scientific ethos propagated by the Royal Society of London is particularly relevant to this point; see Robert K. Merton, *Science, Technology, and Society in Seventeenth-Century England*, pp. 55–79. See also Miller, *The New England Mind: Seventeenth Century*, pp. 221–23.
18 *RSW*, 1:208–12.
19 Drake, *Annals*, p. 272. Moody served as deputy to the General Court in 1677.
20 Cotton Mather, *Diary of Cotton Mather, 1681–1708*, ed. Worthington C. Ford, vols. 7 and 8, 7:163–64; hereafter cited as *Diary* (1) or *Diary* (2).
21 Lawson, *Christ's Fidelity*, p. 99.
22 Mark Van Doren, ed., *Samuel Sewall's Diary*, pp. 28–29.
23 For example, Burr, "New England's Place," p. 207.
24 Perkins, *Discourse*, p. 183.
25 Bernard, *Guide to Grand-Jury Men*, pp. 76–77.
26 George Gifford, *A Dialogue Concerning Witches and Witchcraftes*, sig. H2.
27 Increase Mather, *Remarkable Providences*, pp. 180–81.
28 Cotton Mather, *Wonders*, p. 96.
29 *EQCR*, 4:99.
30 Mather, *Diary* (1), pp. 180–81.
31 See App. A, cases 2 and 3.
32 Drake, *Annals*, pp. 275–277.
33 Perkins, *Discourse*, p. 174.
34 Bernard, *Guide to Grand-Jury Men*, p. 249.
35 Cotton Mather, "Discourse on Witchcraft," in Levin, *What Happened in Salem?* p. 97.
36 The question of what constitutes an adequate explanation for either hysteria or possession is outside the scope of the present analysis. What is relevant is how members oriented themselves to afflictions in the cultural contexts in which they arose. Thus, to understand the public response to afflictions, I have adopted the standpoint of members for whom supernatural forces constituted real objects of social action.
37 Because of this resemblance, control over the definition of afflictions became a closely guarded theological prerogative in seventeenth-century England and New England. That an authentic conversion to God might be misconstrued as demonic possession hardly troubled the clergy at all. It was the obverse error—that the unnatural signs of an affliction would be mistaken for divine inspiration—that necessitated the utmost diagnostic vigilance. For the embattled Protestant minister, the safeguarding of this prerogative served among other uses as a preventive against false prophets, even at the risk of overlooking unheralded saints.
38 Increase Mather, *A Disquisition Concerning Angelical Apparitions*, p. 3. This work was published with *Angelographia* in one volume.
39 Cotton Mather, "Discourse on the Power and Malice of Devils," p. 7; Increase Mather, *Disquisition*, p. 20.
40 The interchangeability between possessions and divine visitations is well illustrated by an incident that Mather relates to Calef. A young woman who claimed to have been visited by an angel began to reprimand her neighbors on advice from this spirit, but because these charges "Endangered the Peace of the Neighborhood," Mather concluded that the visiting spirit was instead a devil; "Mather–Calef Paper," p. 267.

41 Perkins, *Discourse*, p. 124.
42 Excerpted in Alden T. Vaughan, ed., *The Puritan Tradition in America*, p. 96; for further discussion of conversion experience, see Edmund S. Morgan, *Visible Saints*, pp. 69–73.
43 John Whiting, "Letter of John Whiting to Increase Mather," p. 467.
44 Burr, *Narratives*, p. 275.
45 From Samuel Willard's narrative of the case of Elizabeth Knapp, in Samuel A. Green, *Groton in the Witchcraft Times*, p. 17.
46 A demographic profile of these victims is provided in chapter 4.
47 Kittredge, *Witchcraft in Old and New England*, pp. 322–23.
48 John Cotta, *The Tryall of Witchcraft*, pp. 70–76.
49 Meric Casaubon, *A Treatise Concerning Enthusiasme*, p. 23.
50 In this light, it is interesting that the first and only reference to Casaubon's treatise by a New England minister did not appear until after the Salem trials, in Increase Mather's *Angelographia*, p. 18.
51 Green, *Groton in Witchcraft Times*, p. 10.
52 Ibid., p. 11.
53 Ibid., p. 16.
54 Reprinted in Burr, *Narratives*, p. 95. It is noteworthy that Samuel Willard was one of the four signatories. On questions of doctrine, Willard and Mather were in public agreement. The differences between the two men occurred within the framework of shared beliefs. Both acknowledged the immediacy of Satan and the need to impose strong sanctions against those who had allied themselves with Satan. Moreover, both perceived in the affliction a communication of providential design.
55 Mather's narrative on the affliction of Margaret Rule was published in Calef, *More Wonders*. Quote is from Burr, *Narratives*, p. 312.
56 Mather was also one of the very few ministers against whom threats of malefic witchcraft were directed. His considerable receptivity to popular beliefs collapsed status boundaries as well as boundaries between competing cosmologies. Ordinarily, ministers and other members of the gentry were immune from such forms of retaliation; see entry for March 28, 1693, in Mather, *Diary* (1), pp. 163–64.
57 Whiting, "Letter," p. 467.
58 In this light, it is interesting to discover that one of the afflicted girls, whom King James exposed as an impostor in 1602, later confessed that she had acted on instructions from her father. According to her testimony, he desired to discredit a woman in her neighborhood with whom he had once had an argument; reported in Kittredge, *Witchcraft in Old and New England*, p. 322.
59 Green, *Groton in Witchcraft Times*, p. 6, quoting Willard's sermon, *Useful Instructions*.
60 Ibid.
61 Lawson, *Christ's Fidelity*, p. 53.
62 For example, the four signatories to Mather's narrative of the Goodwin children attested to the preternatural significance of the afflictions but mentioned nothing about witchcraft.
63 Green, *Groton in Witchcraft Times*, p. 8.
64 Burr, *Narratives*, p. 183.
65 Samuel Willard, *Some Miscellany Observations on Our Present Debates Respecting Witchcraft: A Dialogue between S. and B.* This work was originally published under the pseudonym "P.E. and J.A." The initials refer to Philip English and John Alden, two prominent fugitives from the law during the Salem trials.

Eventually, this short treatise was included in Willard's *Body of Divinity*, a posthumous collection of his complete works published in 1726.

66 Burr, *Narratives*, p. 274.
67 Ibid., p. 311.
68 Cotton Mather, *Magnalia*, 1:205; Burr, *Narratives*, pp. 389, 390.
69 Burr, *Narratives*, pp. 128-29.
70 For an extended discussion of the decline of rituals of exorcism, see Thomas, *Religion and the Decline of Magic*, pp. 477-92.
71 Perkins, *Discourse*, p. 232.
72 Green, *Groton in Witchcraft Times*, p. 20.
73 Burr, *Narratives*, p. 276.
74 Ibid., p. 318.
75 There are many examples of this vicious cycle during the Salem trials. One witness against Susanna Martin claimed to have been subsequently attacked by a large cat while he was sleeping; see *RSW*, 1:226-27.
76 For example, there are indications that the notorious method of "swimming the witch" was applied to at least three suspects during this period. This practice rested on the belief that water would repel the body of a witch; if the suspect successfully floated above the water, he or she was guilty, but if the suspect sank below the surface, he or she was innocent. For evidence of the use of this test, see Charles Hoadly, "A Case of Witchcraft in Hartford," pp. 557-61.

6 THE IDENTIFICATION OF THE MALEFIC WITCH

1 Most notably, the works of Alan Macfarlane (*Witchcraft in Tudor and Stuart England*), and Keith Thomas (*Religion and the Decline of Magic*). For a review of their contribution, see Lucy Mair, "Witchcraft," pp. 109-16.
2 See App. A, cases 5a-c and 31.
3 See App. A, cases 12 and 13.
4 See App. A, cases 21 and 30.
5 For some examples of hard financial bargaining between widows and widowers, see Morgan, *Puritan Family*, pp. 58-59.
6 For supporting documentation, see App. A, case 25; App. B, case 12.
7 See App. B, case 11; App. C, case of Susanna Martin.
8 John Winthrop, *The History of New England, 1630-1649*, ed. James Savage, 1:321, 330; 2:35, 32.
9 Ibid., 2:31, 36.
10 William Hubbard, *A General History of New England from the Discovery to 1680*, ed. William T. Harris, p. 575.
11 The transcript of Ann Hibbins's excommunication is reprinted in John Demos, ed., *Remarkable Providences, 1600-1760*, pp. 221-39.
12 See App. A, cases 11a, 11b. For an extended discussion of this case, see John Demos, "John Godfrey and His Neighbors," pp. 242-65.
13 See App. A, case 24.
14 Massachusetts Archives, vol. 135, doc. 18.
15 See App. A, cases 4, 5a-c, 10, 21, 30; App. B, case 7.
16 See App. A, case 8. This is John Godfrey of Hampton as distinguished from John Godfrey, the suspected witch.
17 See App. A, case 30.

18 For historical background on New England poor relief, I have relied primarily upon Stephen Foster, *Their Solitary Way*, pp. 134–52.

19 Ibid., p. 136.

20 Ibid., pp. 139–40.

21 Ibid., p. 137. This interpretation differs from that offered by Foster. I have attempted to show that low rates of taxation in the New England colonies were indications not of lack of poverty but rather of public policy toward the poor.

22 Robert Kelso, *The History of Public Poor Relief in Massachusetts, 1620–1920*, chap. 3.

23 Ibid., p. 35.

24 Josiah Henry Benton, *Warning Out in New England*, pp. 41–42.

25 Ibid., pp. 27–28.

26 See Kelso, *Public Poor Relief*, pp. 38–39, for examples.

27 Benton, *Warning Out*, pp. 19–39 et passim; Foster, *Their Solitary Way*, p. 141.

28 Benton, *Warning Out*, pp. 51–56.

29 Foster, *Their Solitary Way*, pp. 142–43, n. 48.

30 Kelso, *Public Poor Relief*, pp. 94–95.

31 See App. A, case 5a–c.

32 Kelso, *Public Poor Relief*, p. 102.

33 John Winthrop's "Modell of Christian Charity," a lay sermon delivered in midvoyage aboard the *Arbella*, well illustrates the early colonial emphasis upon organic unity. In this impassioned oration, the organic analogue of the body politic was invoked to define the desired relationship between members; see *Winthrop Papers*, 2:282–95.

34 For a brief profile of demographic characteristics of the first generation, see Demos, *Remarkable Providences*, intro., pp. 6–7; for a more detailed and extended statement, see T. H. Breen and Stephen Foster, "Moving to the New World," pp. 187–221.

35 For a discussion of political harmony in Dedham, see Kenneth Lockridge, *A New England Town*, chap. 3; for Hingham, see John J. Waters, "Hingham, Massachusetts, 1631–1661," pp. 352–70.

36 Lockridge, *New England Town*, p. 42.

37 Kenneth Lockridge and A. Krieder, "The Evolution of Massachusetts Town Government, 1640–1740," p. 574, table 2.

38 For example, in Dedham, only 3,000 acres out of a huge allotment of nearly 200 square miles were parceled out in the first twenty years; see Lockridge, *New England Town*, p. 12. In Sudbury, 89 percent of the total plot remained under public control after first allotment; see Sumner Powell, *Puritan Village*, p. 94.

39 Darrett B. Rutman, *Winthrop's Boston*, especially chap. 9.

40 For examples of village partitioning, see Lockridge, *New England Town*, p. 12. A more important example for the present investigation is the conflict between Salem Village and Salem Town discussed in Paul Boyer and Stephen Nissenbaum, *Salem Possessed*, especially pp. 80–109; hereafter cited as Boyer and Nissenbaum (2). The relationship between this town-village schism and the pattern of witchcraft accusations during the Salem trials will be explored further in chapters 8 and 9.

41 Lockridge and Krieder, "Evolution of Town Government," pp. 572–74 et passim.

42 Lockridge, *New England Town*, pp. 82–83, 125; Powell, *Puritan Village*, p. 91.

43 For Dedham litigation, see Edward Cook, "Social Behavior and Changing

Values in Dedham, Massachusetts, 1700–1775," pp. 573–74. Also see David Thomas Konig, *Law and Society in Puritan Massachusetts*. Konig makes the salutary point that neither the declining prospects for unanimity among colonial villagers nor the increase in litigation should be equated with social disorder. The growing reliance on courts to resolve conflict should instead be construed as part of a realignment of institutions to meet altered political and economic realities. In the present investigation, while it may be the case that the courts functioned as sources of social cohesion, it is also argued that the use of formal litigation grew because the inhabitants began to transact less as neighbors than as strangers.

44 Powell, *Puritan Village*, p. 108.

45 Lockridge, *New England Town*, p. 85.

46 John Murrin, "Review Essay," pp. 250–51.

47 The dependent and the witch are both referred to as "she" because the preponderance of dependents and suspects discussed in this chapter were women.

48 See App. A, case 27.

49 See App. A, cases 2 and 3.

50 *EQCR*, 4:99.

51 See App. A, cases 4, 16, 21; App. B, case 7.

52 See App. A, cases 5a–c.

53 See App. A, cases 11a, b.

54 See App. A, case 24.

55 *EQCR*, 4:90; *EQCR*, 6:386.

56 For the charge of witchcraft, see App. B, case 11; for the other charge, see *EQCR*, 4:189.

57 See App. A, case 31.

58 Winthrop, *History of New England*, 2:344–45.

59 *EQCR*, 4:129.

60 See App. B, case 5c.

61 See App. B, case 12.

62 See App. B, case 9b.

63 For a brief discussion of Hooker's viewpoint, see Rutman, *Winthrop's Boston*, p. 218.

64 Levin, *What Happened in Salem?*, p. 102.

65 See App. A, case 31.

66 William Poole, "Witchcraft in Boston," p. 141.

67 See App. A, case 21.

68 See App. A, case 24.

69 See App. C, case of Rachel Clinton.

70 See App. A, case 24. Also Thomas, *Religion and the Decline of Magic*, pp. 557–58, for illustrations drawn from English court records.

71 Ibid., pp. 560–67; Macfarlane, *Witchcraft*, pp. 186–88.

72 See App. A, cases 6 and 19.

73 See App. A, cases 2, 3, and 7.

74 See App. A, case 25.

75 As applied in both chapters 5 and 6, the process of signification refers to the social processes by which members decide which of several possible meanings will be assigned to an event, sign, or set of circumstances.

76 See App. A, case 24.

77 See App. B, cases 7 and 12.

78 This type of petition may be seen as a prototype of the petition that would circulate during the Salem trials.

7   THE OFFICIAL RESPONSE TO POPULAR DEMANDS

1   Essentially, the churches and the courts were structurally distinct but functionally interdependent. According to a synod held in Cambridge, "As it is unlawful for the church-officers to meddle with the Sword of the Magistrates, so it is unlawful for the magistrate to meddle with the work proper to church officers"; quoted in Powers, *Crime and Punishment,* p. 107. At the same time, the courts were the fierce defenders of the church. According to the "Body of Liberties" of 1641, the first code of laws to be enacted in the colony, "Civil Authoritie hath power and libertie to see the peace, ordinances and Rules of Christ observed in every church according to his work, so it be done in a Civill and not in an Ecclesiastical Way"; "The Body of Liberties, 1641," in William H. Whitmore, *A Bibliographical Sketch of the Laws of the Massachusetts Colony from 1630 to 1686,* art. 58 (hereafter cited as "Body of Liberties").
2   The discussion of execution sermons is indebted to the rich descriptions provided in Cotton Mather's *Pillars of Salt.* The colonial recipe for bringing the capital offender to the point of public penitence fits nicely into the general model of status demotion developed by Harold Garfinkel in "Conditions of Successful Degradation Ceremonies," pp. 420–24.
3   Mather, *Pillars of Salt,* pp. 68–71.
4   Ibid., pp. 60–62.
5   Burr, *Narratives,* pp. 135–36.
6   Torture was in fact authorized in colonial law but only under special conditions: "No man shall be forced by Torture to confesse any Crime against himselfe nor any other unlesse it be in some Capitall case, where he first fullie convicted by clear and sufficcint evidence to be guilty. After which if the cause be of that nature, That it is very apparent there be other conspirators or confederates with him, Then he may be tortured, yet not with such Tortures as be Barbarous and inhumane"; in "Body of Liberties," art. 45. This provision may well have furnished the legal justification for torture during the Salem trials; see chapter 9, below.
7   Macfarlane, *Witchcraft,* p. 20; Thomas, *Religion and the Decline of Magic,* p. 518.
8   The figure of seventy indictments includes the total cases in Massachusetts and Connecticut before 1692.
9   Thomas, *Religion and the Decline of Magic,* p. 460.
10   Possibly the most influential guide, following those of Perkins and Bernard, was Robert Filmer's *Advertisement to the Jurymen of England.* Filmer dispensed with presumptions altogether but maintained Perkins's recommendations for convictions. Keble's work was published in two editions in 1683 and 1689. For a discussion of the sequence of English guides, see Burr, *Narratives,* p. 163, n. 2.
11   Perkins, *Discourse,* p. 213.
12   Bernard, *Guide to Grand-Jury Men,* pp. 212–21.
13   Ibid., pp. 200–11.
14   Perkins, *Discourse,* p. 204.
15   This evidence was included among presumptions by Perkins and Bernard.

16 Bernard, *Guide to Grand-Jury Men*, pp. 223–24.
17 Perkins, *Discourse*, p. 204; Bernard, *Guide to Grand-Jury Men*, p. 234.
18 Michael Dalton, *Countrey Justice*, p. 273.
19 Among the pre-Salem suspects in Massachusetts, the following were searched for witch's marks: Mary Glover, Ann Hibbins, Margaret Jones, Hugh Parsons, Mary Parsons, and Mary Webster. See App. A for further information on these cases. For the use of this test in Salem trials, see chapter 9.
20 See App. A, case 31.
21 For a brief discussion of the response of medical authorities in England, see Thomas, *Religion and the Decline of Magic*, pp. 535–37. Thomas Ady bluntly maintained that explanations of misfortune in terms of witchcraft served as "a cloak for a physician's ignorance"; Thomas Ady, *A Candle in the Dark*, p. 115.
22 For a discussion of William Harvey's probable skepticism, see Notestein, *History*, pp. 160–63. I am indebted to Sanford Fox's provocative work, *Science and Justice*, pp. 88–89, for this example.
23 Matthew Hopkins, *The Discovery of Witches*, ed. Montague Summers, p. 53.
24 Ibid., p. 52. To further reduce the possibility of error in detection, Hopkins claimed to have employed a dozen examiners for each of the cases.
25 It may occur to the reader to ask where the colonial physician was during the witchcraft trials. In point of fact, what few skilled medical practitioners there were in seventeenth-century New England tended to belong to the clergy rather than to the medical profession. Indeed, the eminent medical historian Richard Shryock has argued convincingly that Cotton Mather himself was without peer in medical expertise in New England for most of his life. See Otho Beall, Jr., and Richard H. Shryock, *Cotton Mather*.
    Certainly, the notes from the medical ledger of Zerubabel Endicott, a seventeenth-century Salem physician, suggest that the gap in learning between midwives and bona fide doctors may have been quite small. For example, Endicott proposed as a remedy for a distracted woman: "take milk of a Nurce that gives such to a male child and also take a hee Catt and a Cut of one of his Ears of a peece of it and Lett it blede into the milk and then Lett the sick woman Drink it doe this three Times." It is unlikely that the substitution of Endicott for a skilled folk healer in the examinations for witch's marks would have significantly altered the findings. Endicott's recipe is quoted in George Francis Dow, *Everyday Life in the Massachusetts Bay Colony*, pp. 183–84.
26 "Witchcraft Records Relating to Topsfield," pp. 52–53.
27 *Records of the Colony or Jurisdiction of New Haven, from May 1653 to the Union*, ed. C. J. Hoadly, p. 77.
28 "Witchcraft Records Relating to Topsfield," p. 56.
29 The decision of the Connecticut magistrates is reprinted in John Taylor, *The Witchcraft Delusion in Colonial Connecticut*, p. 75.
30 Hopkins, *The Discovery of Witches*, p. 54.
31 See App. A, case 16.
32 Increase Mather, *Remarkable Providences*, pp. 201–5.
33 Taylor, *Witchcraft Delusion*, p. 41.
34 Ibid.
35 Burr, *Narratives*, p. 21. Increase Mather reported the use of the water test in 1662 on William Ayres and his wife to determine whether they were responsible for the affliction of Ann Cole. The test confirmed guilt in both cases although the Ayreses managed to leave the colony before legal reprisal.

36 The ordeal by touch was also applied to Goodwife Ayres after the death of Elizabeth Kelley. For discussion, see Charles J. Hoadly, "Some Early Post-Mortem Examinations in New England," p. 213.

37 See App. A, cases 16 and 17.

38 Reported in Joseph A. Smith, ed., *Colonial Justice in Western Massachusetts, 1639–1702*, p. 22.

39 Ibid., p. 23.

40 See App. A, case 13.

41 Quoted in Poole, "Witchcraft in Boston," p. 139.

42 See App. A and B for five legal actions involving John Godfrey.

43 *Records of the Court of Assistants of the Colony of the Massachusetts Bay, 1630–1692*, 3:151–52; hereafter cited as *RCA*.

44 See App. A, cases 5a–c.

45 Quoted in Joseph Dow, *History of the Town of Hampton, New Hampshire*, 1:80.

46 Drake, *Annals*, p. 101.

47 See App. A, case 27.

48 C. H. Levermore, "Witchcraft in Connecticut," p. 806.

49 See Taylor, *Witchcraft Delusion*, pp. 47–61.

50 Ibid., p. 57.

51 William Bradford, *Of Plymouth Plantation, 1620–1647*, ed. Samuel Eliot Morison, app. 10, pp. 404–5 et passim. The three ministers cited Deut. 17:6: "At the mouth of two witnesses or three witnesses, shall he that is worthy of death be put to death; but at the mouth of one witness he shall not be put to death."

52 Two witness rule included in "Body of Liberties," art. 48. For further discussion of the background of this rule, see William H. McBratney, "The One-Witness Rule in Massachusetts," pp. 155–60.

53 Accusations of Joan Francis and John Graves reprinted in Taylor, *Witchcraft Delusion*, pp. 52–53.

54 Ibid., p. 58.

55 *Public Records of Connecticut*, 2:132.

56 For detailed information on expenses, see Drake, *Annals*, pp. 289–96.

57 Ibid., p. 146.

58 Massachusetts Archives, vol. 135, doc. 18, no. 2.

59 Hale, *Modest Inquiry*, pp. 22–23.

60 *RCA*, 1:190.

61 The point here is to suggest that while there was a shift in judicial policy there is little evidence of judicial inconsistency.

62 See App. A, case 10.

8 THE FRAMEWORK FOR OFFICIAL INITIATIVE

1 For reconstruction of events that immediately preceded the trials, I have relied upon Deodat Lawson, *A Brief and True Narrative of Witchcraft at Salem Village*, in Burr, Narratives, pp. 145–64, and Calef, *More Wonders*, also in Burr, *Narratives*, pp. 341–45. Calef himself drew upon Lawson's account for discussion of early phases of trials.

2 For a list of legal actions against witchcraft during the Salem prosecutions, see App. C.

3 Records of decisions of the Superior Court of Judicature are reprinted in

"Some Documentary Fragments Touching the Witchcraft Episode of 1692," pp. 23–26.

4 Probably the two most famous literary works to make use of the Salem prosecutions are still Nathaniel Hawthorne's *House of Seven Gables* of 1851 and Arthur Miller's play, *The Crucible*, of 1953. Since 1950 alone, however, the Salem witchcrafts of 1692 have provided the setting for at least four other plays: James L. Bray, *To Burn a Witch* (1963); L. Phelps, *The Gospel Witch* (Cambridge: Harvard University Press, 1955); William Carlos Williams, "Tituba's Children," in *Many Loves and Other Plays* (New York: New Directions, 1971), pp. 225–300; and John W. Zorn, *The Witch's Sabbath* (1966).

5 The quotation is taken from Miller, *The New England Mind: From Colony to Province*, p. 21, but Miller discusses the idea more fully in *The New England Mind: Seventeenth Century*, chaps. 14 and 16.

6 See Winthrop, "Modell of Christian Charity," in *Winthrop Papers*, 2:282–95.

7 Miller, *The New England Mind: From Colony to Province*, p. 28.

8 Ibid., p. 29.

9 Ibid., p. 28.

10 Ibid., p. 173.

11 For a useful historical summary of the intercharter period, see Richard Dunn, *Puritans and Yankees*, pp. 212–57.

12 Powers, *Crime and Punishment*, p. 68.

13 For a discussion of Andros's activities in New England between 1686 and 1689, see Dunn, *Puritans and Yankees*, pp. 238–51.

14 The incident is reported in Wertenbaker, *Puritan Oligarchy*, pp. 246–49.

15 Ibid., p. 249.

16 Powers, *Crime and Punishment*, p. 69; Dunn, *Puritans and Yankees*, pp. 255–56.

17 For an analysis of political and ecclesiastical response to the new charter, see Susan B. Reed, "Church and State in Massachusetts, 1691–1740," pp. 480–85, 644–45, et passim.

18 For a discussion of the French and Indian War during the period of the Salem trials, I have drawn primarily upon Philip S. Haffenden, *New England in the English Nation, 1689–1713*, pp. 72–119.

19 Ibid., pp. 100–101.

20 Drake, *Annals*, p. 201.

21 Burr, *Narratives*, p. 282.

22 Cotton Mather, "Discourse on the Power and Malice of Devils," p. 19.

23 Haffenden, *New England*, p. 147.

24 Ibid., p. 146.

25 Joshua Scottow, *Narrative of the Planting*, p. 3.

26 Lawson, "Appendix to Christ's Fidelity," p. 99.

27 Lawson, *Christ's Fidelity*, p. 29.

28 Ibid., p. 86.

29 Ibid., p. 71.

30 Ibid., p. lv.

31 For an extended analysis of the schism, see Boyer and Nissenbaum (2), pp. 80–109 et passim.

32 Some questions regarding the extent of correspondence between the membership in the two factions and the form of participation are raised in the following chapter.

33 For my discussion of Parris's sermons, I have profited from the interpretation contained in Boyer and Nissenbaum (2), pp. 153–78.

34 Transcript of sermon included in Boyer and Nissenbaum (1), p. 130. The title is an allusion to John 6:70: "Have I not chosen you twelve, and one of you is a devil?"

35 Burr, *Narratives*, p. 162.

36 Ibid., p. 346.

37 Charles B. Rice, *History of the First Parish at Salem Village*, p. 42.

38 Boyer and Nissenbaum (1), p. 132.

39 Ibid., p. 134.

40 Ibid., p. 133.

41 Ibid., p. 132.

42 Cotton Mather, *Wonders*, pp. 74–75.

43 Ibid., p. 10.

44 Ibid., pp. 14, 44.

45 Ibid., p. 69.

46 Ibid., p. 63.

47 Ibid., p. 74.

9 THE DISCOVERY OF CONSPIRACY

1 Parris presented himself as a sponsor of the afflicted in six cases, as computed from "Salem Witchcraft, 1692," verbatim transcripts of Salem Witchcraft Papers, vols. 1, 2, and 3; hereafter cited as SWP.

2 Bridget Bishop, Dorcas Hoar, and Sarah Wilds. See *RSW*, 1:153–57, 2:245–48; and "Witchcraft Records Relating to Topsfield," pp. 91, 92.

3 Burr, *Narratives*, pp. 369, 361–62.

4 It should be mentioned that Mather's one public appearance at the trials had characteristic dramatic intensity. After a moving speech by one of the convicted witches just before his execution on August 19, 1692, Mather apparently proceeded ex tempore to defend the actions of the court. Later Mather acknowledged that one of his objectives in writing *Wonders of the Invisible World* was to prevent a popular insurrection against the court. It may well be that the experience of August 19 alerted him to this possibility. For an account of Mather's activities on that day, see Burr, *Narratives*, pp. 360–61.

5 Burr, Marion Starkey, and Wertenbaker are among the principal proponents of this interpretation. From this vantage point, the nonparticipation of the clergy is viewed as passive support for the court.

6 These are among the central premises contained in Lawson's *Christ's Fidelity*. The sermon was delivered on March 24, 1692, in Salem Village before an audience that included several magistrates. Six prominent ministers, including Increase Mather, Cotton Mather, and Samuel Willard, endorsed the sermon in its published form.

7 Tituba's activities are recounted by John Hale and by Lawson, both in Burr, *Narratives*, pp. 413 and 147.

8 *RSW*, 1:43.

9 See Boyer and Nissenbaum (2), pp. 203–4, for further information on Good's background.

10 *RSW*, 1:19, 24–29, et passim.

11   Boyer and Nissenbaum (2), pp. 193–94; *RSW*, 1:19.
12   *RSW*, 1:58.
13   Boyer and Nissenbaum (2), p. 146; see also Sidney Perley, *The History of Salem, Massachusetts*, 1:193, and 3:292.
14   Boyer and Nissenbaum (2), pp. 152–54.
15   Ibid., p. 34; SWP, vol. 2.
16   Boyer and Nissenbaum (1), pp. 21–22; *RSW*, 1:83.
17   SWP, vol. 1.
18   Ibid., vol. 2; from William Good's petition for reparation.
19   *RSW*, 1:140–46 ff.
20   Boyer and Nissenbaum (2), p. 56; Boyer and Nissenbaum (1), pp. 174–79.
21   *RSW*, 2:114.
22   Ibid., p. 110, for responses of the afflicted; pp. 119–20, for reports of extraordinary strength.
23   Hale's testimony is recorded in ibid., 1:245–48.
24   Ibid., 2:104–5.
25   Ibid., pp. 66–68. In his testimony in her behalf, Dane reported, "That there was suspicion of Goodwife Carrier among some of us before she was apprehended, I know."
26   Boyer and Nissenbaum (2), pp. 202–3, for background.
27   *EQCR*, 3:458, 4:425, 6:384, 7:100.
28   Upham, *Salem Witchcraft*, 2:185–86, for background.
29   *RSW*, 2:15–16.
30   Ibid., pp. 166–71.
31   Ibid., pp. 80–94; Mather, *Wonders*, p. 150.
32   Those suspects against whom popular allegations were directed are indicated in App. C.
33   These figures have been computed directly from SWD, vols. 1, 2, and 3.
34   Boyer and Nissenbaum (2), pp. 116, 182.
35   Ibid., pp. 131–32.
36   Some caution is recommended in the interpretation of these findings. For present purposes, the efforts of Boyer and Nissenbaum to relate the pattern of accusations to the dynamics of village conflict are useful insofar as the authors account for the selection of suspects in Salem Village and Salem Town who thoroughly contradicted popular expectations. At the same time, it is clear that only a small proportion of the overall distribution of legal actions can be linked to factional conflict. Even before May 31, only a minority of the suspects can be shown to have maintained direct or indirect ties with the anti-Parris group.

Moreover, even within the context of Salem Village, there are embarrassing discrepancies between the expected distribution of accusations and the actual distribution of accusations. While the afflicted accused some of the peripheral members of the anti-Parris faction as well as some of the wives of the leaders, the leaders themselves were not accused. Neither Francis Nurse nor any of the Porters or their blood relatives were ever formally charged with witchcraft.

The authors are aware of the discrepancies, and they suggest that the afflicted were inhibited from accusing the Porters through habits of deference: "it is revealing that the three Porter brothers, none of whom was accused, were all longtime Village residents who had been born to wealth and respectability, while the one member of the family who actually was accused, their brother-in-law, Daniel Andrew, was a comparative newcomer to the Village who had been born in obscurity"; Boyer and Nissenbaum (2), p. 187. This solution raises another problem, however, since the afflicted did accuse persons like English and others who may have surpassed the Porters in wealth and social prestige. To rescue their original hypothesis once again, the authors introduce another explanation: that the afflicted were constrained by habits of deference only within Salem Village (ibid., p. 188). By this time, it is already clear that, even within Salem Village and Salem Town, there were factors involved in the focusing of witchcraft accusations apart from participation in a factional dispute.

37 Burr, *Narratives*, p. 353.

38 Ibid., p. 354.

39 Massachusetts Archives, vol. 135, doc. 25.

40 Burr, *Narratives*, pp. 371-72.

41 For an estimate of population, see Philip Greven, Jr., *Four Generations*, pp. 103-4, 179.

42 SWP, vol. 1.

43 Dane's daughter-in-law, Deliverance, was also accused, most likely in September. Another daughter, Elizabeth Johnson, Sr., was accused on August 29. Regarding his granddaughter, Elizabeth Johnson, Jr., Dane conceded that she was "But simplish at best" (*RSW*, 2:68). For an account of the Dane family during the trials, see Charles M. Fuess, "Witches at Andover," p. 14.

44 Burr, *Narratives*, p. 372.

45 In Andover as well as in Salem Village, accusations tended to be directed first at the wife and then, if at all, at her husband.

46 Burr, *Narratives*, p. 372.

47 See *RSW*, 1:43-48, for Tituba's interrogation.

48 Ibid., p. 122.

49 A similar note is contained at the end of Deliverance Hobbs's examination on April 22: "All the sufferers free from affliction during her examination after once she began to confesse, tho at sundry time they were much afflicted till then" (ibid., 2:190).

50 In Andover, suspects also had an incentive to confess, and it is sometimes difficult to decide from the records who was a confessor and who was a victim of bewitchment. In general, the confessors defined the other suspects as confederates, whereas the afflicted defined the suspects as their tormentors. In several instances, however, notably in the case of Tituba and John Indian, the responses of the confessor are virtually indistinguishable from those of the afflicted.

51 The six were Sarah Vibber, Sarah Bridges, Sarah Churchill, John Indian, Tituba, and Mary Warren; see App. F.

52 Burr, *Narratives*, p. 154.

53 Ibid., p. 423. Hale noted in his *Modest Inquiry* that the "Number of afflicted by Satan dayly increased till about Fifty persons were thus vexed by the Devil." Writing some six years after the trials, the minister cited this increase as evidence that the methods of the court aggravated rather than reduced the problem of witchcraft.

54 For the accusation against Willard, see Burr, *Narratives*, p. 360. William Sargent, Samuel Sewall, and Wait Winthrop, members of the Court of Oyer and Terminer, belonged to Willard's congregation; ibid., p. 186, n. 3.

55 See Boyer and Nissenbaum (2), p. 32.

56 For the accusation against the secretary, see Hansen, *Witchcraft at Salem*, p. 205; for the accusation against Bradstreet, see Burr, *Narratives*, p. 372.

57 Burr, *Narratives*, p. 201, n. 2.

58 Ibid., p. 186. Brattle's letter of October 8 refers to a "Reverend person in Boston" who has expressed disagreement with the court. As Burr has speculated, it is almost certain the person referred to is Samuel Willard.

59 Ibid., p. 201, n. 2.

60 Ibid., p. 360.

61 Ibid., pp. 177–78, for the accusations against Thatcher, and p. 369, n. 1, for the accusation against Hale's wife.

62 Ibid., pp. 177–78.

63 Ibid., p. 373.

64 Ibid., p. 196.

65 For more information on Sewall's legal career, see Powers, *Crime and Punishment*, pp. 476 ff.

66 At least three of the magistrates had prior experience in the handling of witchcraft cases. Gedney, Richards, and Stoughton had served on the Court of Assistants during the case of Elizabeth Morse in 1681.

67 Sewall's presence along with his brother Stephen and three other members of the General Council noted in Marion Starkey, *The Devil in Massachusetts*, p. 91.

68 For an example of the evidences collected for purposes of prosecution, see *RSW*, 1:274.

69 Burr, *Narratives*, p. 170; Lawson, "Appendix to Christ's Fidelity," p. 102.

70 Lawson, "Appendix to Christ's Fidelity," pp. 102–3; Cotton Mather, *Wonders*, p. 163.

71 Burr, *Narratives*, p. 171.

72 Cotton Mather, *Selected Letters*, pp. 36, 39.

73 For materials in the case of Bridget Bishop, see *RSW*, 1:135–72. Interestingly enough, after a search for witch's marks, a panel of examiners declared Bridget "in a clear and free state from any praeternatural excrescence" (ibid., p. 147).

74 Boyer and Nissenbaum (1), p. 118.

75 Burr, *Narratives*, p. 184.

76 The cross-pressures that were experienced by Mather were also experienced by his fellow ministers. Mather's ambivalent response is notable only because it was expressed so openly. The other ministers who signed the "Return of Several Ministers Consulted" were caught in the same predicament of how to challenge the policies of the court and yet not discredit the men who had formulated those policies.

In this context, Mather's strategy of "damning the act while praising the doer" may be more fully appreciated. For example, in his letter to John Foster of August 17, Mather began with a note of caution on the use of spectral evidence: "I do still think that when there is not further evidence against a person but only this, that a specter in their shape does afflict a neighbor, that evidence is not enough to convict the [word missing] of witchcraft" (Cotton Mather, *Selected Letters*, p. 41). These doubts were then followed with lavish praise for the magistrates: "And our honorable judges are so eminent for their justice, wisdom, and goodness, that whatever their own particular sense may be, yet they will not proceed capitally against any, upon a principle contested with great odds on the other side in the learned and godly world" (ibid.).

Unfortunately for Mather, the magistrates appear to have accepted his praise but not to have responded to his recommendations to disqualify or deemphasize spectral evidence. And, also unhappily, a number of his contemporaries, most notably Robert Calef, assumed that because he supported the authority of the magistrates he endorsed their policies as well.

In later writings, particularly in *Wonders of the Invisible World*, it may well be that Mather himself could no longer sustain the delicate balance between deference to judicial authority and dissent from judicial policy. In his attempt to justify the executions as fully warranted by the evidence and in his failure to mention the judicial reliance on spectral evidence, it is not unfair to suggest that he had become a victim of his own strategy, that, in fact, he had become an apologist for decisions that in previous communications he had deplored.

77 Cotton Mather, *Selected Letters*, p. 36.
78 Burr, *Narratives*, p. 359.
79 Ibid., p. 350.
80 That this test as well as the test for witch's marks could only incriminate the suspect but never clear the suspect further demonstrates the judicial predisposition toward conviction. A successful rendering of the Lord's Prayer did not establish the suspect's innocence.
81 Burr, *Narratives*, p. 351.
82 Ibid., p. 363.
83 Ibid., p. 358.
84 See App. D for dates of confessions.
85 Cotton Mather, *Selected Letters*, p. 40.
86 Other benefits conferred on confessors were the removal of leg fetters and confinement in prison rather than in the dungeon.
87 In addition, one of the condemned persons escaped prison just before her scheduled execution, and another was reprieved because of her pregnancy.
88 See Burr, *Narratives*, pp. 177, 366–68; *RSW*, 2.148–50.
89 Burr, *Narratives*, p. 364, n. 2.
90 See *SWP*, vol. 2, for petition of September 21 to Gov. Phips for stay of execution, signed by John Hale, Nicholas Noyes, Daniel Epes, and John Emerson, Jr.
91 Burr, *Narratives*, p. 375.
92 "Recantation of Confessors of Witchcraft," p. 224.
93 Burr, *Narratives*, p. 368.
94 Cotton Mather, *Selected Letters*, p. 40.
95 Burr, *Narratives*, pp. 374, 188, 424.
96 Ibid., p. 181.
97 For example, see *RSW*, 2:130.

10   THE INVISIBLE WORLD AT THE VANISHING POINT

1   *RSW*, 1:188–89.
2   Ibid., 2:76–78.
3   Boyer and Nissenbaum (1), p. 34.
4   *RSW*, 1:72, 73, 115.
5   Ibid., p. 72.
6   Ibid., 2:172.
7   Burr, *Narratives*, p. 366.
8   "Some Documentary Fragments," pp. 17–20.
9   Burr, *Narratives*, p. 355.
10 Ibid., p. 352.
11 For information on other escapes, see ibid., pp. 352–55, 370. Perhaps the most

unusual escape of all was that of Elizabeth Colson, as reported by the sheriff who attempted to arrest her: "I sett my dog at her, and he ran round about her, but would not touch her, and runing litle further there was a stone wall and on ye other side of it a few bushes that tooke my sight from her a litle, being but litle behind her and when I came up to said Bushes I lookt into them, and Could see no thing of her, and running on further there was great Cat running towards me." The outcome of the chase was that the cat and suspect disappeared ("Some Documentary Fragments," p. 15).

12 George H. Moore, "Notes on the Bibliography of Witchcraft in Massachusetts," pp. 246–47.

13 Burr, *Narratives*, pp. 360–61.

14 Massachusetts Archives, vol. 135, doc. 59.

15 Ibid., doc. 61.

16 "Recantation of Confessors of Witchcraft," pp. 221–25.

17 George H. Moore, "Notes on the History of Witchcraft in Massachusetts," p. 172.

18 Quoted in ibid., p. 173.

19 Ibid.

20 Burr, *Narratives*, p. 200.

21 Ibid., pp. 178–79.

22 "Reply of the Dutch and French Ministers of the Province of New York," pp. 353–58.

23 Burr, *Narratives*, p. 190.

24 Ibid., p. 197. Phips complained in his letter of October 12 that "the Persons who have soe ill improvement of these matters are seeking to turne it all upon me."

25 Ibid.

26 Ibid., p. 382.

27 Ibid.

28 For records and summary of proceedings of this court, see "Some Documentary Fragments," pp. 23–26.

29 Burr, *Narratives*, p. 201.

30 Ibid.

31 Ibid., p. 422.

32 Cotton Mather, *Selected Letters*, p. 45.

33 Ibid., p. 46. "Moses and Aaron" refers to magistrates and ministers.

34 For background on production of Mather's treatise, see Burr, *Narratives*, pp. 209–10, n. 2.

35 For example, Mather wrote that the testimonies of the bewitched had been treated merely as preliminary suspicions in the trial of George Burroughs. It was on the basis of other evidences, such as the accusation of a confessed witch and reports concerning his prodigious strength, that a verdict of guilty was returned; Cotton Mather, *Wonders*, pp. 121, 124. Similarly, according to Mather, spectral evidence was used only to justify further investigation in the case of Susanna Martin: "The Court accounted themselves alarum'd by these things [the torments of the afflicted] to enquire further into the Conversation of the Prisoner"; ibid., p. 140.

36 Ibid., p. 255.

37 Ibid., p. 288.

38 Boyer and Nissenbaum (2), p. 70.

39 Ibid., p. 71.

40 Boyer and Nissenbaum (1), p. 307.
41 Boyer and Nissenbaum (2), p. 75. By this time, even Increase Mather had recommended that Parris be removed.
42 Ibid.
43 Ibid., p. 78.
44 Boyer and Nissenbaum (1), p. 298.
45 Ibid.
46 Ibid.
47 Boyer and Nissenbaum (2), p. 73.
48 As mentioned in the various proposals for a Day of Humiliation.
49 Moore, "Notes on the History of Witchcraft," p. 173.
50 Calef, *More Wonders*, pp. 96–97.
51 Moore, "Notes on the History of Witchcraft," pp. 174–75.
52 On the debate over the proposal, Sewall noted: "I doe not know that ever I saw the Council run upon with such a height of rage before." For information on the debate, see ibid., pp. 177–78.
53 Burr, *Narratives*, pp. 386–87, n. 2.
54 Ibid., pp. 387–88.
55 Quoted in Moore, "Notes on the Bibliography of Witchcraft," p. 264.
56 Massachusetts Archives, vol. 135, doc. 109.
57 Ibid., doc. 123.
58 *Mass. Historical Society Collections*, 4th series, VIII, p. 646.
59 Massachusetts Archives, vol. 135, doc. 125, 126.
60 Copy of reversal of attainder included in *RSW*, 2:216–18.
61 Notice and payments and acknowledgments of receipt included in *RSW*, 2: 219–32.
62 Included with Cotton Mather's *Wonders*, pp. 255 ff.
63 Ibid., p. 258 ff.
64 Ibid., p. 283.
65 Ibid., p. 285.
66 Burr, *Narratives*, p. 389.
67 Hale, *Modest Inquiry*, pp. 162–65.
68 Burr, *Narratives*, p. 421.
69 Hale, *Modest Inquiry*, p. 40.
70 Hale may have overestimated the involvement of the clergy in these cases; see chapter 7, above.
71 Burr, *Narratives*, p. 426.
72 Hale, *Modest Inquiry*, p. 81.
73 Ibid., p. 69.
74 Calef, *More Wonders*, pp. 92–94.
75 Interestingly, the only case in which the new rules of evidence were applied occurred in Connecticut in 1693. A young woman who had been convicted on the basis of spectral evidence, the water test, popular allegations, and positive findings in the search for witch's marks, was reprieved by the governor of the colony. Increase Mather's *Cases of Conscience* was cited as part of the justification for reversing the decision of the court. See Taylor, *Witchcraft Delusion*, pp. 62–78.
76 Burr, *Narratives*, pp. 383–84; also W. Watkins, "Mary Watkins," pp. 168–70.
77 For further discussion of survivals of folk belief in witchcraft after the decline of prosecutions, see Herbert Leventhal, *In the Shadow of the Enlightenment*, pp. 66–125.

78 Turell, "Detection of Witchcraft," pp. 10–11.
79 Taylor, *Witchcraft Delusion*, p. 155.
80 With regard to one of the afflicted, Turell wrote: "This little girl had observed what sort of treatment her sisters had met with during their disorders, viz., they seemed to be more the object of their parents' care and love, as well as pity, than ever . . . and, accordingly, she feigned herself afflicted, said and acted as they did, to the very last, without being found out"; Turell, "Detection of Witchcraft," p. 15.

11 WITCHCRAFT IN HISTORICAL AND SOCIOLOGICAL PERSPECTIVE

1 Burr, *Narratives*, p. 420. See also confession of Mary Toothaker, *SWP*, vol. 3.
2 I have drawn upon R. G. Willis, "Kamcape: An Anti-Sorcery Movement in South-West Tanzania," pp. 1–15, and "Instant Millennium" by the same author in *Witchcraft Confessions and Accusations*, pp. 129–39 for a general characterization of witch-cleansing or witch-finding movements.
3 Bernard, *Guide to Grand-Jury Men*, pp. 76–79.

Bibliography

Note: The titles in this list include all references cited in the text as well as a few others that merit acknowledgment because of their general importance as background sources. The list is divided into primary and secondary sources. In turn, primary sources have been subdivided into official records and authored writings, respectively. Secondary sources include the many works by historians, sociologists, and anthropologists that were incorporated into the text.

PRIMARY SOURCES

Published and Unpublished Official Records

Documents and Records Relating to the Province of New Hampshire. Vol. I, "Provincial Papers, 1623-1686," ed. Nathaniel Bouton. Concord, 1867.

Massachusetts Archives, Boston. Vol. 135, *Witchcraft, 1656 to 1750.*

New Haven Town Records, 1649-1684. 2 vols. Ed. Franklin Bowditch Dexter. New Haven: Printed for the New Haven Colony Historical Society, 1917-19.

Probate Records of Essex County, Massachusetts, 1635-81. 3 vols. Salem, 1916-20.

Public Records of the Colony of Connecticut. Hartford. Vol. 1, ed. J. Hammond Trumbull. Hartford, 1850.

Records and Files of the Quarterly Courts of Essex County, Massachusetts, 1636-1683. 8 vols. Salem, 1911-21.

Records of the Colony or Jurisdiction of New Haven, from May 1653 to the Union. Ed. C. J. Hoadly. Hartford: Case Lockwood & Co., 1858.

Records of the Court of Assistants of the Colony of the Massachusetts Bay, 1630-1692. 3 vols. Boston: Printed under the supervision of John Noble, 1901-28.

Records of the Governor and Company of the Massachusetts Bay in New England, 1626-1686. 5 vols. Ed. Nathaniel Shurtleff. Boston, 1853-54.

Records of the Particular Court of Connecticut, 1639-1663. Hartford: Connecticut Historical Society, 1928.

"Salem Witchcraft, 1692." 3 vols. Verbatim transcripts of Salem Witchcraft Papers, compiled under the supervision of Archie N. Frost, Clerk of Courts. 1938. Copies are located in the library of the Essex Institute.

Smith, Joseph A., ed. *Colonial Justice in Western Massachusetts, 1639-1702: The Pynchon Court Record.* Cambridge, Mass., 1961.

"Some Documentary Fragments Touching the Witchcraft Episode of 1692." *Publications of the Colonial Society of Massachusetts* 10 (1904):12–27.

Whitmore, William H., ed. *The Colonial Laws of Massachusetts*. Boston: City Council, 1889.

"Witchcraft Records Relating to Topsfield." Topsfield Historical Society, *Historical Collections* 13 (1908):39–142.

Woodward, W. Elliot, ed. *Records of the Salem Witchcraft*. 2 vols. Roxbury, 1864.

Narratives, Texts, Sermons, and Other Primary Materials

Ady, Thomas. *A Candle in the Dark*. London, 1656.

Bernard, Richard. *Guide to Grand-Jury Men*, 2nd ed. London, 1629.

Bradford, William. *Of Plymouth Plantation, 1620–1647*. Ed. Samuel Eliot Morison. New York: Alfred Knopf, 1952.

Brattle, Thomas. Letter, 1692. Reprinted in G. Lincoln Burr, *Narratives of the Witchcraft Cases*, pp. 169–90.

Calef, Robert. *More Wonders of the Invisible World*. 1700. Rpt. Salem, Mass.: Wm. Carlton, 1796.

Casaubon, Meric. *A Treatise Concerning Enthusiasme*. London, 1655.

Cotta, John. *The Tryall of Witchcraft*. London, 1616.

Dalton, Michael. *Countrey Justice*, 4th ed. London, 1630.

Filmer, Robert. *Advertisement to the Jurymen of England*. London, 1653.

Gaule, John. *Select Cases of Conscience*. London, 1646.

Gifford, George. *A Dialogue Concerning Witches and Witchcraftes*. London, 1593.

Glanvill, Joseph. *Saducismus Triumphatus*. London, 1681.

Hale, John. *A Modest Inquiry into the Nature of Witchcraft*. Boston, 1702.

Hopkins, Matthew. *The Discovery of Witches*. Ed. Montague Summers. 1647. Rpt. London: Cayne Press, 1928.

Hubbard, William. *A General History of New England from the Discovery to 1680*. Ed. William T. Harris. 1680. Rpt. Boston, 1848.

Hull, John. Diary. *Archaeologica Americana: Transactions and Collections of the American Antiquarian Society*. Vol. 3. Boston, 1857.

Johnson, Edward. The *Wonder-Working Providence of Sions. Saviour in New England*. Ed. J. Jameson. New York: Charles Scribner's Sons, 1910.

Lawson, Deodat. *A Brief and True Narrative of Witchcraft at Salem Village*. Boston, 1692.

———. *Christ's Fidelity the Only Shield against Satan's Malignity*. 2nd ed. London, 1704.

Lechford, Thomas. *Plaine Dealing; or, Newes from New-England*. London, 1642.

"Mather–Calef Paper on Witchcraft." 1695. Reprinted in *Massachusetts Historical Society Proceedings* 47 (1914):240–68.

Mather, Cotton. "A Brand Pluck'd out of the Burning." 1693. Reprinted in G. Lincoln Burr, *Narratives of the Witchcraft Cases*, pp. 259–87.

———. *Diary of Cotton Mather, 1681–1708.* Ed. Worthington C. Ford. *Massachusetts Historical Society Collections.* 7th ser. Vols. 7 and 8. Boston, 1911–12.

———. "A Discourse on the Power and Malice of Devils." In *Memorable Providences Relating to Witchcrafts and Possessions.* Boston, 1689.

———. *Discourse on Witchcraft.* Boston, 1689.

———. *Magnalia Christi Americana.* London, 1702.

———. *Memorable Providences Relating to Witchcrafts and Possessions.* Boston, 1689.

———. *Pillars of Salt.* Boston, 1699.

———. *Selected Letters of Cotton Mather.* Comp. Kenneth Silverman. Baton Rouge: Louisiana University Press, 1971.

———. *Wonders of the Invisible World.* 1693. Rpt. London: John Russell Smith, 1862.

Mather, Increase. *Angelographia.* Boston, 1696.

———. *Cases of Conscience Concerning Evil Spirits.* 1693. Rpt. London: John Russell Smith, 1862.

———. *A Disquisition Concerning Angelical Apparitions.* Boston, 1696.

———. *Kometographia.* Boston, 1683.

———. *Remarkable Providences.* 1684. Rpt. London: Reeves & Turner, 1890.

Perkins, William. *Discourse on the Damned Art of Witchcraft.* London, 1608.

Phips, Sir William. Letters to the home government, 1692–93. Reprinted in Burr, *Narratives of the Witchcraft Cases,* pp. 196–202.

"Recantation of Confessors of Witchcraft." *Massachusetts Historical Society Collections.* 2nd ser. 3:221–225.

"Reply of the Dutch and French Ministers of the Province of New York." 1692. Reprinted in *Proceedings of the Massachusetts Historical Society,* 2nd ser. 1 (1884):384–85.

Scot, Reginald. *Discoverie of Witchcraft.* 1584. Preface by H. R. Williamson. Rpt. London, 1964.

Scottow, Joshua. *Narrative of the Planting.* Boston, 1694.

Sprenger, Jacob, and Institoris, Heinrich. *Malleus Maleficarum.* Trans. and with introduction by Montague Summers. New York: Benjamin Blom, 1928.

Turell. "Detection of Witchcraft." 1728. Reprinted in Massachusetts Historical Society Collections. 2nd ser. 10 (1833):6–22.

Whiting, John. "Letter of John Whiting to Increase Mather." 1682. Rpt. Massachusetts Historical Society Collections, 4th ser. 8 (1868):466–69.

Wigglesworth, Michael. Diary. Ed. Edmund S. Morgan. *Publications of the Colonial Society of Massachusetts* 35 (1942–46).

Willard, Samuel. *Christian's Exercise against Satan's Temptation.* Boston, 1701.

———. Letter, 1679. "A briefe account of a strange and unusuall Providence of God befallen to Elizabeth Knap of Groton." Reprinted in Samuel Green, *Groton in the Witchcraft Times,* pp. 6–22.

———. *Some Miscellany Observations on Our Present Debates Respecting Witch-*

craft: A Dialogue between S. and B. Philadelphia: Printed by Wm. Bradford for Hezekiah Usher, 1692.

———. *Useful Instructions.* Boston, 1673.

Winthrop, John. *The History of New England 1630–1649.* Ed. James Savage. 2 vols. Boston, 1853.

———. "A Modell of Christian Charity." *Winthrop Papers,* 2:282–95. Boston: Massachusetts Historical Society, 1931.

SECONDARY SOURCES

Adams, James Truslow. *The Founding of New England.* Boston, 1921.

Bancroft, George. *History of the United States of America.* 6 vols. Rev. ed. New York, 1883–85.

Baroja, Julio. *The World of the Witches.* Chicago: University of Chicago Press, 1964.

Beall, Otho, Jr., and Shryock, Richard H. *Cotton Mather: First Significant Figure in American Medicine.* Baltimore: Johns Hopkins Press, 1954.

Beard, George M. *Psychology of the Salem Witchcraft Excitement of 1692.* New York, 1882.

Becker, Howard S. *Outsiders: Studies in the Sociology of Deviance.* New York: Free Press of Glencoe, 1963.

Benton, Josiah Henry. *Warning Out in New England.* Boston, 1911.

Berger, Peter, and Luckmann, Thomas. *The Social Construction of Reality.* Garden City, N.Y.: Doubleday, 1966.

Blake, John B. *Public Health in the Town of Boston, 1630–1822.* Cambridge: Harvard University Press, 1959.

Boyer, Paul, and Nissenbaum, Stephen. *Salem Possessed: The Social Origins of Witchcraft.* Cambridge: Harvard University Press, 1974.

———. *Salem Village Witchcraft: A Documentary Record of Local Conflict in Colonial New England.* Belmont, Calif.: Wadsworth, 1972.

Breen, T. H., and Foster, Stephen. "Moving to the New World." *William and Mary Quarterly* 30, no. 2 (1973):187–221.

Breuer, Joseph, and Freud, Sigmund. *Studies in Hysteria.* 1895. Rpt. Boston: Beacon Press, 1950.

Breward, Ian, ed. *The Works of William Perkins.* Foxton, England: Sutton Courtenay Press, 1970.

Briggs, Katherine. "Some Seventeenth Century Books on Magic." *British Journal of Folklore* 64 (1953):445–62.

Brown, Peter, "Sorcery, Demons, and the Rise of Christianity." In *Witchcraft Confessions and Accusations,* ed. Mary Douglas. ASA monographs, no. 9. London: Tavistock, 1970.

Burr, G. Lincoln, ed. *Narratives of the Witchcraft Cases, 1648–1706.* 1914. Rpt. New York: Barnes & Noble, 1963.

———. "New England's Place in the History of Witchcraft." *Proceedings of the American Antiquarian Society*, new s. 21 (1911):185–217.

Butler, Jon. "Magic, Astrology, and the Early American Religious Heritage, 1600–1760." *American Historical Review* 84, no. 2 (1979):317–46.

Cohn, Norman. *Europe's Inner Demons: An Inquiry Inspired by the Great Witch-Hunt*. New York: Basic Books, 1975.

Conrad, Peter, and Schneider, Joseph W. *Deviance and Medicalization*. St. Louis: C. V. Mosby, 1980.

Cook, Edward. "Social Behavior and Changing Values in Dedham, Massachusetts, 1700–1775." *William and Mary Quarterly* 27, no. 1 (1970):546–80.

Currie, Elliot. "Crimes without Criminals: Witchcraft and Its Control in Renaissance Europe." *Law and Society Review* 3 (1968):7–32.

Demos, John Putnam. *Entertaining Satan: Witchcraft and the Culture of Early New England*. New York: Oxford University Press, 1982.

———. "John Godfrey and His Neighbors: Witchcraft and the Social Web in Colonial Massachusetts. *William and Mary Quarterly* 23 (1976):242–65.

———. *A Little Commonwealth: Family Life in Plymouth Colony*. New York: Oxford University Press, 1970.

———. "Underlying Themes in the Witchcraft of Seventeenth Century New England." *American Historical Review* 75, no. 5 (1970):1311–26.

———, ed. *Remarkable Providences, 1600–1760*. New York: Doubleday, 1972.

Deutsch, Albert. *The Mentally Ill in America: A History of Their Care and Treatment from Colonial Times*. 2nd ed. New York: Columbia University Press, 1952.

Douglas, Mary. Introduction to *Witchcraft Confessions and Accusations*, ed. Mary Douglas. ASA Monographs, no. 9. London: Tavistock, 1970.

Dow, George Francis. *Everyday Life in the Massachusetts Bay Colony*. 1935. Rpt. New York: Benjamin Blom, 1967.

Dow, Joseph. *History of the Town of Hampton, New Hampshire*. Vol. 1. Salem, Mass.: Salem Press Publishing Co., 1893.

Drake, Frederick C. "Witchcraft in the American Colonies, 1647–62." *American Quarterly* 20, no. 4 (1968):694–725.

Drake, Samuel G. *Annals of Witchcraft in New England*. Boston, 1869.

Duffy, John. *Epidemics in Colonial America*. New York: Kennikat Press, 1972.

Dunn, Richard. *Puritans and Yankees: The Winthrop Dynasty of New England, 1630–1717*. New York: W. W. Norton, 1971.

Erikson, Kai T. "Notes on the Sociology of Deviance." *Social Problems* 9 (1962): 307–14.

———. *Wayward Puritans: A Study in the Sociology of Deviance*. New York: John Wiley & Sons, 1966.

Evans-Pritchard, E. E. *Witchcraft, Oracles, and Magic among the Azanda*. 2nd ed. Oxford: Clarendon Press, 1950.

Ewen, E. L'Estrange. *Witchcraft and Demonianism*. London: Heath, Cranton, 1933.

———. *Witch Hunting and Witch Trials*. London: Kegan & Paul, 1929.

Flaherty, David, ed. *Essays in the History of Early American Law*. Chapel Hill, N.C.: University of North Carolina Press for the Institute of Early American History and Culture, 1969.

Foster, Stephen. *Their Solitary Way: The Puritan Social Ethic in the First Century of Settlement*. New Haven: Yale University Press, 1971.

Fox, Sanford. *Science and Justice: The Massachusetts Witchcraft Trials*. Baltimore: Johns Hopkins Press, 1968.

Fuess, Charles M. "Witches at Andover." *Proceedings of the Massachusetts Historical Society* 70 (1953):14.

Garfinkel, Harold. "Conditions of Successful Degradation Ceremonies." *American Journal of Sociology* 61 (1956):420–24.

———. *Studies in Ethnomethodology*. Englewood Cliffs, N.J.: Prentice-Hall, 1967.

Gellner, Ernest. "Concepts and Society." In *Rationality*, ed. Bryan Wilson, pp. 18–49. New York: Harper & Row, 1970.

Gilsdorf, A. T. B. "The Puritan Apocalypse: New England Eschatology in the Seventeenth Century." Diss., Yale University, 1965.

Goode, William. *Religion among the Primitives*. Glencoe, Ill.: Free Press, 1951.

Gove, Walter R., ed. *The Labelling of Deviance: Evaluating a Perspective*. New York: John Wiley & Sons, 1975.

Green, Samuel A. *Groton in the Witchcraft Times*. Groton, Mass., 1883.

Greene, Evarts B., and Harrington, V. D. *American Population before the Federal Census of 1790*. New York: Columbia University Press, 1932.

Greven, Philip, Jr. *Four Generations: Population, Lands, and Family in Colonial Andover, Massachusetts*. Ithaca: Cornell University Press, 1970.

Haffenden, Philip S. *New England in the English Nation, 1689–1713*. Oxford: Clarendon Press, 1974.

Hammond, Dorothy. "Magic: A Problem in Semantics." *American Anthropologist* 72, no. 6 (1970):1349–56.

Hansen, Chadwick. *Witchcraft at Salem*. New York: George Braziller, 1969.

Harner, Michael J., ed. *Hallucinogens and Shamanism*. New York: Oxford University Press, 1973.

Harris, Marvin. *Cows, Pigs, Wars, and Witches: The Riddles of Culture*. New York: Random House, 1974.

Haskins, George L. "Ecclesiastical Antecedents of Criminal Punishment in Early Massachusetts." *Proceedings of the Massachusetts Historical Society* 72 (1957–60): 21–35.

———. *Law and Authority in Early Massachusetts*. New York: Macmillan, 1960.

Hoadly, Charles J. "A Case of Witchcraft in Hartford." *Connecticut Magazine* 5 (1899):557–61.

————. "Some Early Post-Mortem Examinations in New England." *Proceedings of the Connecticut State Medical Society* 69 (1892):207–17.

Holmes, Thomas J. *Cotton Mather: A Bibliography of His Works.* 3 vols. Cambridge: Harvard University Press, 1940.

Horsley, Richard A. "Who Were the Witches? The Social Roles of the Accused in the European Witch Trials." *Journal of Interdisciplinary History* 9, no. 4 (1979):689–715.

Hutchinson, Thomas. *The History of the Colony and Province of Massachusetts Bay.* New ed., 3 vols. Cambridge, Mass., 1936.

————. "The Witchcraft Delusion of 1692." Communicated with notes by W. F. Poole, in *New England Historical and Genealogical Register* 24 (1870):380–92.

Jackson, Stanley, and Jackson, Joan K. "Primitive Medicine and the Historiography of Psychiatry." In *Psychiatry and Its History,* ed. George Mora and Jeanne L. Brand. Springfield, Ill.: Charles C. Thomas & Co., 1970.

Jacob, James R. " 'The Phantastick Air': The Idea of the Praeternatural in Colonial New England." M.A. thesis, Rice University, 1964.

Kelso, Robert. *The History of Public Poor Relief in Massachusetts, 1620–1920.* Series in Criminology, Law Enforcement, and Social Problems, no. 31. 1922. Rpt. Montclair, N.J.: Patterson Smith Reprint, 1969.

Kieckhefer, Richard. *European Witch Trials.* Berkeley and Los Angeles: University of California Press, 1976.

Kittredge, George L. *Witchcraft in Old and New England.* New York: Russell & Russell, 1956.

Kluckhohn, Clyde. *Navaho Witchcraft.* Cambridge, Mass.: The Museum, 1944.

Konig, David Thomas. *Law and Society in Puritan Massachusetts: Essex County, 1629–1692.* Chapel Hill: University of North Carolina Press, 1979.

Lea, H. C. *History of the Inquisition in the Middle Ages.* 3 vols. London: Sampson Low, 1888.

————. *Materials towards a History of Witchcraft.* 3 vols. New York: T. Yoseleff, 1957.

Leventhal, Herbert. *In the Shadow of the Enlightenment: Occultism and Renaissance Science in Eighteenth Century America.* New York: New York University Press, 1976.

Levermore, C. H. "Witchcraft in Connecticut." *New Englander* 44 (1885): 792–812.

Levin, David, ed. *What Happened in Salem?* 2nd ed. New York: Harcourt Brace, 1960.

Lewis, I. M. "A Structural Approach to Witchcraft and Spirit-Possession." In *Witchcraft Confessions and Accusations,* ed. Mary Douglas, pp. 293–311. ASA Monographs, no. 9. London: Tavistock, 1970.

Lockridge, Kenneth. *A New England Town: The First Hundred Years.* New York: W. W. Norton & Co., 1970.

Lockridge, Kenneth, and Krieder, A. "The Evolution of Massachusetts Town Government, 1640–1740." *William and Mary Quarterly* 23, no. 4 (1966):549–74.

Lukes, Stephen. "Some Problems about Rationality." In *Rationality*, ed. Bryan Wilson, pp. 194–213. New York: Harper & Row, 1970.

McBratney, William H. "The One-Witness Rule in Massachusetts." *American Journal of Legal History* 2 (1958):155–60.

Macfarlane, Alan. *Witchcraft in Tudor and Stuart England*. New York: Harper & Row, 1970.

Mair, Lucy. *Witchcraft*. New York: McGraw-Hill, 1969.

———. "Witchcraft." *British Journal of Sociology* 22, no. 1 (1972):109–16.

Mandrou, Robert. *Magistrats et sorciers en France au XVIIe siecle*. Paris: Librairie Plon, 1968.

Marwick, Max. *Sorcery in Its Social Setting*. Manchester: Manchester University Press, 1965.

———, ed. *Witchcraft and Sorcery*. Middlesex, England: Penguin Books, 1970.

Matza, David. *Becoming Deviant*. Englewood Cliffs, N.J.: Prentice-Hall, 1969.

Merrifield, Ralph. "Witch Bottles and Magical Jugs." *British Journal of Folklore* 66 (1955):195–207.

Merton, Robert K. *Science, Technology, and Society in Seventeenth-Century England*. 1938. Rpt. New York: Harper & Row, 1970.

Middlekauff, Robert. *The Mathers: Three Generations of Puritan Intellectuals, 1596–1728*. New York: Oxford University Press, 1971.

Middleton, J. F. M. *Lugbara Religion*. London: Oxford University Press, 1960.

Middleton, T., and Winter, E., eds. *Witchcraft and Sorcery in East Africa*. London: Routledge & Kegan Paul, 1960.

Midelfort, Hans C. Erik. "The Social and Intellectual Foundations of Witch-Hunting in Southwestern Germany, 1562–1684." Diss., Yale University, 1970.

———. "Were There Really Witches?" In *Transitions and Revolution: Problems and Issues of European Renaissance and Reformation History*, ed. R. M. Kingdon. Minneapolis: Burgess, 1974.

———. *Witchhunting in Southwestern Germany, 1562–1684*. Stanford, Calif.: Stanford University Press, 1972.

Miller, Perry. *Errand into the Wilderness*. 1956. Rpt. New York: Harper Torchbooks, 1964.

———. *The New England Mind: From Colony to Province*. 1953. Rpt. Boston: Beacon Press, 1961.

———. *The New England Mind: The Seventeenth Century*. Cambridge: Harvard University Press, 1939.

———. *Orthodoxy in Massachusetts*. Boston: Beacon Press, 1959.

Monter, E. William. *Witchcraft in France and Switzerland*. Ithaca: Cornell University Press, 1976.

———, ed. *European Witchcraft*. New York: Wiley, 1969.

Moore, George H. "Notes on the Bibliography of Witchcraft in Massachusetts." *Proceedings of the American Antiquarian Society*, n.s. 5 (1888):249–72.

————. "Notes on the History of Witchcraft in Massachusetts." *Proceedings of the American Antiquarian Society*, n.s. 2 (1882):162–81.

Morgan, Edmund S. *The Puritan Family*. New ed. New York: Harper & Row, 1966.

————. *Visible Saints*. Ithaca: Cornell University Press, 1965.

Morison, Samuel Eliot. *Harvard College in the Seventeenth Century*. 2 vols. Cambridge: Harvard University Press, 1936.

Morris, Richard B. *Studies in the History of American Law*. 2nd ed. New York: Octagon Books, 1964.

Murray, Margaret Alice Mary. *The Witch-Cult in Western Europe*. London, 1921.

Murrin, John. "Review Essay." *History and Theory* 11, no. 2 (1972):226–75.

Nevins, Winfield S. *Witchcraft in Salem Village in 1692*. Salem, Mass.: Salem Press Publishing Co., 1916.

Notestein, Wallace. *A History of Witchcraft in England from 1558 to 1718*. 1911. Rpt. New York: Russell & Russell, 1965.

Oberholzer, Emil, Jr. *Delinquent Saints: Disciplinary Actions in the Early Congregational Churches of Massachusetts*. New York: Columbia University Press, 1956.

Oesterreich, T. K. *Possession, Demoniacal and Other, among Primitive Races, in Antiquity, the Middle Ages, and Modern Times*. London: Kegan Paul, French, Trubner, & Co., 1930.

Paige, Lucius. *History of Cambridge*. Cambridge, Mass.: Riverside Press, 1892.

Parsons, Talcott. *The Structure of Social Action*. New York: Free Press, 1949.

Perley, Sidney. *The History of Salem, Massachusetts*. 3 vols. Salem, 1924–28.

Pollner, Melvin. "Constitutive and Mundane Versions of the Labeling Theory." *Human Studies* 1 (1978):269–88.

Poole, W. F. "Cotton Mather and Salem Witchcraft." *North American Review* 223 (1869):337–97.

————. "Witchcraft in Boston." In *Memorial History of Boston*, ed. Justin Winsor, 1:131–72. Boston, 1881.

Powell, Sumner. *Puritan Village: The Formation of a New England Town*. Middletown, Conn.: Wesleyan University Press, 1963.

Powers, Edwin. *Crime and Punishment in Early Massachusetts, 1620–1692*. Boston: Beacon Press, 1966.

Prior, Moody E. "Joseph Glanvill, Witchcraft, and Seventeenth-Century Science." *Modern Philology* 30, no. 2 (1932):167–92.

Putnam, Allen. *Witchcraft in New England Explained by Modern Spiritualism*. Boston: Colby & Rich, 1888.

Rains, Prudence. "Imputations of Deviance: A Retrospective Essay on the Labeling Perspective." *Social Problems* 23 (1975):1–11.

Reed, Susan B. *Church and State in Massachusetts, 1691–1740*. University of Illinois Studies in the Social Sciences, 9:461–655. 1914.

Rice, Charles B. *History of the First Parish at Salem Village.* Boston: Congregational Publishing House, 1874.

Robbins, Rossell. *Encyclopedia of Witchcraft and Demonology.* New York: Crown, 1959.

Rock, Paul, and McIntosh, Mary, eds. *Deviance and Social Control.* London: Tavistock, 1974.

Rose, Elliot. *A Razor for a Goat.* Toronto: University of Toronto Press, 1962.

Rosen, George. *Madness in Society: Chapters in the Historical Sociology of Mental Illness.* New York: Harper & Row, 1968.

Runeberg, Arne. *Witches, Demons, and Fertility Magic: Analysis of Their Significance and Mutual Relations in West European Folk Religion.* Societas Scientarium Fennica Commentiones Humanarum Litterarum, vol. 25. Helsinki, 1947.

Russell, Jeffrey Burton. *Witchcraft in the Middle Ages.* Ithaca: Cornell University Press, 1972.

Rutman, Darrett B. *American Puritanism: Faith and Practice.* New York: Lippincott & Co., 1970.

————. "The Mirror of Puritan Authority." In *Law and Authority in Colonial America*, ed. George A. Billias, pp. 149–67. Barre, Mass.: Barre Publishers, 1965.

————. *Winthrop's Boston.* New York: W. W. Norton & Co., 1972.

Schoeneman, Thomas J. "The Role of Mental Illness in the European Witch Hunts of the Sixteenth and Seventeenth Centuries: An Assessment." *Journal of the History of the Behavioral Sciences* 13 (1977):337–51.

Schur, Edwin M. *Interpreting Deviance: A Sociological Introduction.* New York: Harper & Row, 1979.

————. *Labelling Deviant Behavior.* New York: Harper & Row, 1971.

Shipton, Clifford. "The New England Clergy in the Glacial Age." *Publications of the Colonial Society of Massachusetts* 32 (1933):24–54.

Shryock, Richard H. *Medicine and Society in America, 1660–1860.* New York: New York University Press, 1960.

Stahlman, William D. "Astrology in Colonial America: An Extended Query." *William and Mary Quarterly*, ser. 3, 13 (1956):551–63.

Starkey, Marion. *The Devil in Massachusetts.* 1949. Rpt. Garden City, N.Y.: Doubleday & Co., 1969.

Stearns, R. P. "Colonial Fellows of the Royal Society of London, 1661–1788." *William and Mary Quarterly*, 3rd ser. 3 (1946):208–68.

Szasz, Thomas. *The Manufacture of Madness.* New York: Harper & Row, 1970.

Taylor, John. *The Witchcraft Delusion in Colonial Connecticut.* New York: Grafton Press, 1908.

Teall, John L. "Witchcraft and Calvinism in Elizabethan England: Divine Power and Human Agency." *Journal of the History of Ideas* 23 (1962):21–36.

Thomas, Keith. "The Relevance of Social Anthropology to the Historical Study of English Witchcraft." In *Witchcraft Confessions and Accusations*, ed. Mary Douglas. ASA Publications, no. 9. London: Tavistock, 1970.

————. *Religion and the Decline of Magic.* London: Weidenfeld & Nicolson, 1971.

Trefz, Edward K. "A Study of Satan with Particular Emphasis upon His Role in the Preaching of Certain New England Puritans." Diss., Union Theological Seminary, 1952.

Trevor-Roper, H. R. *Religion, Reformation, and Social Change.* New York: Macmillan, 1967.

Trumbull, James Russell. *History of Northampton.* Vol. 1. Northampton, Mass., 1898.

Turner, Victor W. *Schism and Continuity in an African Society.* Manchester: Manchester University Press, 1957.

————. "Witchcraft and Sorcery: Taxonomy versus Dynamics." *Africa* 34, no. 4 (1964):314–25.

U.S. Bureau of the Census. *Historical Statistics of the U.S.: Colonial Times to 1957.* Washington, D.C.: Government Printing Office, 1960.

Upham, Charles W. *Lectures on Witchcraft.* Boston, 1831.

————. *Salem Witchcraft.* 2 vols. Boston: Wiggins & Lunt, 1867.

Van Doren, Mark, ed. *Samuel Sewall's Diary.* New York: Russell & Russell, 1963.

Vaughan, Alden T., ed. *The Puritan Tradition in America.* New York: Harper & Row, 1972.

Vieth, Ilza. *Hysteria: The History of a Disease.* Chicago: University of Chicago Press, 1965.

Walker, Deward E., Jr., "Nez Perce Sorcery," *Ethnology* 6, no. 1 (1967):66–96.

Walker, D. P. *Spiritual and Demonic Magic from Ficino to Campanella.* London: Warberg Institute, 1958.

Wall, Robert. *Massachusetts Bay: The Crucial Decade, 1640–1650.* New Haven: Yale University Press, 1972.

Warren, Carol A. B., and Johnson, John M. "A Critique of Labelling Theory from the Phenomenological Perspective." In *Theoretical Perspectives on Deviance,* ed. Robert Scott and Jack D. Douglas. New York: Basic Books, 1972.

Waters, John J. "Hingham, Massachusetts, 1631–1661." *Journal of Social History* 1 (1967–68):352–70.

Watkins, W. "Mary Watkins: A Discolored History of Witchcraft, Cleansed by Modern Research." *New England Historical and Genealogical Register* 44 (1890): 168–70.

Wendell, Barrett. "Were the Salem Witches Guiltless?" Essex Institute Historical Collections, no. 29, pp. 129–47.

Werking, Richard H. " 'Reformation Is Our Only Preservation'; Cotton Mather and Salem Witchcraft." *William and Mary Quarterly* 29, no. 2 (1972):281–90.

Wertenbaker, Thomas J. *The Puritan Oligarchy.* New York: Charles Scribner's Sons, 1947.

Whitmore, William H. *A Bibliographical Sketch of the Laws of the Massachusetts Colony from 1630 to 1686.* Boston, 1890.

Willis, R. G. "Instant Millennium: The Sociology of African Witch-Cleansing Cults." In *Witchcraft Confessions and Accusations,* ed. Mary Douglas. ASA monographs, no. 9. London: Tavistock, 1970.

———. "Kamcape: An Anti-Sorcery Movement in South-West Tanzania." *Africa* 38 (1968):1–15.

Zilboorg, Gregory. *The Medical Man and the Witch during the Renaissance.* Baltimore: The Johns Hopkins University Press, 1935.

Subject Index

Afflictions: management of, 61–70, 183;
role of, in Salem trials, 132–34, 144–48;
social distribution of, 50–52. *See also*
Bewitchment; Possession
Age: of accusers, 51; of afflicted, 51;
of witches during pre-Salem trials,
76–78; of witches during Salem trials,
137–38
Astrology, 55, 56

Bewitchment: compared with ordinary
witchcraft, 47–49; defined, 43; distinguished from possession, 62. *See
also* Afflictions

Confessions of witchcraft, 96, 189; role
of, in Salem trials, 154–59
Continental witchcraft, 8–11. *See also*
Witchcraft accusations; Witchcraft
prosecutions
Covenant theology, 120–23; and aftermath of Salem trials, 166–68, 172–76;
and Salem trials, 126–30. *See also*
Puritan beliefs

Defamation suits, 93, 94

English witchcraft, 12–14. *See also*
Witchcraft accusations; Witchcraft
prosecutions
Evidence in witchcraft cases: in aftermath of Salem trials, 176–82; during
Salem trials, 148–54; in pre-Salem
trials, 98–105. *See also* Spectral evidence; Witch's marks

Laws against witchcraft, 12–14

Magistrates, role of: in aftermath of
Salem trials, 168–69; in pre-Salem
trials, 105–12; in Salem trials, 132–35,
148–59. *See also* Witchcraft prosecutions

Ordeals, 104

Possession (by Satan), distinguished
from bewitchment, 62. *See also*
Afflictions; Bewitchment
Poverty and witchcraft, 80–83, 88–90,
139–40
Puritan beliefs: on afflictions, 61–70;
on astrology, 55–56; on magic, 54–57;
on Satan, 25–29; on witchcraft, 23–38,
57–61, 126–31. *See also* Covenant
theology

Satan, 25–29, 127, 129–31, 189
Sex: of accusers, 50, 51; of afflicted, 50,
51; of witches in pre-Salem trials, 76–
78, 91; of witches in Salem trials, 135
Social anthropology and witchcraft, 3–6
Sociology as related to investigation, 2,
3, 184, 189
Spectral evidence, 104, 150–52, 166, 170,
171, 177. *See also* Evidence in witchcraft cases

Witchcraft accusations: logic of, 42–49;
negotiation of accusations, 91–95;
relationship between accusers and
suspects in pre-Salem trials, 78, 79,
83–91; relationship between accusers
and suspects in Salem trials, 127, 128,
135–48

Witchcraft and social position: and accused in pre-Salem trials, 76–78, 80–83; 91–95; and accused in Salem trials, 135–44, 146–48; and accusers, 49–52. *See also* Poverty and witchcraft

Witchcraft beliefs: and popular magic, 54–57; and relationship between popular and theological approaches, 53–72; and religion, 23–38. *See also* Covenant theology; Puritan beliefs

Witchcraft prosecutions: Anglo-American and Continental patterns of, compared, 11–14; decline of, 182, 183; European and African patterns of, compared, 4–6; patterns of, in pre-Salem trials, 105–12; patterns of, in Salem trials, 154–59; in pre-Salem and Salem trials, compared, 184, 185, 187, 188. *See also* Magistrates, role of

Witch's marks, 101–3, 150. *See also* Evidence in witchcraft cases

Name Index

Ady, Thomas, 101
Alden, Capt. John, 142, 161, 163, 165, 169
Allen, James, 162
Ames, William, 31
Andrew, Daniel, 141, 162
Andros, Sir Edmond, 124
Ayres, Goodwife, 46

Babson, Ebenezer, 125
Baxter, Richard, 180
Becker, Howard S., 2
Beman, Symon, 89
Bernard, Richard, 35, 59, 61, 71, 99, 100, 112, 154, 180, 187
Bishop, Bridget, 86, 138, 139, 152, 153, 156, 160, 170
Boyer, Paul, 6, 128, 133, 141
Bradbury, Mary, 140, 162, 163
Bradford, William, 109
Bradstreet, Dudley, 143, 146, 147
Bradstreet, John, 86, 90, 144
Bradstreet, Simon, 124
Branch, William, 89
Brattle, Thomas, 135, 151, 159, 161, 165, 166, 168
Brown, Christopher, 86, 90
Buckley, Sarah, 139
Buckley, William, 139
Burr, G. H., 7, 16–20
Burroughs, George, 138, 156, 157, 163, 170, 176, 180
Burt, Goodwife, 86, 88

Calef, Robert, 27, 33, 36, 68, 128, 133, 144, 147, 153, 157, 158, 163, 168, 171, 174
Carr, James, 49
Carrier, Martha, 139, 143, 170
Carrier, sons of Martha, 143
Cary, Nathaniel, 155
Casaubon, Meric, 65, 101
Chase, John, 79
Clinton, Lawrence, 140
Clinton, Rachel, 89, 140
Cloyce, Peter, 141
Cloyce, Sarah, 128, 141, 149
Cole, Ann, 63, 66, 67
Cole, Eunice, 76, 82, 86, 106, 107, 108
Corey, Giles, 137
Corey, Martha, 136, 137
Corwin, Jonathan, 147, 153
Cotta, John, 64, 156

Dalton, Michael, 99, 101
Dane, Francis, Sr., 139, 143
Dane (daughter and granddaughter), 143
Davis, Zachery, 89
Demos, John, 16, 50
Dorchester, Anthony, 44, 45
Drake, Alexander, 86
Dudley, Joseph, 123, 124
Durkheim, Emile, 2
Dyer, Mary, 29

Easty, Mary, 158
Edmonds, Anna, 90
Edwards, Mary, 89
Ela, Daniel, 87
English, Mary, 142, 163

English, Philip, 142, 161, 163, 165, 176
Evans-Pritchard, E., 4
Ewen, C. L'Estrange, 13, 14
Fanning, William, 79
Foster, Ann, 143
Francis, Joan, 109
Fuller, James, 90
Fuller, Rachel, 79, 104

Gaule, John, 42
Gedney, Bartholomew, 142, 148, 149
Gifford, George, 59
Glanvill, Joseph, 32, 33
Glover, Mary, 66, 68, 113, 114
Godfrey, John (accused witch), 43, 44,
    77, 86, 87, 88, 106, 107, 108
Godfrey, John (accuser), 79
Good, Dorcas, 138
Good, Sarah, 136, 137, 138, 139, 156, 160
Good, William, 136
Goodwin children, 66, 67, 68
Goodwin, John, 68
Graves, John, 109
Greensmith, Rebecca, 66
Griggs, William, 117

Hale, John, 112, 133, 139, 169, 178, 179,
    180, 181, 188
Hale, Mary, 76
Hale, Mrs. John, 47
Harris, Marvin, 1
Harrison, Katherine, 108, 109, 110, 111
Harvey, William, 102
Hathorne, William, 136, 137, 155
Hibbins, Ann, 76, 77, 88, 106, 113, 180
Hoadly, Charles, 46
Hoar, Dorcas, 139, 157
Holman, Winifred, 86, 93, 94
Hooker, Thomas, 87
Hopkins, Matthew, 101, 102, 103
Horton, John, 87
How, Elizabeth, 140, 159, 162, 170, 171
Hubbard, Elizabeth, 45, 46
Hubbard, William, 24
Hull, John, 59
Hutchinson, Anne, 29
Hutchinson, Thomas, 106, 147

Ingersoll, Nathaniel, 141

Institoris, Heinrich. See Malleus
    Maleficarum

Jacobs, George, 162
Jacobs, George, Sr., 156, 157
Jacobs, Margaret, 156, 157
James I (king of England), 12, 64
James, Jane, 87
Johnson, Mary, 97
Jones, Margaret, 86, 103, 105, 180
Jones, William, 104

Keble, Joseph, 99
Kelley, Elizabeth, 46
Kelley, John, 46
Kendal, Mrs., 106
Kittredge, George, 7, 16–20
Knapp, Elizabeth, 65, 67, 69
Knight, Jacob, 49

Lake, Mrs. H., 90, 106
Lawson, Deodat, 25, 26, 28, 33, 35, 36,
    37, 40, 58, 67, 117, 126, 127, 128, 130,
    133, 145
Lea, H. C., 17
Lewis, Mercy, 45, 141
Lombroso, Cesare, 2

MacFarlane, Alan, 13, 89, 98
Malleus Maleficarum, 8–11, 53, 54
Mandrou, Robert, 11
Martin, Susanna, 58, 77, 86, 87, 160, 165,
    170
Marwick, Max, 48
Mather, Cotton, 23, 24, 27, 28, 32, 33,
    34, 35, 36, 37, 41, 58, 59, 60, 61, 63, 65,
    66, 87, 97, 113, 125, 126, 127, 129, 130,
    131, 133, 141, 151, 152, 153, 156, 158,
    163, 170, 171, 174, 175
Mather, Increase, 23, 24, 25, 31, 33, 41,
    56, 60, 62, 67, 68, 69, 71, 104, 152, 164,
    166, 170, 171, 173, 175, 177, 178, 179,
    180, 181, 182, 189
Matza, David, 2
Merrifield, Henry, 81
Merton, Robert, 56
Midelfort, H. C., 4
Milborne, Rev. Mr., 163
Miller, Perry, 24, 30, 121, 122, 123
Monter, E. William, 11

Moody, Caleb, 58, 78
Morse, Elizabeth, 58, 76, 78, 79, 85, 86,
    88, 89, 99, 108, 111, 112
Morse, William, 78, 79, 85, 112
Murray, Margaret, 9

Newton, Thomas, 142
Nissenbaum, Stephen, 6, 128, 133, 141
Noyes, Nicholas, 133, 156
Nurse, Francis, 137, 141
Nurse, Rebecca, 103, 128, 137, 141, 153,
    154, 159, 161, 162, 165

Osborne, Alexander, 136
Osborne, Sarah, 136, 137

Paison, Edward, 162
Parris, Elizabeth, 117, 141
Parris, Samuel, 35, 117, 126, 127, 128,
    129, 130, 131, 133, 134, 136, 141, 142,
    146, 172, 173
Parsons, Hugh, 44, 45, 78, 86, 88, 89, 93,
    106
Parsons, Mary, 93, 106
Parsons, Mrs. J., 15, 77, 87, 90, 93, 94
Perkins, William, 27, 36, 37, 55, 59, 61,
    63, 68, 71, 99, 100, 112, 154, 187
Philips, Samuel, 162
Phips, Lady, 146, 147
Phips, Sir William, 118, 148, 152, 163,
    166, 167, 169, 170, 171, 172, 175
Pike, Robert, 162
Porter, Elizabeth and Israel, 137, 141,
    142
Powell, Caleb, 85, 108
Pressy, John and Mary, 58
Preston, John, 31
Proctor, Elizabeth, 162, 175
Proctor, John, 142, 155, 162
Pudeator, Ann, 140
Putnam, Ann, Jr., 45, 141
Putnam, Ann, Sr., 141
Putnam, Edward, 45, 46, 141
Putnam, John, 141
Putnam, Nathaniel, 141
Putnam, Thomas, 45, 46, 141

Reed, Wilmot, 139, 165
Remington, John, 86
Richards, John, 148, 151, 154

Rowe, Nicholas, 79
Rule, Margaret, 66, 68, 69
Russell, Jeffrey Burton, 8

Saltonstall, Nathaniel, 146, 147, 148, 153
Sargent, William, 87, 148
Schur, Edwin, 2
Scot, Reginald, 11, 12
Scottow, Joshua, 126
Sewall, Samuel, 58, 148, 149, 163, 164,
    175, 179, 181
Sewall, Stephen, 129
Shephard, Thomas, 63
Short, Mercy, 63, 68, 69
Sibley, Mary, 136
Singletarry, Jonathan, 43, 44
Smith, Philip, 28, 87
Sprenger, Jakob. *See* Malleus
    Maleficarum
Stoughton, William, 129, 148, 149, 157,
    169

Thacher, Mrs. Margaret, 147
Thomas, Keith, 6, 55, 70
Tituba, 136, 139, 144
Turell, Ebenezer, 183

Walcott, Jonathan, 141
Walcott, Mary, 45, 141
Walford, Jane, 76, 79
Wardwell, Mercy, 157
Wardwell, Samuel, 156, 157
Wardwell, Sarah, 157
Warren, Mary, 142, 144, 145
Watkins, Mary, 182
Webster, Mary, 76, 86, 87, 101
Wells, Thomas, 60, 86
Wheeler, David, 89
White, Thomas, 140
Wigglesworth, Michael, 30, 59, 166, 175,
    176
Wilds, Ephraim, 161
Wilds, Sarah, 161, 162
Willard, John, 45, 156, 157
Willard, Samuel, 25, 27, 65, 66, 67, 68,
    69, 127, 135, 146, 147, 166, 168, 175
Williams, Abigail, 45, 117, 141
Winthrop, John, 24, 83, 86, 106, 108, 121
Winthrop, Wait, 148